EMILY AUSTIN *of* TEXAS
1795-1851

Emily as Mrs. James F. Perry. Courtesy of the the Brazoria County Historical Commission.

EMILY AUSTIN *of* TEXAS
1795-1851

by LIGHT TOWNSEND CUMMINS

THE TEXAS BIOGRAPHY SERIES ★ NUMBER 1

A Joint Project of the Center for Texas Studies at TCU
And TCU Press ★ Fort Worth, Texas

Library of Congress Cataloging-in-Publication Data

Cummins, Light Townsend.
Emily Austin of Texas, 1795-1851 / by Light Townsend Cummins.
p. cm.
Includes bibliographical references and index.
ISBN 978-0-87565-351-8
1. Perry, Emily Austin Bryan, 1795-1851. 2. Women pioneers--Texas--
Biography. 3. Pioneers--Texas--Biography. 4. Frontier and pioneer life--Texas.
5. Austin, Stephen F. (Stephen Fuller), 1793-1836--Family. 6. Texas--History--
Revolution, 1835-1836. 7. Texas--History--To 1846--Biography. I. Title.
F389.P48C86 2009
976.4'04092--dc22
[B]
2008034699

TCU Press
P. O. Box 298300
Fort Worth, Texas 76129
817.257.7822
http://www.prs.tcu.edu

To order books: 800.826.8911

Design/Margie Adkins Graphic Design

FOR

Victoria Hennessey Cummins

Katherine Anne Cummins

Leslie Johanna Cummins

TABLE OF CONTENTS

EDITOR'S FOREWORD

Throughout its rich and colorful history, Texas has been home to countless fascinating figures. Some of the state's great works of historical literature, such as Eugene C. Barker's biography of Stephen F. Austin and Marquis James' study of Sam Houston, have chronicled the lives of Texas' larger-than-life leaders. However, there remain many important personalities who have not yet found their biographer and many more whose stories are in need of fresh examination in a scholarly biography. The Texas Biography Series, published by TCU Press and the Center for Texas Studies at TCU, offers a new venue for telling their stories. Another major goal of the series is to broaden the body of biographical literature in Texas historiography beyond its traditionally heavy emphasis on the "great men" (which has often meant "great white men on horseback"). While the series will certainly include biographies of nineteenth-century political and military leaders, it will strive to encourage biographers to examine the full range of historical actors who have shaped the destiny of the Lone Star State, including women and members of racial and ethnic minorities, as well as figures from the worlds of business, the arts, science, religion, and even sports. In doing so, the series will contribute to keeping the field of Texas history vital and relevant as it moves into the twenty-first century.

It is with particular pride that we inaugurate the Texas Biography Series with the publication of *Emily Austin of Texas*. In this finely drawn study, Light Townsend Cummins admirably fulfills one of the principal aims of the series, which is to place well-known Texas personalities in modern historiographical context utilizing recent scholarly knowledge.

Professor Cummins has done just that, using concepts from modern women's historiography—including the ideas of patriarchy and separate spheres—to illuminate the life of a woman who was heretofore known mainly as the sister of Stephen F. Austin. Professor Cummins has revealed Emily as much more than just a relative of the "Father of Texas"; she emerges in these pages as a remarkable historical actor in her own right, often stepping outside the gendered boundaries of her era to take an exceptionally active role in managing her family's complex business affairs and asserting her independence in family and marital matters. Emily Austin, we learn, was no stereotypical southern belle on the proverbial pedestal. By exploring her life, Light Cummins has also succeeded in adding to our knowledge of Texas colonization, the Texas Revolution and Republic, the era of early statehood, and the growth of the plantation economy.

This book and its successors in the Texas Biography Series owe their existence to three important institutions. TCU Press and its staff have furnished the editorial and production expertise to create books equal to those of the leading national publishing houses. The Center for Texas Studies at TCU is a critical partner in launching, funding, and publicizing the series. And finally, Houston Endowment has provided a generous grant underwriting much of the cost of *Emily Austin* and the next several titles in the series. As series editor, I am grateful to all of these partners who have made the series a reality.

Gregg Cantrell
Erma and Ralph Lowe Chair in Texas History
Texas Christian University

INTRODUCTION

Biography as a form of analysis seeks to understand the relationship between the normal and the unusual in the life of its subject. The public deeds and the private life of the individual are the traditional domains of the biographer. Each must be balanced against the other to provide a synthesis that relates the person to the larger framework of history. This can be a complex process, especially in deciding exactly how the public and the private are to be defined in tandem with the classification of the typical and the atypical. In the case of elite southern women of the antebellum era, those who were married in particular, there might be a temptation to view them from a perspective emphasizing the private and typical in their lives. The following chapters will show that Emily Austin was in many respects a typical woman of her era, one who oftentimes was restrained within the private sphere, although she also stepped outside these boundaries in public ways that made her exceptional for her time. In addition to the public and the private, any consideration of Emily Austin's life must focus on the concept of family as a building block of history. "Family figures as a central metaphor for southern society as a whole," Elizabeth Fox-Genovese has pointed out, and provides "the personal and social relations through which individuals defined these identities and understood their lives. Women, especially, relied upon family relationships to define their identities." As historian Rebecca Sharpless has written about a later generation of nineteenth-century Texas women, "within their networks of families, women...lived as wives, mothers, daughters, and sisters, defining themselves in their relationships to others." Complex family relationships provided a constant frame of reference for elite southern women across the nineteenth century, and such was certainly the case for Emily Austin, who was the daughter of Moses Austin and the sister of Stephen F. Austin. The story of her life is entwined with a network of family ties that held together her existence as a person. For her, the daily reality of family was the fundamental fabric of her universe, the centerpiece of her worldview. At the same time, she was very much her own woman, with strong, well-articulated personal feelings centered on a steely personality. Her rock-solid resolve for action enabled her to survive almost six decades of frontier hardship.[1]

Through all of these decades, Emily Austin was first and foremost a southerner in her outlook and lived as member of that society. Both Missouri and Texas, the two places where she spent most of her life, had close ties to the older parts of the antebellum South and in many respects represented the westernmost geographical extension of its culture. For that reason, the value structures and philosophical assumptions of early nineteenth-century southern life, especially among the slaveholding elite, provided the social context in which Emily Austin lived. In that society, southern men tended to view women of their class as delicate, submissive helpmates who embodied the virtues of purity, humility, and devotion to familial duty. Many women consciously and unconsciously lived within these social conventions. As historian Anne Scott has observed, "Women, along with children and slaves, were expected to recognize their proper and subordinate place and to be obedient to the head of the family." Under such circumstances, many married women from Emily Austin's social class in the South related to the world through the framework provided by the men in their lives. Anya Jabour has characterized these women by noting that "from the mid-nineteenth century forward, observers have commented upon certain similarities between the status of women in antebellum America and the position of slaves in the Old South." Some elite women and the slaves living on southern plantations thus held mutual sympathies in their respective subordinations to a male-dominated society. At the same time, however, there were a few southern plantation women who resented their slaves and treated them in a harsh manner in spite of any theoretical commonalities between them. Emily Austin was not one of these latter women. Instead, she belonged to the group of plantation mistresses who treated their slaves with respect and sympathy, although her writings provide no historical clues to her motivations for so doing.[2]

Emily lived all of her life within the parameters of the gendered subordination so pervasive throughout the antebellum South, and she did so without complaint. She in fact relished being a wife and caring mother, while maintaining a firm command over the domestic sphere at Peach Point Plantation, toiling diligently as a plantation mistress. She fulfilled admirably the traditional roles expected of any married woman from her class and background. Her life functioned successfully under these circumstances because of her commitment to the concept of family. Above all else, Emily Austin was the touchstone at the center of an extended family that provided a common point of reference for four generations of Austins, Bryans, and Perrys, beginning with her parents and extending to her grandchildren.[3]

Emily began her life as a young person of privilege in two different towns that had been founded by her father, Moses Austin. A pampered child and vivacious adolescent, she lived in a frontier mansion with all the advantages that the fruits of her father's business entrepreneurship could provide. As a young girl, Emily attended boarding schools both in Kentucky and New York. She enjoyed a teenaged social life that included contact with bright young people, not only among the elite families of

Missouri, but in such diverse places as Lexington, Philadelphia, New Haven, and New York City. Marriage at age eighteen to James Bryan, a Missouri merchant and mine owner, saw the direction of her life turn drastically away from the gentility to which she had been raised. While a young mother in her twenties, a series of profound setbacks forced her to develop a greater self-assertion and independence of mind than otherwise might have been the case. After only a few years of marriage, she experienced the death of two children and the untimely passing of her husband. She also witnessed the collapse of the Austin family businesses in Missouri and the resultant unraveling of their financial affairs, which brought all of them (including Emily and her children) to the brink of penury. The death of her father, Moses Austin, left widowed Emily with the added responsibility of caring for her invalid mother. These adversities began a period of constant hardship and material deprivation, during which time she was the sole breadwinner for both her mother and her children. Steeled by these events into a resolute woman of independent viewpoint and practical action, Emily eventually married James Franklin Perry Jr., a man with whom she started a second family and a new life. However, she never surrendered the personal resolve and self-direction she had acquired as a young widow.[4]

After her marriage to Perry in 1824, Emily and her husband lived in Missouri for almost eight years before moving to Texas, where they established a plantation that would be home for the rest of their lives. It was fortunate that Emily's second husband was a man who understood her personality and relished the companionate nature of their marriage. By the time she became mistress of Peach Point Plantation in the early 1830s, Emily had completed her transformation from an inexperienced young wife into an articulate, hardworking, and very active woman in her own right. Most notably, she was a person of thoughtful, strong opinions. Of her own volition, Emily routinely made personal sacrifices for her children, sometimes at the peril of her health and well-being. She had a firm understanding of her place in the world and earned a reputation as a consummate hostess in the Texas plantation belt. She appreciated the beauty of nature, loved music, and had a deep religious commitment. Emily also staunchly valued education. Not only did she insist that all of her children be well educated, she was a generous early supporter of schools in antebellum Texas. In all of these matters, she was highly organized and task oriented. That was a useful characteristic since, as the sole surviving legal heir of Moses and Stephen F. Austin, Emily had become by the mid-1830s one of the largest individual landholders in Texas and indisputably its richest woman.

Perhaps the most significant reason for Emily's uniqueness rests on her personal wealth, which gave her an autonomous perspective and a privileged social standing that provided an identity beyond her marital status as Mrs. James F. Perry. The laws of Texas permitted married women to retain personal ownership of any assets they might inherit as individuals, while they shared with their husbands one-half of all property that resulted from marriage. After 1836, Emily Austin owned thousands of acres of Texas land that legally was hers alone by inheritance, and she also shared in her husband's community property. As a married woman, Emily was constrained by the doctrine of *feme covert* under the Law of Coverture in Texas, a legal stricture that prohibited married women from entering into contracts in their own name apart from that of their husband. For that reason, James Perry served as her legal agent and as the named party in managing her landed wealth. Nevertheless, at every turn she participated fully in all matters touching on her considerable amount of property. The two fashioned a very successful partnership in which James honored her wishes regarding her property while Emily sought his counsel in its management. Accordingly, she involved herself in various land development schemes and other business ventures, including the organization of a railroad company.

This personal wealth, coupled with her earlier experiences as a widow, gave Emily a self-reliant spirit that expressed itself in numerous ways during the years she lived at Peach Point. In addition to business matters regarding her Austin inheritance, Emily's participation in other activities showed her to be her own woman. For example, in the era of the Texas Revolution, she assisted her brother Stephen F. Austin in various matters related to his imprisonment in Mexico between 1834 and 1835, helped him in his political leadership during the revolt, and worked on his behalf in maintaining political alliances in the partisan rivalries of the infant Republic of Texas. Starting in the late 1830s, she also began traveling extensively and independently throughout the United States, personally arranging for the education of her children at boarding schools in West Virginia, Ohio, and Kentucky. She spent long periods of time away from her husband in the company of her children, especially after one of them developed a chronic illness. Emily and the child were forced to travel widely to seek medical treatment. Under these circumstances, she made independent decisions about medical care and educational matters for the family, and she participated by letter in the long-distance management of Peach Point. During the 1840s, she also became a motivating force in the establishment of the Episcopal Church in Texas and a major benefactor in founding one of the first colleges in the young state.

Emily enjoyed unique relationships with the men in her family. Her successful survival as a young widow gave her an autonomy that emancipated her from male supervision, although she had to act legally through the auspices of her husband in decisions regarding her assets. It is interesting to note that the male members of her family, beginning in childhood with her father and ending with her sons after her death, wrote much of the correspondence that speaks to Emily's life, particularly outside the domestic sphere. The historian must sometimes view her personality through the historical lens these men provided in their letters and other documents. Nonetheless, a clear picture of Emily Austin and her multifaceted personality, both in its public and private manifestations, emerges for anyone who reads the extended correspondence that passed among the members her family.[5]

An overt examination of Emily's life, given the variety of her experiences during adulthood, could superficially highlight the historical viewpoint that men and women in the antebellum South inhabited separate spheres of existence. That interpretive perspective, as historians Cathy N. Davidson and Jessamyn Hatcher have noted, "is a metaphor that has been used by scholars to describe a historically constituted ideology of gender relations that holds that men and women occupy distinct social, affective, and occupational realms. According to the separate spheres metaphor, there is a public sphere inhabited by men and a private sphere that is in the domain of women." A number of historians have characterized antebellum women such as Emily Austin as existing within spheres of responsibility and action different from those experienced by the men in their society, centering mostly on domestic concerns. This perspective was pervasive during Emily's own lifetime. "Many early nineteenth-century southerners, like their northern contemporaries," Cynthia A. Kierner reminds us, "celebrated the ideal of sexually defined 'separate spheres,' which gave men exclusive access to the public world outside the home while endowing women with special moral authority and influence within it." A detailed analysis of Emily Austin, however, belies the model of separate spheres as a metaphor for understanding her life as a southern woman of the elite class. She was active, involved, and fully engaged in the world around her on her own terms. Emily's concerns as such were "intimately intertwined and mutually constitutive" with the men in her adult life.[6]

Moreover, Emily's experiences as a young widow, her subsequent partnership in a companionate marriage, her work as a plantation mistress, her legal status as the sole heir of her brother's estate, and the eventual financial independence created by that inheritance successively provided for continuing intersections between the private and the public. In these activities, Emily became adept at using her highly visible domestic existence as a platform from which to influence public concerns, especially during her marriage to James Perry. He was a willing supporter of her having a voice that reached beyond the quietness of domesticity. This was not entirely atypical for the time, most notably in the antebellum South. As historian Robert L. Griswold pointed out, many southern men from the planter class intertwined their lives with those of their wives in ways that negated the separate spheres. Perry, like other men of his era, took an active role in the household and the rearing of children, no doubt because he saw himself in a companionate relationship with his wife. "Marriage became less a union of families and more a bond of companionship between two people," Griswold noted of southern men, and "these sentiments carried over to father-child relations." For that reason, some historians believe that separate spheres in the antebellum South were not entirely immutable in the lives of plantation mistresses. Historian Joan E. Cashin is accurate when she contends that "white men and women led highly segregated lives in the antebellum South" and there existed a distinct women's culture in the region that stood apart from its male counterpart. Even so, a consideration of Emily Austin indicates that distinctiveness did not imply separation into a different sphere than the men in her life.[7]

This biography of Emily Austin owes a tremendous scholarly debt to a number of historical studies that deal with southern women, especially those who lived during the antebellum period. The notes upon which this biography rests contain many references to significant history books and interpretive articles that provide a conceptual foundation for viewing the life of Emily Austin. A considerable amount of this important historical literature is of relatively recent vintage, having been published over the last several decades. As historian Laura F. Edwards has noted, historical research and writing about the women of the South, starting in the early 1970s, "has grown from a small outpost in the subfield of southern history into a field of its own, complete with its own professional organization (Southern Association for Women Historians) and a triennial national conference." The portrait of Emily Austin that appears in the following pages is based on many of the interpretive underpinnings about southern women as characterized in these studies.[8]

This is the case regarding studies of elite women on southern plantations. It was as the work-a-day mistress of Peach Point Plantation that Emily Austin made her individual mark on history in concert with her planter husband, James F. Perry. They labored for almost twenty years on the land and in its household, fully participating in the antebellum world of the southern plantation. Two scholarly studies in particular inform the pages below. In many ways, Emily's life as an elite southern woman in antebellum Texas fits the patterns of plantation existence as described in Catherine Clinton's landmark study *The Plantation Mistress*. Although Clinton does not specifically address Emily Austin as an historical person, a number of women similar to Emily can be found in that volume, some of whom were likewise descended from families of power and prestige. In *Within the Plantation Household: Black and White Women of the Old South,* Elizabeth Fox-Genovese examines the gendered relationships that existed on the antebellum plantation. This study also provides a useful framework for examining Emily's life.[9]

Fox-Genovese points out an important distinction among white women of the plantation elite: "The terms 'woman' and 'lady' evoke mature female identity, but in different forms. 'Woman' suggests at once a more inclusive and more private female nature, whereas 'lady' evokes the public representation of that nature. To be a lady is to have a public presence, to accept a public responsibility." Not all plantation mistresses accepted such public responsibilities, but Emily Austin most certainly did. She was in every way a lady as described by Elizabeth Fox-Genovese. In large part, Emily's status as a lady during her adult life in Missouri and Texas depended on widespread public recognition that she was a member of the Moses Austin family. She clearly preferred to be perceived within that context rather than merely as the wife of her planter husband. Unlike many southern women of her class and family origins, Emily's prestige as an Austin consistently distinguished her as a member of the "first family" in any locality where she lived during adulthood. She fully embraced this public identity and, even as a married woman, often defined herself as the daughter of Moses Austin and the sister of Stephen F. Austin. Nonetheless, Emily alternately embraced the more private identity attached to the sphere of her husband as mistress of Peach Point Plantation. Hence, Emily's life serves as an object lesson in the manner by which elite southern women fashioned their own place within a male-dominated world. The historical perspective of household and family, balanced by her public persona as a member of the Austin family of Texas, yields a two-faceted point of reference for understanding the life of Emily Austin.[10]

CHAPTER 1 FRONTIER BEGINNINGS

Once a year on a Saturday morning in the early summer, over a hundred people gather in a small country churchyard located a few miles from where the Brazos River flows into the Gulf of Mexico on the coastal plain of Texas. They have done so for many decades and will most likely continue for years to come. These people have not gathered to worship at the small church, but instead to attend a family reunion. Some of them carry personal copies of a big red book that chronicles the genealogy of their family, with the occasional notation marking the birth and passing of relatives. A cemetery on the grounds, which lies a few steps beyond the church, was first used in August of 1833 when a child from this family died of cholera. The graveyard there remains an active place of burial today. Some of the attendees stroll quietly under the shade of massive trees that stand sentinel over hundreds of the graves before they greet each other at the reunion. Many of them first pause before the empty tomb of a man who died in 1836. That grave has been vacant since 1910 when officials of the state of Texas moved his remains to the State Cemetery in Austin. Nearby, another grave invariably attracts the respectful attention of those attending the annual reunion. It is the final resting place for the sister of the man whose grave is now empty. She has special meaning to those at the reunion, as almost everyone there has a direct tie to her as their common ancestor. She was Emily Margaret Brown Austin, who lived from 1795 to 1851. She was the daughter of Moses Austin and the sister of Stephen Fuller Austin, the man who once occupied the grave nearby. He now rests in a place of honor in the city that bears his name.[1]

The Gulf Prairie Presbyterian Church and its burial ground sit on a plot of land initially carved out of Peach Point Plantation, an agricultural enterprise founded by Emily and her husband James F. Perry in late 1832. The death of Emily's daughter Mary Elizabeth in August of the following year made the creation of the cemetery necessary. Today, descendants of Emily and James Perry still own the nearby plantation house at Peach Point, rebuilt early in the twentieth century after hurricanes destroyed most of the original residence. Only one wing of the 1830s-era home remains. It contains the historic rooms that served as the office and bedchamber of Emily's bachelor brother, Stephen F. Austin. He made his official residence with his sister's family and considered Peach Point to be his home. The group of descendants that gathers from across the nation each year on the church grounds calls itself the Austin/Bryan/Perry family. They come from all walks of life, have diverse histories, and represent a cross section of people who define what it means to be Texan and to be American.[2]

The woman they honor, Emily Margaret Brown Austin, was a child of the westward-moving Anglo-American frontier. Emily was born to Moses and Maria Brown Austin on June 22, 1795, at a fledgling village nestled in the shadow of Virginia's western mountains. It was named Austinville by her father. He founded the town in anticipation that it would become a commercial center for the small lead mining district in western Virginia. Only twenty-five years earlier, the region had seen the tramping of American rebels who helped win independence from Great Britain while opening the Ohio River Valley to settlement. Emily Austin eventually followed the paths blazed by the expansive frontier folk who went on to settle the Mississippi Valley and Gulf Coast during the early nineteenth century.[3]

Hence, the life that began for Emily Austin in the foothills of Virginia was one of great diversity and constant growth. She traveled westbound rivers to new lands and a series of homes in Spanish Louisiana, American Missouri, and finally Texas, where she lived from the Mexican era, through the years of the Republic, and into the period of antebellum statehood. Emily undertook all of these travels within the context of her large and extended family. Much of her adult personality was influenced by the fact that she was a member of a family that included strong-willed and active people who made enduring marks on the history of their era. Emily's family seemed to specialize in entrepreneurial men such as her father, Moses, and brother Stephen F. Austin, along with the two men who would become her husbands, James Bryan and James F. Perry. Four of her sons lived to adulthood, each of them making important historical contributions. All of these exceptional men had grand vision and earned widespread recognition during times of rapid westward expansion. Emily learned to hold her own place among them.

Emily Austin's pride in her family constituted an important part of her worldview. She learned about their extended American genealogy as a girl and proudly communicated it to her own children. The Austins had a long heritage deeply rooted in the British colonial experience in North America. John Winthrop's Massachusetts Bay Colony had been established less than a decade when the first members of the Austin clan came from England to take up residence. Richard Austin had no way of knowing that his arrival in the Bay Colony during July of 1638 would begin the establishment of a family line that produced scores of descendants, including Emily Austin, born four generations later. Richard's son Anthony manifested the peripatetic nature that characterized many of the Austins. Upon reaching manhood, he settled in the town of Suffield, Massachusetts, which became part of Connecticut in 1749 when the two colonies adjusted their border. There Anthony met and married Esther Hudgins in 1664 and built a home that stands today. He and Esther had three sons who carried on the family line. Of these, Richard, who was born in 1666, became Emily's great-grandfather.[4]

Emily's grandfather, Elias Austin, grew up surrounded by numerous brothers and sisters, many of whom started families during the years of his childhood and adolescence. By the 1740s, at least a dozen Austin households existed in Suffield, creating an impressive enclave of over sixty relatives. In 1743, on the day of his twenty-fifth birthday, Elias purchased a town lot in the village of Durham, Connecticut, some forty miles to the south. He began his own family there in 1746 when he married Eunice Phelps of Suffield, a young woman he presumably knew while growing up. Their youngest child would become well known to American history and one day be Emily's father. He was Moses Austin, born on October 4, 1761, in a bedroom of the home in Durham.[5]

Moses Austin spent his childhood in the Durham house before making his way in the world as a fifteen-year-old business apprentice in his older brother-in-law's general store, located in a neighboring Connecticut town. Becoming a merchant in his own right, Moses moved to Philadelphia in his early twenties and worked in his brother Stephen's mercantile business. He was filled with ambition and grand designs for future success. A personable young man, Moses attracted the attention of Philadelphia's better families, especially their daughters. This proved to be the case for Maria Brown, whose first name was pronounced in the English manner, as "Ma-rye-ah," after the fashion of the day. She would become Emily's mother. Moses and Maria met in one of the city's salons and soon developed a romantic relationship. Maria was several years younger, having been born on January 1, 1768, in New Jersey. She was the oldest child of Abia and Margaret Sharp Brown, the latter of whom descended from the Sharp family that arrived in the area with William Penn. Maria's first American ancestor on her father's side, Abraham Brown, had been an original patentee of Monmouth County, New Jersey. The Browns were all of Quaker stock, although Maria lived her life as an Episcopalian. For Emily and her brothers, the combined parental heritage of Puritan New England and Quaker New Jersey fostered an ingrained austerity, a solid work ethic, and a lifelong suspicion of frivolity. Emily in particular displayed a seriousness and intensity in all her endeavors, something that could also be seen in her older brother, Stephen.[6]

After a proper courtship, Maria Brown married Moses Austin in a grand ceremony at the Anglican parish of Philadelphia's Christ Church on September 8, 1785. The young couple formed a bond that carried them through the trials, hardships, joys, and satisfactions of almost four decades of life as husband and wife. Their marriage provided far more than a foundation for an extended family of descendants; upon it rested the expansion of the nation itself. Together, Moses and Maria materially assisted in pushing the lines of American settlement westward. True to the Austin family tradition of action and activity, Moses was eager to start his new life with Maria. On the day following their wedding, they moved to Richmond, Virginia. There he cast about for new mercantile ventures while Maria began their domestic existence, one saddened over the ensuing years by the loss of two infants. Moses' driving ambition for financial success eventually carried him beyond Richmond's limited mercantile economy. After a few years in the Virginia capital, he found a more lucrative business possibility in the New River Valley, located approximately 250 miles to the west on the frontier line. That area had become the center of a small lead mining and smelting industry several decades earlier. Lead mining intrigued Moses Austin as a possible avenue to wealth.[7]

During the summer of 1789, Moses left Maria at their home in Richmond and made a trip to the New River mines to assess their potential for development. This was the couple's first separation since their wedding. While he journeyed to the mines, Maria wrote one of the few surviving letters to her husband, telling him that she was "continuously tortured with distressing reflections of one kind or another." She wrote that "at this moment I am thinking of the absurdity of looking for happiness in this world, when in fact there is no such thing to be found." She continued by observing that "adversity and misfortune we are taught to expect on our passage through life." Maria's letter displayed a melancholy state of mind that was reflected from time to time in her own children. It was not pathological, but the adult correspondence of Emily and her brothers—especially Stephen— routinely manifested a measure of self-pity that often did not seem justified by the circumstances of their lives. Such a state of mind may well have come from their mother if Maria's 1789 letter to Moses serves as an accurate indication of her personal perspective on life, even if it was only transitory. Maria's unhappiness after losing two children, coupled with Moses' desire for a more promising business venture, may have yielded unspoken motives for the Austins' move west to the frontier. By early the next year, Moses was engaged in full-scale development of the lead mines.[8]

By late 1790, Moses Austin supervised some sixty men working at the mines. His financial successes convinced him to establish a formal settlement on the New River. Although people had been living in the vicinity for almost thirty years, there had never been an organized town at the mines. Moses therefore founded the town of Austinville, named appropriately for his family. He applied to the United States Post Office for an official designation, and it was speedily granted. Charles Austin, the son of Moses' brother Stephen, moved to Austinville as the town's first postmaster. Moses constructed houses, stores, shops, and other buildings to sell to those moving to the new town. Most houses and businesses clustered around the lead furnace located on the south side of the river. Several side streets branched at right angles from Main Street, which ran uphill perpendicularly from the river to the furnace. Moses built his own home nearby on a hill that provided a commanding presence over the town. This house was the place of Emily Austin's birth several years after its construction.[9]

It was at Austinville that Moses and Maria once again started their family after the loss of two infants in Richmond. Maria bore a son on November 3, 1793. They named him Stephen after Moses' brother, giving him the middle name Fuller to honor the man in whose home Maria lived during her adolescent years. "Relatively little is known of the domestic environment in which Stephen F. Austin lived for the first few years of his life," biographer Gregg Cantrell wrote of the years at Austinville. It is nonetheless safe to assume that Stephen had a satisfactory childhood. "The early part of my life," he recalled years later, "was spent happily in the quiet enjoyments of home." Just before his second birthday, a younger sister, Emily Margaret Brown Austin, joined Stephen in the household. By all accounts, it was a happy family circle and she became a welcome part. Maria attended to her growing family with love and devotion. Driven by ambition and the desire to amass a fortune, Moses left the concerns of child rearing to his wife and was minimally present in the daily lives of his children. This pattern of paternal involvement held true for the rest of Moses' life. Moses, at the least, was a good provider for his family. Emily's birth came at a time when Austinville was beginning to prosper. The town had a general store, several taverns, a pottery, and the lead smelter, along with a gristmill, clothing store, and hat shop. Moses operated a commercial ferry service across the New River that provided regular contact with areas to the east and west of the town. Austinville was also an agricultural center since local residents raised most of the food they consumed. It was here that Emily learned to walk and observe the world beyond the confines of her family home. She also first encountered the institution of slavery at Austinville, although she might have been too young to understand its nature or the implications that it would have for her life. Moses had purchased a house servant while living in Richmond, and he bought several additional slaves to work in the mines at Austinville. As historian David Gracy II noted of Moses by the early 1790s, "Austin had adopted the ways of the Southern upper class as his own." These southern viewpoints, especially regarding slavery, shaped the lives of his children as well.[10]

The natural beauty of Austinville and its vicinity had a profound impact on Emily during her early childhood. For the remainder of her life, she had an appreciation for flowers and the splendor of nature. She excelled in creating gardens throughout her adult years and marked her passage through the western frontier by planting a considerable number of trees. No image of Austinville remains from the specific years of Emily's life there, but one landscape painting does exist from the early nineteenth century. It shows Austinville as viewed from the north, looking across the New River southward to the lead smelters. In this bucolic scene, a winding tree-lined road meanders down to the river, passing well-maintained homes and farms. Cattle and other livestock shade themselves in verdant pastures. Across the river, the neat buildings of Austinville, some of them several stories high, are nestled against a high bluff that formed the southern boundary of the New River Valley.[11]

As a toddler in Austinville, Emily found herself surrounded by her immediate family and various relatives. In addition to her older cousin Charles Austin, the local postmaster, her father influenced others from the extended Connecticut family to settle at the mines. James Austin, an older cousin, moved to the town and served as bookkeeper for the family mining company. Emily's uncle by marriage, Moses Bates, also

Austinville, Virginia, Emily's birthplace. Courtesy of Archives Department,
Wytheville Community College Library, Virginia.

came to Austinville with his children. One of them, Elias Bates, who
was an adult, served as Moses' chief assistant at the mines and in the
smelter. In this atmosphere of family and rural splendor, Emily began to
form some of her basic values, especially what would become a lifelong
commitment to religion and matters of faith. Maria Austin ensured the
religious development of her children in spite of Austinville's isolated
location. She insisted, for example, that Stephen and Emily were
baptized, although Moses probably did not have strong feelings on the
matter. The historical record does not note the denomination of the
minister who performed these baptisms. It was most likely an Anglican
clergyman, as ministers from that denomination routinely traveled the
Virginia countryside, in some cases founding tiny "chapels of ease"
where communicants could regularly say morning and evening prayers

without clergy. Baptism in the Episcopal Church remained consistent with Maria Austin's staunch Anglicanism. Like many devout Anglicans of that era, Maria may have led her children in daily devotions from the *Book of Common Prayer* and read them the Jacobean beseechments from the Rite of Evensong at the close of day. Emily would prefer to participate in Episcopal worship for the remainder of her life, although she lived far from an Episcopal parish during many of her subsequent years.[12]

By the time Emily reached her second birthday, prospects for long-term financial success had begun to evade Moses at the lead mines. Profits declined while the bills mounted. He accordingly turned his attention to potentially lucrative lead mines located far to the west in Spanish Louisiana. This area was initially settled by the French, who established towns at Cahokia, Kaskaskia, and Ste. Genevieve on the Mississippi River. It became Spanish territory after the American Revolution. Moses apparently read a description of these mines written by a Frenchman named Pierre de Hault de Lassus, who noted, "There is in this country a great quantity of iron, lead and copper ores." In December of 1797, armed with letters of recommendation to several Spanish officials in the region, Moses Austin left his wife and young family in order to visit the lead mining district of Upper Louisiana. Once at Ste. Genevieve, he signed an agreement with the Spanish commandant to develop the mines in return for a grant of land in the vicinity.[13]

Moses Austin hastened back to Virginia to close his affairs at the New River mines and make preparations to relocate. A new life was beginning for Emily. She and her family were about to embark on her first great adventure to a home in Spanish territory south of St. Louis, a region then known as Upper Louisiana. Moses crafted elaborate plans for moving his family and a large group of settlers from Austinville to the new enterprise in the West. He busily collected supplies, purchasing some $6,400 in goods for the journey. Rather than go by land along the Wilderness Road as he had done on his recent trip to inspect the mines, Moses decided to travel down the inland waterways of the Ohio and Mississippi Rivers. This would be an easier trip for Maria, Stephen, and Emily. Their projected route began at a boatyard on the Kanawha River. They would travel on flatboats down the Kanawha to the Ohio and continue to its junction with the Mississippi. They planned to follow the "Father of Waters" northwest to Ste. Genevieve. Maria and the children would stay there temporarily while Moses continued his journey inland to Mine á Breton to make preparations for the family's permanent home. During May 1797, Moses and Maria supervised the transfer by wagon of their household goods, personal possessions, and supplies to the boatyard on the Kanawha. No doubt these preparations excited Stephen and Emily, who, although too young to have a firm concept of what was happening in their lives, certainly understood that great changes were in store for them.[14]

Finally, on June 8, 1798, all preparations were completed. The traveling party left the mines of the New River Valley at Austinville and embarked on their journey to fresh prospects in Upper Louisiana. Almost three years of age, Emily found herself seated in a carriage and on her way to a new life. In addition to Moses, Maria, Stephen, and Emily, several relatives, including the family of Moses Bates, traveled with the group. Both the Austin and Bates families took approximately a dozen of their slaves with them. Furthermore, many of Moses' employees from Austinville decided to join him in this new venture. A total of fifty people and nine heavily loaded wagons left that day for the Upper Louisiana mining country. In some respects, this was no ordinary expedition of common frontier folk. Maria and her children traveled in a formal coach drawn by four horses, a relatively regal conveyance not normally used by westward-moving migrants. They arrived at the boatyard without incident, loaded their possessions onto the flatboats Moses had engaged for the trip, and floated down the Ohio River to the great Falls of the Ohio located at Louisville. This was Emily's first trip by boat, a mode of transportation she would employ many times throughout her life. Once at Louisville, the group marked the Fourth of July with a patriotic celebration. The trip proved unproblematic until they arrived at the Falls of the Ohio, a formidable obstacle that could not be navigated easily by boats loaded with cargo and people. The Austin party therefore stopped in the town, unloaded the cargo, and went downstream to calmer water, where they watched river pilots shoot their empty vessels through the falls. This must have been an interesting and exciting process for Emily and Stephen to witness. However, a tragic event indelibly fixed this moment in Emily's memory forever. Her cousin and playmate, young Henry Bates, fell into the water while the boats were coming through. He drowned in spite of the adults' valiant efforts to save him. This naturally sobered the entire group and no doubt prompted Maria Austin to keep a closer watch on her children. Once their shock and sadness had somewhat abated, the group continued the journey. Their trials, unfortunately, had not come to an end. Although the historical record fails to document exactly what happened to them, Henry Bates' mother and his brother Parson also died on the trip at some point after departing from the Louisville area. They most likely succumbed to illness in the vicinity of Kaskaskia. Moses Austin later recorded that sickness, probably malaria, which was endemic in the region, struck at that time and all of them suffered badly from it during the rest of the journey. Most became ill after the flatboats moved down the Ohio and made their northwesterly turn into the Mississippi, where they began the upstream voyage to their destination. All the travelers arrived at Ste. Genevieve "sick and debilitated" during September. Some were too weak to walk ashore unassisted.[15]

Moses found lodging for Maria, Emily, and Stephen in Ste. Genevieve. They would live there for almost a year before following him to Mine á Breton, as Moses did not want his family to move to the mines until he had built a suitable home for them. Hence, the sleepy river town founded several decades earlier by the French became Emily Austin's first home in Upper Louisiana. Ste. Genevieve on the Mississippi served as an agricultural center for the area while providing a convenient point of access for miners traveling to and from the lead mining districts located some thirty miles inland. It must have seemed an interesting place to Emily and Stephen, even though they were little more than toddlers. The center of Ste. Genevieve consisted of a main street that paralleled the Mississippi, with minor streets intersecting at right angles from the landed side of the town. A new church had been built in 1794, along with a small fort for protection. Most of the buildings lined the banks of a creek that flowed from the hills down to the Mississippi. Although Ste. Genevieve had a central square, many of its haphazardly placed homes

Emily's home in Ste. Genevieve, Missouri.
Courtesy of the the Brazoria County Historical Museum.

were not oriented to the street grid. Visitors to the town immediately noticed its "helter-skelter" and "ad hoc" atmosphere.[16]

Maria, Emily, and Stephen found the town to be different from what they had experienced in Virginia. Many, if not most, of the people spoke French. The houses were built in the French style, rectangular with broad porches, and were frequently raised off the ground on stilts. They had thatched roofs, wattle and dab walls, and were surrounded by wood palisade fences that obstructed all view of them from the street. Perhaps more unusual to the Austins was the fact that, following the French and Spanish models of settlement, everyone lived in the town and not in the countryside. Local farmers walked each day in European fashion to the outlying fields and returned to town at night. The only church in Ste. Genevieve was the Roman Catholic parish, and everyone in the town belonged to it. Its priest was a person of great local importance. Maria and the children attended the Mass there, which, except for its Latin language, was liturgically similar to the Anglican services Emily's mother had known in Pennsylvania and Virginia. Emily surely noticed the relatively large number of slaves at Ste. Genevieve, as persons of bondage had a much greater presence there than in frontier Virginia. "Plantation slavery never developed in Missouri," historian Diane Mutti Burke noted, due to the area's relatively short growing season. Nonetheless, much of the lead mining and agricultural labor was accomplished by slaves. Within a short time, slave labor would become ubiquitous at Mine á Breton as well, because Moses Austin sought every possible advantage to turn a profit from his mining enterprises. Along with her extended circle of Austin family relations, slavery would be another constant presence in Emily's life. Indeed, there was never a time during which she did not have the labor of slaves available to her. It was at Ste. Genevieve that, as a toddler, Emily most likely recognized slaves as persons of bondage with a different social status and began her personal reconciliation with the institution.[17]

As Maria, Emily, and Stephen settled into their temporary home, Moses shuttled between Ste. Genevieve and his holdings at Mine á Breton. As had been the case at Austinville, Moses left the child rearing to his wife and threw himself vigorously into work at the mines. Within a few months, he was routinely sending wagonloads of lead ingots to Ste. Genevieve, where they were loaded on boats for shipment down the river to markets at New Orleans and along the Atlantic Coast. Moses had been working at the mines for only a few months when he was struck by a bad case of the "bilious fever," which incapacitated him. This gave Stephen and Emily the happy opportunity to spend more time with their father while he recuperated at Ste. Genevieve. This was not the first time, nor would it be the last, that illness intervened as Moses worked under the great strain of his various business ventures. These intermittent illnesses, trying as they were to his stamina, seldom derailed him for long. Such was the case for this illness at Ste. Genevieve in 1798. After several months of recuperation, Moses was heartened to learn that the grand home he had been constructing for his family at Mine á Breton was ready for them. He promptly named his new residence Durham Hall in honor of his

Durham Hall, the Austin home in Potosi, Missouri.
Courtesy of the the Brazoria County Historical Museum.

birthplace in Connecticut. This home was certainly the finest structure built at that time by an Anglo-American settler west of the Mississippi River. The solid two-story edifice sat on a large rock foundation with a stone wall surrounding the front elevation. It was located on a bluff overlooking the area, giving it a stately presence when seen from the smelter district that lay to the south across a creek. The home eventually boasted some twenty rooms with a formal porch graced by high columns. As a concession to the demands of frontier life during that era, Durham Hall had stone parapets and gun ports to protect against possible attacks.[18]

The Austin family moved to Durham Hall in June of 1798. It would remain Emily's home until her marriage, except for several periods when she was attending boarding school in the East. Four years old at the time, a relative later characterized Emily as a "brown haired and delicately featured" child who was "naturally slight and not too tall." She was quiet, respectful, and overshadowed by her vocal and sometimes demanding mother. Many traits of her childhood physical appearance stayed with Emily into adulthood. A portrait from late middle age showed her to have been a very thin woman with finely delineated facial features, and her coloring retained a darkish cast even after she turned gray as an elderly person.[19]

The move to Durham Hall marked the start of a period of stability in Emily's life after her two early years at Austinville, the arduous journey across the western frontier to Upper Louisiana, and a year in the French atmosphere of Ste. Genevieve. For the time, her travels had come to an end. Emily would grow to womanhood in the lead country of Spanish Louisiana and witness it become American Missouri. The violent, hardscrabble frontier spirit of the Ozark Plateau mines and the ribald miners who lived in the lead country undoubtedly influenced Emily's personality, giving her a practicality and toughness that she subsequently called upon many times during her adult life. Durham Hall became the center of her world. There she amassed vivid memories from her early childhood, Indian attacks ranking chief among them. Hostile Osage Indians struck the mining settlements at Mine á Breton several times. Perhaps the most dangerous moment for the Austins came in May of 1802 when a party of Osage warriors attacked Durham Hall. The family, including six-year-old Emily, and nine men in Moses' employ took refuge behind the brick walls of the home, where they withstood a direct assault. The decisive factor that saved the Austin family and drove the Indians away that day was the vigorous, noisy firing of a three-pound canon Moses had mounted on the front parapet. These attacks by hostile Indians were not the only violent events that Emily remembered from Durham Hall. The small mining settlement had a rough-and-tumble atmosphere since it tended to attract an unruly and ungovernable element. Some of these residents proved to be a problem for the Austins. The construction of Durham Hall provoked disaffected French miners who believed that Moses Austin's land grant had cheated them out of their earlier holdings. As a result, when the family occupied the house, a recalcitrant group of French residents built rude huts across the road in protest. These squatters sometimes made threatening gestures to Emily, Stephen, and their parents when they passed in their carriage, occasionally blocking the road. In addition, a rival miner constructed a crude lead smelter near Durham Hall that often belched smoke and foul odors into the house. Eventually Moses mollified the protesters, bringing peace and quiet to the neighborhood.[20]

These experiences with the French miners convinced Moses to found an Anglo-American settlement north of the creek to counterbalance the rowdy Gallic settlement at Mine á Breton. This became the town of Potosi, which Austin named in honor of the rich mining settlement in Spain's Viceroyalty of Rio de la Plata in South America. Within a year, he constructed a sawmill, distillery, blacksmith shop, and a small shot factory at Potosi, thus beginning the process of neutralizing the older French settlement. One observer would later characterize Potosi as a village "pleasantly situated in the center of the mining district. Built to a better style than the villages in the county generally, it has a thriving appearance, and contains several handsome edifices." Most of the people who settled in Potosi were Anglo-American migrants. As more of them arrived, the residents of Potosi quickly constituted a small but close-knit community. A number of these families would be associated with the Austins for many decades to come, both in the lead country of Missouri and later in Texas. By the time Emily approached in age the end of her first decade, she lived in a well-defined, English-speaking neighborhood. Down the road from Durham Hall and across the creek lived the Perry family, who operated a general store. William Ashby resided close by and ran a small gunpowder factory near the home of Andrew Hagan and his family. Ashby and Hagan would later go into business together and reap great riches from trading on the Oregon Trail. Another neighbor on the Mine á Breton side of the creek was Pedro Vidal, a French miner who knew Emily during her childhood years. Vidal would help develop the Santa Fe Trail. John Rice Jones, one of Moses' business partners in the development of the lead mines, also lived nearby with his three sons. Emily knew them at Ste. Genevieve before they moved to the mining district. Jones, a native Welshman, earned degrees in both law and medicine prior to migrating to America. His sons became playmates for Emily and Stephen. One of them, John Rice Jones Jr., later followed the Austins to Texas and settled in Brazoria County near Emily's future home at Peach Point Plantation. These were the people inhabiting Emily Austin's childhood world. She and her brother often walked down the main street of the mining district to visit them. The local residents called this dusty thoroughfare Barefoot Street, a fanciful name that no doubt

Potosi, Missouri, in 1819. Durham Hall is the large home with the portico in the upper right.

captured the attention of young children such as Emily and Stephen. This street ran parallel to the creek on the other side from Durham Hall. The Austin children reached Barefoot Street by way of a bridge that Moses constructed. They often crossed it when walking to the Austin smelter to visit their father. And, if they were like children of other eras, they enjoyed playing in the rocks and crags of the creek bed under its sheltering arch. It was this bridge to Barefoot Street that at stood at the center of young Emily's childhood universe.[21]

Potosi therefore became a pleasant, stable town and a far more sedate settlement than the Austins encountered at Mine á Breton on their initial arrival. By 1808, Potosi had two gristmills, a sawmill, a small school, and several stores and churches. The Austins directly prospered from the growth of the lead mines and the civic expansion of Potosi. The family circle increased again on October 3, 1803, when a brother joined young Stephen and Emily. He was named James Elijah Brown Austin, and the family thereafter affectionately called him Brown. Lacking an Episcopal church, Maria had the newborn baptized in the

Roman Catholic parish in Ste. Genevieve. Brown Austin's birth marked the start of a new era for the family, as several months later they became aware of a momentous political event that touched all of their lives: the Louisiana Purchase. By the stroke of a diplomat's pen at negotiations thousands of miles away, the Austins once again became citizens of the United States.[22]

Thus, by the time she was nine years of age, Emily Margaret Brown Austin was very familiar with the expanding frontier. Born on the western fringes of the Virginia settlement line, she had floated the Ohio and Mississippi Rivers to upper Spanish Louisiana, which was now becoming known as Missouri. Her childhood years witnessed the transition from a rough frontier to the relatively stable existence of a growing town. Nonetheless, from the more genteel perspective of Maria Austin, her three young children lived on the unrefined edge of civilization. Maria considered herself a person of good breeding, refined tastes, and respectable social standing. She had known the drawing rooms of Pennsylvania society as a girl in Philadelphia and led a life closely linked to the educated business establishment. As a teenager, Maria Brown once attended a Philadelphia reception where she was presented formally to George Washington. For the rest of her life, she treasured the set of silver shoe buckles she wore on that occasion. It is not surprising that even in the Missouri mining towns, Maria Austin manifested an aristocratic bearing and an air of exalted social status. She was never completely at home on the frontier. In contrast, Moses Austin seemed a warm, gregarious person and attracted great loyalty from many people who came into contact with him. The inveterate traveler Henry Schoolcraft wrote of a visit to Potosi, "Mr. Austin was a gentleman of general information, easy and polite manners, and enthusiastic character. He was a man of very dedicated enterprise, inclined to the manner of the old-school gentleman. His family has been from an early day the first and important of civilization in the country." The Austin parents clearly saw themselves as leaders in a frontier aristocracy with a duty to set the example for more plebian residents at Potosi. They communicated such a viewpoint to Emily and her brothers. This concept of familial place was not entirely inaccurate since the Austins were in fact the "first family" of Potosi, as they had been in Austinville. Emily, until she went away to boarding school, had lived all but one year of her life—the time at Ste. Genevieve—in towns founded by her father. Given these orientations of class and status, it was not surprising that Moses and especially Maria wanted their children to attend boarding schools in the East, as opposed to the small school at Potosi. The family's economic success made this course of action possible, while Maria's social predilections demanded it. Stephen F. Austin was the first of the children to leave home when his parents enrolled him at the Bacon Academy in Connecticut.[23]

Moses and Maria then turned their attention to the matter of Emily's schooling. They decided that their daughter should also attend boarding school, although she was only nine years of age, soon to celebrate her tenth birthday. This decision was typical for the era among well-to-do families who lived in the South, of which southeastern Missouri was culturally a part. One historian of southern women noted, "Elite southern families valued their daughter's education highly," especially in the arts and classics. The female academy movement swept the South in the generation after the American Revolution, making the Austins' desire to send Emily away to school very much in vogue with the times. The Austins chose a school located in Lexington, Kentucky, operated by Mary Messier Beck, one of the more accomplished artists and educators on the frontier. Lexington proved to be a convenient choice because it was one of the larger towns west of the Appalachians and could be easily reached from Missouri. The Austin family had connections there. Maria journeyed to Lexington to enroll Emily at Mrs. Beck's School, as the establishment was known formally. The young girl traveled with her mother from Ste. Genevieve down the Mississippi, up the Ohio, and on to Louisville, passing the spot where her cousin had drowned on the family's earlier trip to Missouri. From there, they went by stagecoach to Lexington, and Maria left Emily at the school. Mary Beck would have a profound and enduring impact on the young girl, particularly in awakening her to the arts, literature, and high culture. Beck and her husband had cosmopolitan backgrounds unique to the early Kentucky frontier. Born in England, Mary Messier was the daughter of a Member of Parliament. George Beck, a recognized artist in England who studied with the accomplished British landscape painter Richard Wilson, married Mary Messier in 1786. Mary was a budding artist herself, having shown her paintings at London's Royal Academy during 1790 and 1791. One friend described her as a woman "accomplished in mind, inspired in reciprocity of taste and sentiment." Mrs. Beck attempted to instill these characteristics in her pupils, including Emily.[24]

Emily found that her new schoolmistress had definite ideas about what constituted progressive education for young ladies. "The moral parts," Beck noted about her curriculum, "must begin with the first rudiments and be controlled in such a manner as to instruct the feelings, excite the curiosity, and awaken sympathy, benevolence, and generosity." Mary Beck stressed the arts and music. Emily excelled at playing the piano, and for the remainder of her life, she never lived in a home without one. Beck and her teachers also offered instruction in science, logic, and history, subjects that were not routine staples in the education of young women during that era. One of Emily's favorite teachers was Charlotte Minnelli, who, several years later, opened a female academy in Lexington where Mary Todd Lincoln studied as a young girl. A highlight of Mary Beck's academic program was the public recitation and performance in which her pupils participated twice a year. Prominent Kentuckians, including Henry Clay, served as judges at these exhibitions. Emily participated on a regular basis between 1805 and 1808, judged by Senator Clay and other luminaries. Emily's mother visited Lexington periodically, and it may be that she also attended these public recitations.[25]

Although no student record remains regarding Emily's individual progress at the school, it can be inferred that she participated in the entire curriculum, especially music courses. Her time as a student at Mrs. Beck's markedly refined her personal tastes regarding the arts, music, and literature. The public declamations in which she participated undoubtedly helped to mitigate any childhood shyness. As an adult, Emily would have a confident and plainspoken manner. She remained a student at Mrs. Beck's for almost three years, during which time she traveled back and forth between Lexington and Potosi for holidays and visits with her family.[26]

As Emily entered her adolescent years, the Austins determined that she should return home permanently in order to save money for Stephen's educational expenses, as he had enrolled at Transylvania University in Lexington. Emily thus returned to live at Durham Hall in late 1808 or early 1809, and there she would remain for the next three years. An attractive and vivacious young woman, it can be assumed that these were happy and satisfying times for her. "It is likely that many a boy and girl affair," recalled one of Emily's descendants, "sprung up through the various hospitalities of Durham Hall." One of the individuals who began calling with increasing frequency was a young man named James Bryan. Emily quickly developed a special fondness for him, but Moses and Maria did not approve of their growing romantic relationship. They worried that twenty-year-old James might be too old for their daughter, who was fifteen at the time. In addition, Maria Austin most likely had marital aspirations for Emily much grander and socially prestigious than someone such as James Bryan, a young merchant plying his way in the rural lead belt of Missouri.[27]

As the months passed, the romantic bond between Emily and James became increasingly visible to everyone at Durham Hall. Emily played an active role in encouraging affection from him. Many girls of that era had a firm belief in the concept of romantic love and assumed that it was in a "marriage based on romantic love that individuals would discover their true selves and find true happiness." William Bryan, James' brother who often visited Potosi on business, squarely put responsibility for the relationship on Emily's shoulders when he penned a letter of advice to James. "As to your going to get a wife I would think of that a while first," he wrote. "She talks of getting you; if she is for getting, I would be for quitting, for a wife is a thing easy to get any time." William's counsel to cool the growing relationship apparently did not dissuade James, nor did the opposition of Emily's parents. That may have been, in part, because Moses Austin did not have an unfavorable opinion of James Bryan as a person and local businessman. The elder Austin seemed to like him in most ways, except for the possibility that he might become a son-in-law. James Bryan did have impressive business and family connections for a young man on the Missouri frontier. He was descended from William Bryan, a successful English businessman who migrated to Bucks County, Pennsylvania, in the early eighteenth century. William's son Guy, in turn, opened a mercantile house in Philadelphia during the 1760s and, after the American Revolution, became one of the most prosperous merchants in the city. In 1790, Guy Bryan decided to open trade with the expanding western areas, especially along the Ohio and Mississippi Rivers. He took as his partner in this venture a brother-in-law, William Morrison. Bryan and Morrison opened several frontier stores in the upper Mississippi Valley during the first decade of the nineteenth century. In 1806, they decided to establish a lead mine and store somewhere in the district around Potosi. They bought land along a small creek known as Hazel Run, which flowed into the Bonne Terre Creek and eventually into Big River northwest of Ste. Genevieve. Bryan and Morrison sent their teenage nephew, James Bryan, to this new establishment at Hazel Run to take charge of mining operations and operate the general store. "It was a good place for a store," one modern commentator noted of Hazel Run, since "the land was for the most part high and healthy, well watered, and well timbered." James already had experience in the mining districts, having worked for a year or two at Bryan and Morrison's Ste. Genevieve branch.[28]

James Bryan selected a home site on the sloping west bank of Hazel Run, approximately a quarter mile north of where it flowed into the larger Bonne Terre Creek. He built a house that overlooked a peaceful valley surrounded by a bucolic countryside, and he later constructed a small dam that powered a water wheel. He located good lead-ore-bearing deposits several miles to the north and soon set miners to work digging mining pits. James began making business trips to other towns in the area, including Potosi, where he met Moses Austin and sold him supplies for the mine and smelter. Emily, having returned from school in Lexington, likely met James Bryan on one of these business visits, although history fails to pinpoint the time and place of their first meeting. The rhythm of life in the area surely provided many opportunities for this to have occurred. Merchants and mine owners routinely traveled throughout the lead country. Surviving correspondence from a number of families indicates that they often visited one another in the various settlements, as well as in the river towns such as Ste. Genevieve. Bryan's visits to Durham Hall had become routine by the time Emily reached her sixteenth birthday.[29]

Emily's burgeoning romantic feelings for James Bryan began a period of great change in her life. Born to live a life of privileged status as the beneficiary of all that her hardworking parents could provide, she had an orthodox upbringing designed to prepare her for becoming an upper-class wife and mother. Family relationships existed at the center of her universe. "A dense web of family ties eased young women's passage into adulthood," historian Laura F. Edwards noted, and "extended families served as a vital social and economic support system." Within this context, Emily's childhood provided her with everything she needed to live at the pinnacle of her society. The coming years, however, would see drastic changes that made for something more difficult, and unanticipated events called her to tap deep wellsprings of strength in her character. Rather than becoming what her parents intended, Emily had a much harder future in store. She would have to deal with the eventual bankruptcy of the family, the dislocations caused by economic depression, and illness and death in her close familial circle. She was, on the surface of things, seemingly ill equipped by her education to deal with these coming hardships. Nonetheless, she would do so in an impressive and successful fashion. Her romance and eventual marriage to James Bryan while still an adolescent marked the point of her transition from a typical upper-class young woman to a self-sufficient person who would meet the tribulations of life on her own terms.[30]

CHAPTER 2 A MISSOURI MARRIAGE

While the relationship grew deeper between Emily and James Bryan, the Austin family's financial situation at Potosi began to change for the worse. Always short of cash and liquid resources, Moses suffered a series of business losses. In order to economize, Stephen left Transylvania University in the spring of 1810 and returned to Durham Hall, his years of formal education at an end. Falling lead prices and unanticipated expenses at the mines did nothing to improve the family's finances. Moses also became involved in heated controversies and feuds with other local miners and business people. Maria and the children sometimes found themselves the objects of harassment perpetrated by Moses' enemies. On one occasion in early 1811, the family was at Durham Hall when gunfire erupted outside on the road. As a rain of bullets shattered the windows of the mansion, everyone dove for cover. This experience must have reminded Emily of the similar Indian attacks and miner protests that had occurred at Durham Hall in her early childhood. Although no one was injured in this latest incident, Moses was understandably incensed and reacted with much complaining and vituperation directed at his enemies. In newspapers throughout the mid-Mississippi Valley, he offered a reward for the capture of the unknown assailants, but nothing ever came of it. In the months thereafter, Stephen became involved in the quarrelling. At one point, Maria warned her son that he should avoid being provoked into a fatal duel with a person she identified only as "WS," apparently a villain who had insulted Moses. Maria worried a good deal about this person doing harm to Stephen, and happily for her, the confrontation she feared never occurred.[1]

James Bryan, as Emily's suitor and as a local businessman, publicly stood by the Austin family during these controversies at Potosi. Bryan's resolve to support the Austins was no doubt bolstered by the fact that Stephen F. Austin liked him and the young men had come to consider each other friends. Moses and especially Stephen increasingly engaged in regular business dealings with James Bryan during 1810 and 1811, both at Hazel Run and Potosi. The younger Austin and Bryan became partners in several transactions involving the buying of supplies and the selling of lead, some of which may have been arranged during James' courting visits to Durham Hall. Moses clearly trusted Bryan as a merchant. As a sign of business confidence, he left James in charge of arranging the lead shipments for the Austin mines during an 1810 trip to New York City, where the elder Austin hoped to cultivate new business contacts.[2]

James Bryan must have been encouraged by the growing confidence that Emily's father and brother showed him at the time when his relationship with her was becoming serious. Family tradition, as perpetuated by Emily's descendants, holds that sometime in early 1811, James Bryan proposed marriage to Emily and that she eagerly accepted. Her mother did not approve of this and raised staunch objections to the relationship. Given that Moses and Stephen had favorable opinions of Bryan as a person and a businessman, Maria turned to a new objection, basing her concerns on what she felt was the Bryan family's lack of proper social standing in Philadelphia. They were not among the established elite of the city, she contended, and thus James was not socially suitable for Emily as a husband. This constituted an egregious case of grasping on her part since Uncle Guy Bryan was a wealthy and respected merchant there. Whatever the reality of the Bryan family's social situation, Maria Austin clearly had higher hopes for her daughter than marriage to James Bryan.[3]

In 1811, Maria decided to send Emily east to attend finishing school. This decision was no doubt prompted by her strong desire to separate sixteen-year-old Emily and twenty-one-year-old James, but there were additional reasons for it. Maria Austin was continually unhappy about living on the isolated and rude Missouri frontier, an existence about which she sometimes complained. As a young woman who had eagerly participated in the social whirl of late eighteenth-century Philadelphia, Maria never completely accustomed herself to the relative social deprivations of life at Austinville and Potosi. She badly missed her friends and family in Philadelphia, whom she had not visited since marrying Moses and moving to Richmond years earlier. By late 1811, her longstanding desire to visit back East was strengthened by the deteriorated state of her health. As was the case with Moses, she had recurring bouts of minor illness. In particular, she had recently experienced loss of weight and chronic muscle pain. A change of scenery and a visit to her family might improve her health. In addition, both Austin parents had begun to think about a proper education for their youngest son, Brown, who was born in 1803 at Potosi and had never been east. Therefore, during the late spring of 1811, the family made plans for Maria to travel. She would enroll Emily and Brown in boarding schools while Moses and Stephen remained in Missouri. Maria planned to be absent for a period of many months, if not over a year. She would visit her family in Philadelphia and the Austin relations in New Haven. These relatives would advise her on possible schools where Emily and Brown could enroll as boarding students. Moses engaged the services of Elijah Lewis, a relative who was then living at Potosi, to serve as chaperone to Maria, Emily, and young Brown. It was also Lewis' duty to superintend a shipment of lead and other goods that Moses was sending along with them, the sale of which in New York City would pay for the trip.[4]

All preparations had been made by May of 1811. Emily, Brown, and their mother left Missouri and traveled down the Mississippi to

New Orleans, catching a packet to the East Coast. They arrived at Baltimore. Maria and the children traveled north to Philadelphia, their first destination. Lewis continued to New York City, where he planned to sell the cargo, eventually reimbursing Maria with the funds from this transaction. Maria and the children took temporary lodgings at the home of her sister Rebecca in Camden, New Jersey, across the river from Philadelphia. This was Emily's first glimpse of the wider world of a major American city. The town of Lexington, Kentucky, of course, had a measure of urban substance compared to Potosi, but the Pennsylvania capital represented one of the most urbane and sophisticated places in the nation, if not the entire English-speaking world. Maria Austin proved to be well connected and well suited to give Emily a full appreciation of its civic benefits and urban wonders. Philadelphia's art museums, libraries, and musical performances must have made an enduring impression on Emily, who would visit the city many times in her adult life. Although Maria had planned to stay in Philadelphia with her sister—Emily's aunt—for only a short while, the weeks flowed into months, and the visitors from Missouri remained there for most of the summer. The outbreak of a contagion of fever finally convinced them to leave the Pennsylvania capital and travel to New Haven, where the Austin family relations lived. There the sea breezes of Long Island Sound might provide a more healthful climate than that of fever-ridden Philadelphia.[5]

Maria also wanted to visit New Haven because she, Emily, and Brown were running out of money. She hoped to collect funds from their traveling companion and relative, Elijah Lewis, who was living at New Haven and had, months earlier, supposedly sold in New York City the cargo they had brought from Missouri. Furthermore, the various members of the Austin family living in New Haven could serve as hosts for Maria and assist in finding appropriate schools for Emily and Brown. This reliance on family connections was a longstanding Austin tradition.

At every turn of their lives, Moses and his family sought to maintain connections with their extended network of relations. Maria's arrival at New Haven solidified what would be strong bonds of lifelong association between Emily and her Austin cousins, especially the children of Moses' brother Elisha. Emily never knew her uncle Elisha Austin, as he died in 1794. His involvement in maritime commerce with China had brought him great wealth, and as one historian noted, "it opened a new era in American trade with China and gave New Haven the chance to get ahead of other ports." Elisha's sudden death threw his family onto hard economic times, but by the time Emily arrived in New Haven with her mother and brother, most of the family's fortunes had been restored by Elisha's son, Henry Austin. He had achieved financial success as a merchant with his own trading house located in New York City.[6]

Cousin Henry Austin, who would later settle near Emily and her adult family in Texas during the 1830s, played a continuing role in her life for as long as he lived. Thirteen years older than Emily, he had first opted for a career at sea as a common sailor. In 1795, the year of Emily's birth, Henry signed aboard the brig *Neptune* for a voyage around the world. It was at this time that he met and befriended the older Elijah Lewis, who later became his stepfather. By the early 1800s, Henry had decided upon a career as a merchant. As part of his training for this occupation, he decided to visit his uncle Moses in Missouri during 1805. There he first met his younger cousins Stephen, Emily, and Brown. After a brief time in the lead country, where he took his commercial lessons from Moses to heart, Henry moved to New York City and opened a merchant house. This establishment served as the New York corresponding agent for the sale of considerable amounts of Missouri lead consigned to it by Moses Austin and other mine operators Henry had met during his sojourn at Potosi. By the time of Emily's arrival in Connecticut in 1811, Henry was so prosperous that he maintained a home in New Haven and one in

Manhattan, dividing his time between the two cities.[7]

In addition to Henry Austin, Emily reestablished herself on this trip to New Haven with another Austin relation who had earlier visited Missouri before returning to Connecticut: Timothy Phelps. By all accounts, he was a "lively, sociable man, who liked to be open-handed and free with his money." The Phelps home was considered to be one of the city's liveliest places of domestic entertainment for elite families. Built in an imposing style of filigree brickwork, his large, stately house and nearby stables faced the main green of New Haven just across from Yale College, near the corner of Church and Chapel Streets. A number of Phelps and Austin family members, along with their friends, could be found at the house on a daily basis. It was here that Maria and the children stayed upon their arrival in New Haven. Sixteen-year-old Emily clearly enjoyed the social excitement and entertainments available to her in the orbit of the Phelps household. She soon fell into a circle of young people and developed firm friendships with several girls her own age, continuing a gossip-filled correspondence with some of them for many years thereafter.[8]

It was also during this visit to New Haven that Emily came into prolonged contact with Henry's sister, her cousin Mary Austin Holley, the daughter of Elisha and Esther Austin. The two female cousins may have met at some earlier point in the past, although family correspondence does not record it. Eleven years older than Emily, Mary Austin had been born in 1784, attended New Haven schools, and become accomplished in the study of music and languages. She lived in the Timothy Phelps home after the death of her father, Elisha. It was there that she met young Horace Holley, then a Yale student. He eventually graduated with a ministerial degree. In January 1805, Mary Austin married Horace, who was recognized as a scholarly, dynamic young man full of potential. In 1808, the Reverend Horace Holley became the minister of the Hollis

Street Church, one of the largest and most prestigious Congregational pulpits in Boston, where he established himself as a person of great ministerial standing. Mary had an exuberant spirit and was a person of deep faith. She quickly developed a strong bond of kinship with her cousin during Emily's stay in the Phelps home. They seemed to have much in common in terms of their personalities, tastes, and interests. Both were very social individuals who enjoyed the company of others in formal and informal situations. They got along well and would do so for decades, although temporary quarrels and family disputes occasionally had a fleeting negative impact on their relationship as cousins.[9]

While Emily enjoyed the adolescent social whirl of New Haven, Maria Austin turned her motherly attention to enrolling both of her children in boarding school. These efforts had been hampered by the fact that Elijah Lewis had not given her the money from the sale of the Missouri goods, which, in truth, he had squandered. This infuriated Maria. Henry Austin, however, came to the rescue when he advanced her the needed funds. With this money now in hand, Maria placed Brown Austin in a school operated by an Episcopal minister, the Reverend Samuel Whittlesey, in Washington, Connecticut. After some investigation, Maria decided to enroll Emily in the Hermitage Academy in New York City, where she would be near Henry Austin's other home and major place of business. The academy was located in the Bowery section of lower Manhattan on the premises of a colonial manor house, the former home of a wealthy merchant who had lost his fortune. This grand house thereafter became a "dame school" for boarders and was renamed the Hermitage Academy, denoting the elegant nature of its location. A Miss Hall served as the lead teacher with several assistants, while all of their female pupils lived in the house.[10]

The curricular goals at the Hermitage corresponded closely with the Austin parents' sentiments regarding the sort of school in which their only daughter should enroll. Moses had precise desires about what he wished Emily to accomplish. In one of his first letters after she was settled in New York City, Moses showed himself to be a doting father who had Emily's best interests very much at heart. Education should be preparation for life, Moses wrote her. His advice seemed almost prosaic, as he acknowledged that "now is the time to examine well the things of nature and art." He also wrote "that all things in this life are under an all wise creator who has ordered all things to answer to his great intentions." The Hermitage Academy gave Emily full rein to develop herself into a cultivated young woman. She enjoyed the many opportunities for personal enrichment that New York City presented to a sixteen-year-old girl with pronounced interests in art, music, and culture. Students at the Hermitage Academy took full advantage of being in one of the most vibrant urban centers in the nation. Emily proved no exception, gaining a poise and air of sophistication that she would carry for the rest of her life. Yet the Hermitage Academy was an expensive place to study. The tuition alone ran $100 per session plus incidentals, an amount considerably larger than the total annual wages of many working people of that era.[11]

With her children's schooling arranged, Maria returned to her sister's home in Camden, New Jersey. Most of the time, she existed on funds borrowed from family and friends while she waited to receive money from Moses to make up for the funds squandered by Elijah Lewis. Maria attempted to economize but always found herself in financial distress, which was most often relieved by advances from Henry Austin. Hence, by the end of 1812, it was essential that Maria receive funds from home, especially to underwrite Emily's school expenses. Moses had completed the assembly of a new cargo and was ready to send Stephen from Missouri to New York City, where it would be sold through Henry Austin's mercantile house. The shipment consisted mostly of lead, along with other products of the area. Maria, however, could wait no longer for money from home. She made the decision to leave Philadelphia and withdraw Emily from the Hermitage Academy. They both returned to the Phelps home in New Haven and awaited the money from the anticipated sale of Stephen's cargo. Brown Austin would remain at the nearby boarding school under the care of Reverend Whittlesey until the day when Moses could pay his tuition and expenses. Henry Austin promised Maria that he would provide financially for their needs in New Haven until that money came to hand. Once back in Connecticut, Maria lived a much quieter life than she had previously enjoyed in the Pennsylvania capital. Emily quickly reentered the social life of the city's young people. Letters from some of these friends, written after she later returned to Missouri, were filled with gossip and ample news of their adolescent romances. The tone of these letters clearly indicated that by the summer of 1812, Emily had become a popular, self-directed, and active young woman who developed friendships happily and easily. Her decided social grace made her a natural confidant and one of the leaders of her social circle.[12]

Although the historical record fails to indicate if Emily forgot about James Bryan or not during her months in the East, events transpired that autumn that made this consideration moot. In late October, Maria received the surprising news by letter from Moses that James Bryan was traveling east. Ostensibly, he would be visiting his own relations in Philadelphia, but he was also coming to rescue Maria and Emily from their penury. The cargo that Stephen F. Austin had been bringing down the Mississippi foundered on the river above New Orleans when its barge struck a sandbar, and since the cargo had been uninsured, all was lost. There were no funds from Missouri to ease the honorable poverty in which Maria and Emily were living. After visiting his own Philadelphia relations, Bryan would escort both women back to Missouri while

Brown remained at his Connecticut school. By this time, Maria was ready to return to Missouri, so she found this news welcome. Moreover, she had changed her previously critical opinion of Bryan. Maria most likely came to accept James Bryan as Emily's intended husband because, having spent time in Philadelphia, she fully understood the prestige of his family connections there. The fact that Maria now had a good opinion of the Bryan family confirms the important role that family connections played for upper-class parents of the era in approving a daughter's fiancée. As historian Laura F. Edwards noted about families such as the Austins, parents wanted "respectability, social status, financial security, and mastery tempered by compassion" in the person of the intended husband. Romantic love was not enough in the eyes of most fathers and mothers from the elite class, although Emily and James had that as well. Maria's extended stay in Philadelphia had, at the least, convinced her that James Bryan's satisfactory social background, coupled with his own maturity, made him suitable for Emily. Moses agreed and was eager for Bryan to arrive in Philadelphia. Several times that fall, the elder Austin wrote polite and informative letters to Bryan, keeping him fully apprised of business events in Missouri. These letters seemed to reflect genuine affection and consideration for the young suitor.[13]

Bryan arrived in Philadelphia sometime during the mid-fall of 1812. He learned from friends there that Maria and Emily had gone to New Haven and that their financial situation was even more desperate. Bryan called them back to Philadelphia, and they eagerly greeted him as their savior. It appeared that the romantic ardor that James and Emily had for each other in Missouri had not diminished. More importantly, Maria now welcomed James Bryan's affection toward her only daughter. Ever the socially conscious matron, Maria Austin was particularly impressed with the polite attention paid to her by James' very wealthy and prominent uncle, Guy Bryan. Having won the support of the

Austin parents, Bryan once again made a formal proposal of marriage to Emily, who eagerly accepted this offer with her mother's approval. Emily and James decided that they would wait to marry in a formal ceremony until they returned to Potosi, so that most of their immediate family and mutual friends there could attend. That settled, Bryan remained in Philadelphia for a visit with his uncle Guy. In the meantime, Emily and her mother traveled to New York City on a shopping trip, where they bought a complete wedding trousseau for the bride-to-be, probably at the groom's expense. Several fine lace garments were among the purchases. These elegant and imported items, handmade by Swiss craftsmen, would eventually become treasured heirlooms in the hands of Emily's descendants.[14]

By the early spring of 1813, Bryan was ready to begin the trip back to Missouri with Maria and Emily. They left in March and took the Wilderness Road westward to Kentucky, where they embarked on the voyage down the Ohio and up the Mississippi. Moses and Stephen greeted their return to Missouri with great joy and enthusiasm, and Maria made plans for a formal wedding to be held at Durham Hall. Although family letters give no specific description of these festivities, family lore holds that the wedding of James Bryan and Emily Austin on August 13, 1813, constituted one of the most elegant affairs up to that point in the history of Potosi. As one descendant later noted, Maria and Emily were dressed in fashionable clothing "with more regard to the ladies' taste than the country where it would be worn." Emily's cousin James Austin performed the ceremony in his capacity as Justice of the Peace at Potosi, while a number of family members and friends signed the marriage certificate as witnesses, including Moses, Maria, Stephen, and James' brother William Bryan. The newlyweds decided to live at Durham Hall until Bryan could make ready appropriate lodgings for his bride at Hazel Run, still the location of his store and mining operation. Now happily married at age eighteen, Emily settled into a comfortable life as Mrs. James Bryan. James doted on her and seemed to enjoy the company of his in-laws. During the months after the marriage, Bryan greatly increased his involvement in the Austin family business enterprises while simultaneously managing his personal affairs. It became increasingly clear that Bryan had pronounced entrepreneurial skills, and like his father-in-law, Moses, he was willing to take calculated, sometimes rather spectacular, business risks. These qualities set Bryan apart from the more cautious and deliberate personality of his brother-in-law Stephen, with whom he was involved in numerous projects and investments.[15]

While Emily and James lived at Durham Hall as newlyweds, construction continued on the new Bryan home at Hazel Run. James traveled back and forth between Hazel Run, Potosi, and Herculaneum, where the Austins had business interests, sometimes taking Emily with him on these trips. Although the exact date remains uncertain, Emily and James moved to Hazel Run sometime in late 1813 or early 1814, most likely during the Christmas season. By early 1814, they were receiving all letters at the address of their new home, which the family called Hazel Run Cottage. Emily was also pregnant with the couple's first child. The prospective parents and grandparents, along with uncle-to-be Stephen, looked forward to the arrival of the baby. Emily experienced good health during most of the spring, and as her time drew near, she traveled to Durham Hall to be with her mother. During the hot months of June and July, however, Emily began to suffer from the heat. She soon developed, as she later recalled, "a severe nervous complaint that I had in my head which affected my eyes to such a degree that I was neither able to read or write for several weeks." Maria noted that this complaint became "measles of the worst kind and . . . for 10 days she was confined to her bed and had but little hope of ever rising from it." Under these conditions, Emily prematurely gave birth to a baby boy on July 14, 1814. Cheerfully, she called it "the most perfect male infant I ever saw." She and her husband named the baby Stephen Austin in honor of his uncle, Emily's brother. Things seemed to be progressing normally immediately following the birth, but after several days Stephen took ill. Stoically, Maria wrote to Moses, who was away on a trip, that the baby "was seized with this dangerous disease attended with a sore mouth, violent cough, and fever." Stephen Austin Bryan died at approximately four weeks of age. During most of his short life, the infant's young mother had been too sick herself to care for him. As Maria recalled, "owing to Emily's illness, weakness and inability to take charge," she as grandmother was the primary caregiver for her ill-fated grandson. This would not be the last child that Emily lost in her lifetime, but at age nineteen, the unexpected tragedy affected her and the entire family deeply. As historian Sally McMillen noted, "the death of a child can be the most traumatic experience in a parent's life."[16]

The circumstances surrounding Emily's pregnancy and the baby's tragic death highlighted an interesting aspect of her marriage to James Bryan. Although their union was a romantic one, it brought James into the Austin family to a far greater extent than it had made Emily a Bryan. She clearly conceptualized herself as an Austin and not a Bryan or a Morrison. For example, no correspondence exists between Emily and her husband's relatives. James' brother William apparently had minimal contact with the young couple although he had attended the wedding ceremony. Uncle William Morrison at Kaskaskia confined his relations with his nephew to formal business matters. This likely did not indicate any harsh feelings between Emily, Bryan, and his family. It simply indicated a reality of life: namely, James Bryan had married into the Austin family and had become one of them. The Austins, all of them active individuals with vibrant personalities, had strong bonds among them. Perhaps the greatest evidence of this family identity can be seen in the fact that forever after, Moses addressed Bryan as "son," while Stephen called him "brother." This view of family by Emily was an exception for the era. As Catherine Clinton noted, "To nearly all women, marriage meant the acquisition of an entirely new network of kin," but such was not the case for Emily. Instead, it was James Bryan who made the transition to a new family and with apparent willingness.[17]

Even as a married woman, Emily enjoyed a close and unusually explicit bond with her brother Stephen. They were kindred spirits whose relationship had been forged in the shadow of their father's strong personality. One historian observed that Moses was "impetuous, irascible, belligerent, and even litigious in defense of his rights—all of which would, on the one hand, have kept him in a state of perpetual warfare." He was sometimes prideful and never retreated from controversy. The elder Austin saw the world as a never-ending series of obstacles that he had to overcome in order to succeed, often in the face of adversaries. Moses had high expectations for his children, as seen in the advice-filled letters that he periodically wrote to them. At times Moses was heavy handed in his counsel to Emily, as when he told her to "always think that you are only doing your duty when you make all such persons easy and satisfied in your company, and give offense to no person however low their situation and condition in life." He reminded her, "You have now a father that takes great pleasure in laboring that you may enjoy the advantages, yet the time will come when that father will cease to labor for his much esteemed Emily . . . then, you will require all your exertions to rise superior to the frowns of the world." These precepts struck Emily forcefully, and they became watchwords by which she lived.[18]

It is not surprising, given Moses' worldview, that the Austin children developed a conspiratorial perception of the world. They felt, as one of Stephen's biographers observed, "that a hostile world was arrayed against the House of Austin." As adults, Stephen, Emily, and their younger brother, Brown, had a tendency, as did their parents, to view themselves as actors in a common struggle that pitted their family and its goals against the rest of the world. At times, they seemed almost sorrowful, sometimes to the point of self-pity, about this. "My opinion of mankind has," Stephen once noted, "unfortunately perhaps, been as bad as it could be for some years, but the longer I live the worse it grows." This pessimistic view of the world stayed with Stephen, Emily, and Brown throughout their lifetimes, and such sentiments forged a familial bond. No more eloquent example of this viewpoint exists than a letter Brown Austin wrote to Emily in early 1826. He and Stephen were then involved in the settling of Texas and anticipated its success. "Our old Enemies," he told Emily regarding the family's business rivals in Missouri, "will in a few years more dwindle into insignificance and they will lick the dust from our shoes to gain a favor—It will then be a satisfaction—a 'heavenly satisfaction'—for me to assist them—That is the revenge which will be sweet to me." Emily occasionally echoed this unique combination of family pride and self-pity. It solidified her primary identification as an Austin even after her marriage to James Bryan.[19]

This outlook on life was reinforced by the fact that, starting in 1814, hardship began to enter Emily's life in a significant way, something with which she had little previous experience. The tragic death of the infant Stephen Austin Bryan can be seen as a milestone in everyone's lives at Durham Hall due to the fact that his passing coincided with the start of additional troubles for the family. The rather stable and predictable world in which Emily and her family had lived began to unravel, especially in terms of their financial well-being. Constant worries about money, an economic depression in the lead industry, and illnesses in the family altered the lives of the Austins and Bryans over the ensuing years. Although she was not a direct participant in all of these difficult changes, Emily felt their overwhelming impact. They became apparent in the fall of 1814 when James Bryan, along with Moses and Stephen, started to experience serious financial reverses.[20]

The reasons for the Austin family's increasing financial distress were complex. Moses had engaged in new business ventures and drew Bryan into them as well. The elder Austin committed a tremendous amount of money to the long-term lease of several dozen slaves to work his mines, some of whom became house servants at Hazel Run. He and Bryan, as his partner, negotiated for the slaves with a promissory note that would be paid over the ensuing ten years. Moses was optimistic that increasing profits from greater production at the mines would easily cover the debt. "If ever there was a time that would justify a higher price for Negroes," Austin wrote James Bryan, "it is at this moment." Although the arrival of this labor force did permit increased production, the Austins and Bryan soon found that providing room, board, and necessary living expenses for such a large group of slaves drained their operating budget. This move initially seemed full of economic promise, but only until the end of 1814, when a drastic fall in the price of lead brought profound problems to the mining belt of Missouri. By the spring of 1815, the Missouri frontier was experiencing a precipitous financial downturn as the bottom dropped out of the wholesale lead market. Moses Austin was particularly hard hit since most of his mining and mercantile activities were based on credit. Bryan, both as the son-in-law and a commercial figure in his own right, was also badly affected. The family's economic status declined further due to an ill-fated banking adventure in which Moses, Stephen, James, and Emily were involved as investors. Moses, along with a group of businessmen at St. Louis, had decided to found a private bank in 1813. They enthusiastically set about raising capital, and Moses heavily pledged his assets to its organization. He was elected to be on the board of directors when the Bank of St. Louis opened for business in December of 1816. James and Emily had also invested their own funds in the bank, and as long as it remained financially stable, they had high hopes of reaping great profits. Such was not to be the case, however. By the end of the decade, the failure of the Bank of St. Louis brought all of them to the brink of bankruptcy. [21]

While these financial problems occupied Moses and James, the Bryans nonetheless moved forward on the domestic front. The loss of infant Stephen Austin Bryan the previous year was mitigated when Emily gave birth to a healthy, vigorous baby boy on December 14, 1815, at Hazel Run. His parents named him William Joel Bryan. The family called him Joel, the name by which he was known for the rest of his life. The Austin grandparents naturally took great interest in their grandson and followed his progress closely. After his birth, Moses and Maria kept steady pressure on Emily to be with them at Durham Hall on every possible occasion so that they could have contact with the young boy. On one such visit, Emily wrote James, "Our darling boy walks very well and is a very good child yet, but I am afraid that his grandparents will spoil him." Emily could not help but notice on these visits that her parents were in declining health. Moses Austin suffered from various respiratory complaints, while Maria battled debilitating and uncomfortable rheumatism. She suffered a bad fall from which it took her many months to recover. Moses wrote his daughter that Maria's injuries were much worse than was first expected "and that she was in great pain." Maria experienced such bad rheumatism that she had problems using her right arm and wrote letters with great difficulty.[22]

In an effort to ease his financial burdens and possibly recoup some of his lost health, Moses made a major decision that changed the lives of his entire family. In the fall of 1816, he chose to turn the operation of the mines at Potosi over to Stephen and move to Herculaneum, where

Herculaneum, Missouri, in 1819 as Emily and James Bryan knew it.
Courtesy of Harlan Bartholemew Associates and Parson, Inc.

he would pursue other business interests. On October 20, 1816, the father and son created a new partnership styled Stephen F. Austin and Company to operate the Potosi mines. As part of this agreement, Moses leased the mines to his son for a five-year period, during which Stephen agreed to pay him an interest of 20 percent of the lead produced. Stephen worked hard at Potosi in an effort to make the mines profitable. He badly wanted to erase the debt created by the slave lease arrangements and the problems related to the decline of the Bank of St. Louis. He wrote to

Emily, "I am flattering myself with the pleasing hope of being able, by the end of this year, to free the family from every embarrassment." In spite of his high hopes for success, Stephen was sometimes bothered by the fact that he felt alone at Potosi, with his parents in residence at Herculaneum and the Bryans at Hazel Run. He extended a standing invitation for Emily and her son to visit him at Durham Hall whenever they wished. "I hope sister will not desert me but will very often enliven the hall with her society, when left here alone how I shall envy her the company of little Joel; his prattle would be music to me compared to the cheerless, chilling silence which will pervade the hall when deserted by all but a solitary bachelor."[23]

James and Emily, still making their permanent home at Hazel Run Cottage, worked hard to turn a profit in their operations there. At times, Emily worked in the store located next door to the cottage. Shopkeeping apparently agreed with her. The shelves of the Bryan store were stocked with various sundries, including crocks, pine barrels, shoes, boots, and items of clothing, as well as pine boards and nails. Perhaps as an indication of the rigor of life at the mines, the store had a full selection of coffins, an item regularly needed on the rough-and-tumble Missouri mining frontier. James further diversified his interests at Hazel Run by opening a whiskey distillery. The district produced a large amount of corn, the bulk of which could not be shipped cheaply down the shallow Terre Bleu Creek and Big River to the Mississippi. He therefore opened a distillery on the property and began producing what he hoped would be high-quality corn whiskey. Bryan did this legitimately, securing a federal distilling license from the United States government. Many of the local farmers preferred to sell Bryan their corn since he paid a higher price than they could garner by shipping the grain to market. Emily's father became involved in this operation from time to time as sales agent for the distillery. "I returned yesterday from St. Louis," Moses wrote Bryan from Herculaneum in the late summer of 1817, "and after trying every man now in town, I made out to sell the whiskey to Mr. Handley at $70 payable in eight days." Ever the entrepreneur, Bryan also opened a planking mill near the distillery at Hazel Run. Moses again acted as an agent for this enterprise. On one occasion, he sent a Herculaneum resident to Hazel Run to buy a load of milled lumber. Moses used much of Bryan's lumber in the building of his home at Herculaneum. Specifically, in June of 1817, he bought one thousand board feet of flooring plank and another thousand of three-quarter timbers, which Moses noted "will be as much as will make a finish of my house."[24]

The Bryan family continued to grow during these years as James and Emily pressed ahead with the domestic joys of their life at Hazel Cottage. Another son, Moses Austin Bryan, was born on September 25, 1817, at Herculaneum, where Emily had gone so that her mother could assist in her confinement and care for young Joel. The family called this new baby Austin rather than Moses in a probable attempt to avoid confusion between him and his grandfather. With little Austin's birth, Emily and the children began to make prolonged visits to her parents' home at Herculaneum. Moses and Maria added an extra room to the house in order to accommodate their daughter and the two grandchildren. These visits occurred regularly because James Bryan had begun to spend longer periods of time away from home. Shortly after Austin's birth, he embarked on a career as a land speculator in the Arkansas territory, which was just opening to settlement. James also drew his brother-in-law into these speculations. Stephen hoped that they would provide a way to pay off the slave contracts and recover the bad investments in the Bank of St. Louis. Bryan frequently traveled to Arkansas to superintend his affairs, reluctantly leaving Emily and the children behind since there were no proper accommodations for them there. Bryan's prolonged involvement in these schemes meant that Emily and the children spent increasingly longer periods of time alone in Missouri without him.[25]

By the end of 1818, Stephen F. Austin had decided to leave Missouri, move to Arkansas, and go into a business partnership with his brother-in-law. It was their intention to make southwestern Arkansas a way station on the Southwest Trail for an eventual Anglo-American migration into Texas. Bryan bought a farm for Stephen at Long Prairie on the Red River, and the two men began agricultural operations there. Bryan supplied it with a yoke of oxen, four horses, ten cows, and two bulls. He opened a small store at the site of present-day Arkadelphia and purchased a nearby salt works, which had previously failed to turn a profit. He hired an employee, James Cummins, to operate this business for him. By the summer of 1819, the salt works had produced 170 bushels of salt, and the store was selling merchandise shipped from Missouri. Cummins also became a partner with James and Stephen in the land speculations.[26]

Both Emily and her mother were resourceful in their support of James' new ventures in Arkansas. Among other things, they spent hours making sunbonnets and women's hats, which Emily sent to Arkansas for sale at Bryan's store. She also helped manage the business operations at Hazel Run during his long absences. For the most part, however, Emily found herself occupied with the constant demands of caring for children and looking after her mother, whose rheumatism grew progressively worse. Emily's life was now proving to be a hard one, filled with the sorts of chores, work, and responsibilities that were largely unknown to her several years earlier. At this time, Emily turned to her love of music for encouragement and diversion. She had always shown ability in music, which she polished during the years of her formal education in Lexington and New York City. She had a piano in her home at Hazel Run and began keeping a rather elaborate, handwritten book of her favorite music. This book eventually became very involved, with words and music for over one hundred songs. Some of the selections were traditional church hymns well known on the frontier, while others appeared to be original compositions specific to that time and place in Missouri. Many lyrics spoke of the development of moral character, recalled recent events such as the New Madrid earthquakes, or expressed uplifting thoughts by which adversity could be overcome. It is not clear if Emily actually composed some of the locally focused songs; most likely she did not. She had befriended a local music teacher by the name of Bradford, who traveled around the area giving piano and singing lessons. Emily inscribed Bradford's name in the music book along with her own, and it is probable that he was the source of the songs, which may have been copies from elsewhere in the region.[27]

Emily badly needed the solace that music provided her. The Panic of 1819, an economic depression experienced by the entire nation, hit the frontier with full force and ended all hope that James Bryan would be successful with his Arkansas plans. The panic also dashed what remained of Moses and Stephen's personal finances. This economic catastrophe placed the three men in dire financial circumstances that caused them to lose most of their assets. Emily and her mother, along with all the children, now found themselves completely alone in Missouri. James traveled back to Arkansas after the panic struck, valiantly but unsuccessfully attempting to realize something from his ventures. About the same time, Stephen moved to New Orleans, where he began clerking in a law office, and Moses embarked on his attempts to settle an Anglo-American colony in Spanish Texas. The elder Austin hoped that profits from his Texas enterprise would help recoup the family's lost fortune. The absence of all three men from Missouri during 1820 put Maria, Emily, and the children into desperate straits. They lacked a steady source of income and were hounded by debt collectors at Hazel Run and Herculaneum. Their penury was so great that Joseph Hawkins, the attorney for whom Stephen worked at New Orleans, advanced his new employee money, which he sent to Missouri to buy groceries for his mother and sister.[28]

As this was occurring, Moses arrived in San Antonio de Béxar hoping for the success of his Texas plan. After a series of conferences with Governor Antonio Martinez, he received permission to bring three hundred families into Spanish Texas. Moses left San Antonio several days before Christmas 1820 and began his return journey to Missouri to recruit settlers. A respiratory illness that had been variously plaguing him for months struck him down as he traveled. By the time he arrived at a way station on the road to Natchitoches, he was weak, wracked by exhaustion, and appeared to be a shell of his former self. He took to bed and spent a number of days attempting to recuperate. Back in Missouri, Maria Austin had become so worried about her husband that she dispatched a nephew, Elias Bates, to Texas in an effort to search for him. Bates first traveled to New Orleans, where he talked to Stephen, and eventually went to the Natchitoches area. There he found Moses and accompanied him back to Missouri. It was clear that the elder Austin suffered from serious respiratory distress. He coughed up phlegm repeatedly and had difficulty breathing, complaining of bad chest pains. He collapsed into bed upon reaching his home at Herculaneum. Nonetheless, Moses manifested great excitement about the possibilities of his settlement plans for Texas. He envisioned planting a city on the Texas coast where the Colorado River flowed into the Gulf of Mexico. Moses announced that he would name this place Austinia and that it would become a prosperous community of settlers drawn from "people of the first class." In spite of his grand plans, Emily and Maria despaired for Moses because of his weakened condition.[29]

Moses' enthusiasm proved such that he was incapable of resting. He worked relentlessly over the ensuing weeks to set the Texas colonization venture into motion. "Such was his anxiety to arrange all his business in this quarter," Maria noted, "I could not prevail upon him to attend to his health and take those medications necessary to restore it." Barely able to ride a horse, Moses struck out for St. Louis, where he intended to meet with representatives of the Bank of St. Louis and renegotiate his protested accounts. In the meantime, James Bryan had returned to Hazel Run from Arkansas, broke and saddled with bad debt. Emily was no doubt glad to have her husband home but was saddened by his business failures. Moses wrote to his son-in-law from the Missouri capital, "I am sorry to say that I have not yet settled finally with the bank." "I am in a most unpleasant situation without a dollar to get a shirt washed." Having achieved what he could at St. Louis, Moses departed in early May for Herculaneum. He arrived home at Maria's doorstep "spent and exhausted with fatigue." She was horrified by his condition, especially when she learned that he intended to travel to Potosi to make additional arrangements for his Texas venture. She later wrote, "I felt greatly alarmed and did all I could to prevail on him to take my advice and postpone his journey a few days." Moses nonetheless traveled to Potosi and then to Hazel Run, planning to stop for a few days to discuss Texas with James Bryan before continuing his trip back to Herculaneum. Moses' appearance at Hazel Cottage also gave him the happy opportunity to see a new grandson for the first time. Guy Morrison Bryan had been born earlier that year on January 12 at the Austin family home in Herculaneum, where Emily again spent her confinement. She and the children, now joined by her husband, had been back at Hazel Cottage for only a month when the elder Austin appeared there.[30]

Moses arrived at Hazel Run Cottage so exhausted that Emily had to assist him in dismounting his horse. She now had her hands full with a newborn infant in the house and a very sick father as her guest. Emily put Moses directly to bed and sent an express rider to Herculaneum with the news that Maria should come to his bedside immediately. Emily also summoned a local physician, who found Moses' condition "dangerous, it being a violent attack of inflammation on the breast and lungs, attended with a high fever." For the next several days, his condition fluctuated. At times he appeared to be improving, but by June 8, Moses had taken a turn for the worse. At this point, Maria wrote a long letter to Stephen in New Orleans describing recent events at Emily's home in Hazel Run. "Your father had completed all of his business in this quarter," she told her son, "much more to his satisfaction than he ever expected to do." She reported that the ventures he arranged in Texas had great potential for future success. Apparently, she and Moses had already discussed the possibility that Stephen might carry on the Texas plans should something happen to his father. Although gravely ill, Moses clearly conveyed this desire to those present at Hazel Cottage. Maria wrote Stephen that Moses wished "to extend his goodness to you, and enable you to go along with the business in the same way he would have done had not sickness prevented him from accomplishing this. Everyone has the highest opinion of his plans and many are only waiting until they know he's made the establishment, when they mean to follow him." Maria continued, "He begged me to tell you to take his place, tell dear Stephen that it is his dying father's last request to prosecute the enterprise he had commenced." Moses died at Hazel Run Cottage on June 10, 1821. The family buried him on the Bryan property a short distance away from the room where he had spent his last days. Emily could stand in the doorway of her home and see her father's simple grave only a short distance up a small hill, set in an open clearing that eventually gave way to a stand of timber beyond.[31]

The death of Moses Austin drastically altered the lives of his surviving family members, including Brown, who remained at school in the East. Maria Austin never fully recovered from her husband's passing.

She seemed to lose all of the strong attributes of her personality that over the years had made her a person of formidable opinion and decisive action. Almost literally from the moment of Moses' death, she withdrew inside of herself. Maria moved permanently into Hazel Cottage and spent much of her time preoccupied with her illnesses, which were very real and physically overwhelming. Stephen F. Austin took up his father's enterprise of settling Anglo-Americans in Texas. In fact, he did not travel to Missouri at the time of Moses' death, instead leaving New Orleans directly for Texas. Stephen appeared in San Antonio de Béxar several months later, where he talked with officials and set in motion the start of the Empresario era that would be so much a hallmark of his own personality. Stephen F. Austin never returned to Missouri and, for many years thereafter, was an absentee brother to his sister. Emily and James remained at Hazel Run, now with three young children in the house in addition to the infirm grandmother. Emily's family had become, in effect, the keystone that held the Austins together after the passing of its patriarch.

At this time, decisions had to be made concerning Brown Austin, the youngest child of Maria and Moses. He had been away from Missouri at school for almost seven years at the time of his father's death. The difficulties experienced by Moses, Stephen, and Bryan had already placed Brown in dire financial circumstances. Moses had done the best he could to meet Brown's school expenses, but this support was not enough. The elder Austin had therefore attempted to arrange Brown's appointment as a naval officer in 1820 but was unsuccessful. Moses thereafter wrote his youngest son, "I'm sorry, my son, to say that my situation will not allow me to do for you what I could wish, but when I am clear of all of my difficulties, I can then say what I can do for you. In the meantime, I shall forward to you money to pay your bills and clothe you as your station in life requires." After Moses' death, everyone in the family turned to Emily and James Bryan as the people responsible for the young man. This assumption provoked a temporary quarrel between Stephen and James. By late 1821, Stephen apparently felt that the Bryans had not done enough to assist Brown financially, although he never explained why such an expectation had settled on his sister's family instead of him. He did nothing to help his younger brother. In a harsh exchange of letters, Stephen took Bryan to task for what he felt was an abandonment of the young man's needs. This development distressed Emily, who understood that Bryan was experiencing financial problems of his own. Maria took Bryan's part and wrote Stephen that her son-in-law had "an affectionate kindness" and was worthy of his "confidence in friendship." This mollified Stephen, who later wrote his brother-in-law, "I have thought that I had cause to be dissatisfied with you, perhaps I may have been wrong, and perhaps not—be that as it may, let the past be forgotten forever. Your family shall participate fully in what ever advantage I may be able to secure in Texas." After some discussion, Emily and James decided that Brown should join his older brother, Stephen, in Texas, something the young man wanted. The Bryans scraped together enough cash from their meager resources to bring him to Hazel Run, where he stayed until funds could be found that would send him to Texas. Stephen again contributed nothing financially to these efforts, but within the year, Brown did arrive in Texas. He worked diligently to learn Spanish, served as an assistant to his older brother, and eventually embarked on a business career of his own.[32]

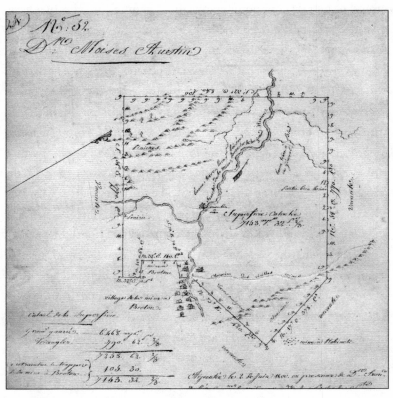

Land plat survey of the Moses Austin holding at Mine á Breton, June 2, 1800. This was the center of Emily's childhood world. The plat is oriented with geographic north pointing toward the upper right-hand corner. The houses located just outside the Austin land in the double row along the south side of the creek (as seen in the lower left) mark the course of Barefoot Street. The houses located just outside the Austin land in the double row along the south side of the creek (as seen in the lower left) mark the course of Barefoot Street. Durham Hall may be seen to their north, located by itself on the other side of the creek. The bridge to Barefoot Street ran between Durham Hall and the Austin forge, located inside the plat directly across the creek, west of the double row of houses. The structure located towards the center of the plat near the creek junction was Austin's mill.
Reprinted from *Opening the Ozarks: A Historical Geography of Missouri's Ste. Genevieve District, 1760-1830* by Walter A. Schroeder, by permission of the University of Missouri Press. Copyright ©2002 by the Curators of the University of Missouri.

THE YEARS AT HAZEL RUN
AND POTOSI

B y early 1822, it was evident that
Emily wanted to move to Texas and reassemble the Austin family there.
James Bryan agreed with this course of action and possibly saw the move
as a solution to his financial woes, which had continued to worsen since
his return from Arkansas. Within months of Brown's arrival in Texas,
Bryan was writing to Stephen about Emily and the rest of the family
joining them. "I may possibly come on myself in the spring though
not certain," he noted. Bryan asked his brother-in-law to select some
suitable land for him and, "if it is possible, to have a building of some
sort put up." James further reported that he was busily involved in
closing out his own financial matters in Missouri, along with those that
were still pending from the estate of Moses Austin. Bryan also noted
that "I am daily hearing of people preparing to move, etc.—you will
have a number of your old acquaintances as settlers." Most importantly
for Stephen, James wrote that Emily was "anxious to see you, and we
flatter ourselves it will not be longer than next autumn before we have
that pleasure." Maria wrote Stephen that Bryan had "not got through
his difficulties, but he thinks it will be in his power to make you a visit
next Spring, when I hope he will make a choice of a situation where
your sister will experience more happiness than she has enjoyed for some
years past." Maria Austin's delicate health and the potential rigors of
such a journey did, however, constitute a stumbling block to these plans.
Nonetheless, Bryan reported that by early 1822, Maria's health seemed
somewhat improved. "Mother's health is much better than it has been
for the last six months," he wrote Stephen, "and if she lives to settle

at the colony I have no doubt that she will enjoy much better health than she would here." Indeed, Maria wrote to Stephen to express her happiness that she, Bryan, Emily, and the children would be moving to Texas. She told her son, "I cannot help anticipating future pleasures and pleasing tranquility of mind in the society of my beloved children." She observed that "nothing is spoken about but the Texas fever, the times are so hard, and the people so dissatisfied with the country, or rather with those who govern it; I really think one half of the farmers will move this year." She happily reported to Stephen that he would very much enjoy the company of his young nephews once the family arrived in Texas. She told him that "they are fine looking boys, but my little Guy is the beauty of the family." Maria also broached with Emily and her sons a subject that weighed heavily on her mind as the Bryans planned the departure from Hazel Run: namely, what to do with the remains of Moses Austin. She hoped "the body could be taken up and placed in another coffin" and moved to a better location. She worried that her husband would remain buried on the land of strangers in Missouri when she and Emily's family left. Maria thus wished to move him to a more suitable grave in a true cemetery.[1]

Bryan had great difficulty in closing out his Missouri affairs during 1822 in preparation for the move to Texas. The inability to meet his financial obligations distressed him greatly, to the point that he borrowed money from his uncle Guy in Philadelphia in order to stay afloat financially. The elder Bryan seemed willing to assist his nephew at this time of need and loaned him $5,000. In spite of this familial bond, however, Guy (a hardened Philadelphia businessman) required that his nephew use the real estate at Hazel Run as collateral for the loan. This Bryan did, pledging "480 acres, the distillery, the dwelling house, and the ownership of several slaves," including the house slaves who assisted Emily in the running of Hazel Cottage. Bryan intended to repay the loan by selling shipments of lead at New Orleans during the spring shipping season. Such a consignment never took place for several reasons, and Bryan's finances continued to decline. Fighting impending bankruptcy, Emily and James decided that all of them would leave Hazel Cottage and take up temporary residence at Moses Austin's vacant home in Herculaneum while Emily prepared for the birth of their fourth child. This move would save them expenses, and James would not be in the environs of Hazel Run should creditors attempt to locate him. Grandmother Maria, of course, went with them to help care for the family and assist with Emily's impending confinement. Maria worried again about leaving the remains of her husband on the heavily mortgaged property along the banks of Hazel Run. She wrote to Stephen in Texas, "The idea of leaving the body of my dear husband on the land of strangers, on an open field, is truly distressing to my feelings." She continued, "I have thought that if it was possible for my dear son to come to this country next fall, the body could be taken up and placed in another coffin. It will be with some satisfaction to us to remove your dear parent from a country where he had been so critically persecuted." Although he expressed sympathy and familial devotion, Stephen seemed remarkably uninterested in providing any sort of assistance to his kinfolk, being fully consumed with his affairs in Texas. He was content to leave all Austin family matters in Missouri to Emily.[2]

By the late spring, Emily and her family were settled at Herculaneum, where Bryan attempted to further untangle his complicated finances while his wife awaited the arrival of the baby. Maria, exercising her prerogative as grandmother, spent a good deal of time with her grandsons. The hot weather of June and July began to take its toll on the Herculaneum residents, and a contagion of fever appeared in the town. It was during the most oppressive heat of the summer that Emily's first daughter was born. They named her Mary Elizabeth. However, the happy event of her birth was tempered by the increasing number of deaths in the town due to the fever's rampage. During her lying-in, Emily learned that several of her friends and neighbors had succumbed to it. Affairs at the Bryan home took a distressing turn when James grew ill several days before the birth of Mary Elizabeth. The house now had two sick rooms: the first where Emily recovered from the birth and the second where James lay fighting a steadily debilitating fever. After ten days of great pain and discomfort, James Bryan died on July 16, 1822. He was thirty-three years of age. Everyone in the house was devastated, especially Emily, who now had to take charge of her aging mother and four children, the youngest a newborn in swaddling blankets. She soon found herself without any financial resources. James was literally bankrupt and had no cash on hand. All of his assets had been collateralized in the loan from Uncle Guy Bryan. Plaintively, Emily wrote Stephen in Texas that she hoped "to secure something for the children, and to be able to pay the debts." Stephen offered her nothing, and Emily learned that many of James' friends were of the fair-weather variety when none of them would help her either.[3]

James Bryan's death thrust Emily into the rigors of a new and completely unanticipated life, one that would test the mettle of her character. She was now a young widow, twenty-seven years of age, upon whose decisions and labors rested the future of her four children and her infirm mother. These circumstances steeled Emily's personality and gave it additional depth of commitment as she held her small, struggling family together in the months after James' death and confronted the public sphere of managing their income. Kirsten E. Wood has noted of elite southern widows that "from the beginning of widowhood, slaveholding women participated in exchange as both consumers and producers." Emily quickly manifested an inner reserve and independence of mind greater than had ever been seen while James Bryan was alive, tapping the wellsprings of her own determination and fortitude. Her absent brothers in Texas seemed not to consider that her problems were their responsibility. Stephen remained in Texas, and although he professed to be sympathetic, he continued to offer no assistance of any kind to his sister or to his mother. In the dismal months after Bryan's death, Maria spent hour after hour reading the Bible and sending letters to her sons in Texas, most of which went unanswered. Meanwhile, Emily took stock of her situation, making a series of bold and definitive decisions. She and the children, along with Maria, would move back to Hazel Run. The house at Herculaneum could be sold for cash, which, although not a large amount, would at least provide them with some resources. The property at Hazel Run and its cottage were, of course, mortgaged to Emily's uncle-in-law Guy Bryan in Philadelphia. She gambled on the supposition that he would not dispossess them and proved to be correct. Emily returned to Hazel Cottage to face grim prospects for the future of her small family, for which she was the sole responsible party and breadwinner. "Grief, poverty, and obligations from a broken business," one of her descendants later recalled about this time, and her obligation to "four small children, and invalid mother, did not daunt Emily Margaret, but on the contrary stimulated her to a Herculean effort." Emily stalwartly threw herself into a determined regime of hard work at Hazel Run designed to keep her family functioning. Emily took in sewing from the men in the neighborhood, moved a boarder into a spare room at Hazel Cottage, and opened a small "dame school" where she taught some of the neighborhood children for a modest tuition fee. She also put everyone in her household to work making handicrafts for sale, such as bonnets, which she and Maria had done as a sideline several years earlier for James' store in Arkansas. Above all, Emily maintained a frugal regime at Hazel Run, cutting expenses in every way possible. We are all living "like hermits," she wrote Stephen in Texas. "By our industry and economy we have endeavored to live tolerably comfortable, but when I say that, I say all."[4]

Stephen never abandoned hope that Emily, her children, and his mother would move to Texas. Almost all of his letters to Emily during the period after James Bryan's death focused on this desire. However, he had somewhat mixed feelings that complicated his planning for such a move. On one hand, he badly wanted to reassemble his family in Texas; on the other, he apparently did not want them to arrive until all the proper arrangements had been made to his satisfaction. Stephen thus vacillated between having Emily come to Texas or remain in Missouri, and plans for the move progressed slowly during 1823. Stephen did not seem to have an accurate understanding of the poverty and hardship in which his sister's family was living. Emily's situation changed drastically when Maria Austin died unexpectedly on January 8, 1824. Maria had never recovered fully from her husband having lost his fortune. The years after his death had not been easy ones for her, and the absence of her two sons in Texas only added to her melancholy disposition. At one point, Emily wrote her brother Stephen, "Mother often says that she will never see Texas or you but expects to lay her bones by the side of father." Emily further reported, "I endeavor to laugh her out of the idea, but it appears to be fixed on her mind; she has become quite religious, and spends much of her time in studying her Bible." Maria's passing proved poignant for the family since Stephen had been, at that very time, making final arrangements to bring his mother, sister, and the Bryan children to Texas. Unaware of his mother's death, he dispatched Brown to Hazel Run to accompany them to the Mexican province. "Be very particular to collect all the little property that Emily has," Stephen advised Brown, "and provide well for them on the journey; bring all their beds and bedding and pots, kettles, and crockery ware and [items] that are of light carriage, and bring all kinds of garden seed and roots." He also told Brown to bring any slaves that James Bryan had owned, and he would settle for them later with the estate. On this trip to get Emily's family, Brown stopped at Natchitoches and found that two letters from Missouri were being held for him in the Louisiana town. The first letter was from Maria, written shortly before her passing. The second, written by a relative at Herculaneum, contained news of his mother's death.[5]

This shocking information compelled Brown to hurry forward to Missouri so that he could bring Emily and the children back to Texas. Once there, he found that Maria had been laid to rest on the small rise above Hazel Run next to the remains of her husband. What Brown learned from Emily at Hazel Cottage, however, proved as astounding as his mother's death. Emily informed her brother that she and the children would not be returning to Texas with him. Instead, Emily planned to marry a local merchant, James Franklin Perry. This news momentarily took Brown aback, and he expressed his profound disappointment at her decision. He wrote to Stephen, "I confess I was as much surprised as you will be, when she informed me of it, a few days ago." Brown noted that "my reply to her was, that she knew whether her marriage with Mr. P. would be conducive to her happiness or not." Although hardly an endorsement of the marriage, Brown further advised his brother, "I acquiesced with cheerfulness and made no doubt you would do the same—I only regret that it will be impossible for us to collect the remains of our unfortunate family together for some years to come, if ever."[6]

Family tradition among Emily's descendants holds that the two Austin brothers did indeed have a negative reaction to the news of their sister's remarriage. Emily perhaps sensed this. "I am fearful," she wrote Stephen, "you will accuse me of ingratitude for not going on with brother and sharing with you and him the hardships of settling a new country." Nevertheless, in a letter to Stephen, Brown characterized James F. Perry as a man whose "standing is high and morals unexceptionable." Stephen and Brown's failure to express fulsome approval of Emily's decision to marry Perry may not have been caused by a low opinion of him, but rather by disappointment that she and the Bryan children would not be coming to Texas. Brown remained in Missouri for some months thereafter. He learned a good deal of information from Emily about financial matters affecting the Austin family. For example, Emily was considering a lawsuit against the current owners of the Moses Austin tract at Mine á Breton for recovery of the property due to the bank's improper actions in dispossessing their father several years earlier. "Durham Hall can be recovered," Brown wrote Stephen, "when our purses are long enough to stand a seven years lawsuit." He also reported on the debts at Little Rock and pending claims regarding Stephen's earlier residence

there. These, he noted, had not been dealt with since Emily "wished nothing done in the business until you came up yourself." Yet both Brown and Stephen appeared content to leave the resolution of these matters in Emily's hands. Emily would expend much effort over the coming years in an unsuccessful attempt to settle these claims on behalf of her older brother, who left all such issues to her.[7]

Emily and James F. Perry were married in the parlor of Hazel Cottage on September

James Franklin Perry

23, 1824, in a ceremony presided over by the Reverend Thomas Donnell. The Bryan children, Brown Austin, members of the Perry family, and several friends attended the ceremony. Shortly afterward, James, Emily, and the children moved to Potosi. Emily seemed brutally frank about her circumstances. She later recalled, "I was poor, having but little property at the time of our marriage and having at the time four small children." She did, however, place much confidence in Perry as the new father and protector of the Bryan children. "My husband, James F. Perry," she noted many years later, "was always kind to my said children, educating them and supporting and treating them as affectionately as if they were his own children." She adopted a mollifying attitude towards her brother Stephen since her marriage meant that there would be no move to Texas. Emily did offer some hope when she advised him that "I have not given up (nor never will) the idea of moving to Texas: I flatter myself that when you visit Missouri that you will prevail on Mr. Perry to join you in Texas. I can assure you that I shall make use of every means to persuade him to go on."[8]

The marriage of Emily and James F. Perry would be successful for the remainder of their lives. James Perry belonged to an important mercantile family that had long been established in the mining country. He was born in Allegheny County, Pennsylvania, on September 19, 1790, one of the eleven children of Hannah and James Franklin Perry. He received a "plain education" as a young man and during the War of 1812 served in the United States Army, from which he received his formal discharge on February 14, 1814. It was shortly thereafter that Perry decided to join his uncle John Perry and his cousins in Potosi, Missouri, although the decision was not made without trepidation. "If you be industrious and attentive to business," his father advised young James, "there is no doubt but that you may with the blessing of God make a living there." At the same time, the elder Perry warned his son, "That is a wild country and you will no doubt be exposed to bad company, which I would beg you to refrain from and behave yourself at all times soberly and have the fear of God always before your eyes." Young James Perry, upon arrival at Potosi, where he joined his relations in business, did find the area to be something less than a garden spot. The prevalence of smoke-shrouded smelters, wagon-track roads that were alternately dusty or mud laden, scarred landscapes where lead digging had been the order of the day, and the relatively rude nature of the isolated mining settlements, at least when compared to towns of western Pennsylvania, apparently gave him pause. Young Perry expressed in his early letters to relatives back home some reservations about his first opinions of the area. One of his sisters responded with commiseration. "Judging by your description of the inhabitants generally," she wrote by return mail, "I draw an unfavorable inference as regards the state of literature and politeness, and would almost be willing to class them among semi-barbarians in their festive enjoyment; I fondly wish you may see some more certain road to fortune and fame than this place could afford you."9

Nonetheless, Perry decided to follow his path to fortune and fame with his uncle and cousins at Potosi, and he threw himself into working at their store on Barefoot Street. The Perrys had already established a solid reputation in the lead country as honest and respected merchants. It was said that "the Perrys came to Missouri with a barrel of beans and a barrel of whiskey. They drank the whiskey and sold the beans— and they were in business." James lived in a back room at the Perry store near his uncle's home. It was a small but close-knit neighborhood that surrounded the complex of Perry buildings. One observer noted that a great "amount of business was transacted by these merchants, as Potosi was then the trading point for the country south of it and extending down into Arkansas, from where people with their pack mules came to trade." Several blocks away and across Mine á Breton Creek stood Durham Hall, where Stephen F. Austin was then attempting to operate his family's business ventures since Moses had already moved to Herculaneum. The Perrys had routine dealings with young Austin, buying and selling lead with him. At one point in 1817, James' cousin Samuel Perry borrowed $500 from Stephen.[10]

James assumed an increasing responsibility for running the Perry store. By 1822, he had negotiated a partnership with his cousin Samuel whereby the two men were joint owners of the mercantile business. Samuel Perry, who had most of the capital, would underwrite the cash expenses of the establishment while James provided the management of the store. Samuel received two-thirds of the firm's annual profits, and James got one-third. James also began to accumulate land, sometimes in partnership with his cousin and uncle. In 1821, for example, he patented four hundred acres in concert with his Perry relations in Potosi, adding another 320 acres to his holdings within the year. In 1824, he took additional patents on 160 acres in his own name as the sole owner. It was very clear by this time that James F. Perry had notable business skills that marked him for financial success. He had established a reputation as "an intelligent, public-spirited man of high character and good business principles."[11]

At this point in 1823, James entered the life of widowed Emily Austin Bryan in a meaningful way. Whatever the nature of their initial contact, the emerging relationship between James and Emily changed dramatically when Maria Austin's illness worsened and she died. James acted as Emily's legal agent in settling Maria's estate, a role at law that Perry would play for his wife many times in the future. Emily's marriage to James Perry, in retrospect, serves as an example of marital conventions that were beginning to characterize relationships between spouses in the early nineteenth century. These new assumptions, known as "companionate marriage," first took hold in the United States in the late eighteenth century and became vogue among many elites during Emily's generation. Companionate marriage revolved around the concept that people married primarily for love and mutual feelings. "In other words," one historian noted, "emotion moved to the center; mutual affection and respect replaced the call of duty and pressure from the community as the main ties that year in and year out bound husbands and wives together." This concept of marriage suited Emily's personality since "the old habit of male command was replaced by shared activities and joint decision making." That became the key factor that governed the remainder of her life. Emily's future activities as a woman had deep roots in the philosophical basis of companionate marriage, making her relatively modern for her era. However, it was still common for the husband to take the ascendancy in matters of mutual spousal concern. As Catherine Kerrison noted of companionate marriage, "it rarely implied an equal partnership. It was clear that men expected to take the initiative and women to follow." This was the case for the Perrys, and although most family concerns were necessarily conducted in the name of James F. Perry, Emily fully participated in all decisions.[12]

The circumstances of Emily's residence as a widow at Hazel Run and her companionate marriage to James Perry provide windows into understanding the strength of her adult character as an individual and as a woman. She had matured considerably since her trip east in 1811, in the process shedding the adolescent concerns of a schoolgirl for the mature responsibilities of a woman who alone supported her family. By the time of her marriage to James Perry, Emily had become a person who lived life on her own terms and set her own personal destiny. This was especially true given the fact that Emily married Perry in the midst of her two brothers' attempts to move her family to Texas and that she embarked on this marriage without bothering to tell them of her plans in advance. She had been the breadwinner at Hazel Run for almost two years before she remarried, while she personally negotiated with the Bryan family in Philadelphia for the settlement of her late husband's estate. During that entire time, she never explicitly asked for monetary assistance from either of her brothers in Texas, nor did they offer any of their own initiative. This lack of support seems somewhat curious since Emily's mother and brothers viewed her as someone whose "disposition is by no means calculated to bear the disappointments that this life is subject to." Stephen F. Austin's opinions about her therefore seem almost misinformed in light of what she had been doing in Missouri for almost the entire time he had been in Texas. From his great distance away, it is likely that Stephen viewed his sister's character and personality through the lens of stereotypical notions about women as refined objects of purity and submissiveness. His assumptions about Emily may have thus been cultural rather than based on specific knowledge of his sister's state of mind or what she was capable of accomplishing on her own initiative. In reality, adversity and years alone in Missouri had made Emily a far more self-directed and complex person than her brother realized.[13]

Emily's resolve to be in control of her own destiny and that of her children showed through when Uncle Guy Bryan made her an offer that she rejected summarily. He offered to cancel the mortgage on Hazel Run if Emily would make him the guardian of his namesake, Guy M. Bryan, and send the young boy to be raised in his grand home in Philadelphia. Such a turn of events would certainly relieve the financial burdens at Hazel Run while providing sterling opportunities for the young boy's future. To the credit of her resolve to keep the children together, even in times of adversity, Emily politely but firmly refused this proposal. Moreover, she flatly rejected the offer over the advice of her brother Brown, who told her, "I would recommend it by all means." Emily knew her own mind and acted accordingly. Her new self-reliance no doubt came from the fact that she had grown accustomed to putting food on the table for her children every day by the labor of her own hands. This would have changed any young woman of the era, and it certainly changed her. Emily was now very much her own woman, even in her marriage to James F. Perry. The wedding ceremony itself hinted at this new self-possession when Emily announced that she would continue to wear James Bryan's wedding ring on her left hand, while the one James Perry gave her would be worn on the right. She wore these wedding rings openly for the rest of her life without brooking any comment or criticism from those who thought it bizarre that a married woman would have two, one on each hand.[14]

The greatest evidence of this profound maturation of Emily's personality after the death of James Bryan and her marriage to James Perry came in the forthright manner by which she dealt with other people. By the time she married James Perry, she was a thoughtful woman of well-formed opinions on most concerns that came to her attention and one who was certainly not demure or subservient. Her letters increasingly reflected definitive viewpoints, and this attitude became a major attribute of her personality. Such strength of opinion was especially apparent in her relationships with family members, manifested in her strident reactions to their behavior and activities. At times, she could seem irritable and critical, if not querulous, in her comments to them and to others, as generally she had no reticence at all about expressing her opinions about anything to anyone. This was often the case in future years on the many occasions when Emily, as a mother and a plantation mistress, wrote to those remaining at home during her various travels. Such letters contained minute instructions for her husband, detailed observations about what should be accomplished in her absence, and—more than occasionally—a healthy measure of moral advice specifically directed to particular members of the household. For example, after their marriage, Emily once learned that James Perry had caught a cold. She wrote him, "You are not half so careful of yourself as you should be; how careless to go out without your hat or coat, I am really astonished at you." A later historical writer (who apparently knew little of Emily's life and therefore assumed too much) incorrectly stereotyped her in a very superficial sketch as having been a southern planter's wife who lived as a "petted and spoiled woman—the only daughter of a man of power and means." Such was not the case at all. Emily was not one of the southern women "placed on pedestals" as delicate objects of male deference, although that indeed might have colored Stephen F. Austin's view of her. This did not mean, either, that Emily lacked the social graces or that she failed to become the perfect hostess in an elite planter society, because that she surely became. Many who knew her over the years would remark on her personal charm, graciousness, absolute kindness, and her concern for hospitality. The years alone with her mother and children at Hazel Run, however, had done something more profound in reshaping her personality: they had taught her how to get along in a man's world on her own terms. That she never lost, even as she became Mrs. James Franklin Perry.[15]

Naturally, because of Emily's proximity to the Perrys when they moved to Potosi in the months after the wedding at Hazel Cottage, she and the Bryan children had much closer contact with their in-laws than had been the case with her first husband's family. Nonetheless, her long-distance relationship with her brothers in Texas allowed her continued identification with the Austins. "I often think of you," Emily wrote Stephen a year after her marriage to Perry, "and think of how much you must suffer in that wilderness." In late 1825, Emily sent Stephen locks of hair from the Bryan children, an action that moved him to make an eloquent reply. He wrote, "I needed nothing to keep me in mind of them, but, it is, notwithstanding a pleasure to have something that

Stephen F. Austin as an empresario in Texas. Courtesy of Austin College.

was once theirs—some keepsake, to represent them in their absence."
He then made a somewhat surprising observation, writing her that "I
never expect to marry and in that event I should adopt our orphans for
my own or a part of them." He further noted, "I hope that it will be
in my power to aid in educating them." In short, Stephen wanted to
adopt one or more of the Bryan sons. Although she graciously never
explicitly rejected this, Emily would not brook any serious discussion of
the matter, reacting to it in the same way she had received a similar offer

from Guy M. Bryan in Philadelphia. Emily was the mother, and that she would remain. On the other hand, the bachelor status of her brothers in Texas was a particular concern for Emily during much of the mid-1820s. "I shall be extremely happy to hear that that one or both of you were married," she wrote them. "You must lead a very disagreeable life the way that you live" without a wife. She especially beseeched Stephen to return to the lead belt in order to find a mate. "I do not like to hear you say, Stephen, that you cannot visit Missouri," she told him. "I think that if you were to come on, that you might find some lady that would please you." His being alone in Texas worried Emily a great deal. On learning that he had been ill on one occasion, she wrote him, "Oh! That I could have taken wings and flown to your sick bed; but, alas I am apprehensive that it is our lot to be separated the remainder of our lives."[16]

Stephen dismissed these concerns by pleading the all-consuming and demanding task of planting a new colony in Texas. "The truth is that both brother and myself," he responded, "are too much unsettled as yet to trammel ourselves with a family, or one of us would have been no doubt married before this." Emily seemed philosophical in observing, "It appears that our family was destined to be immured in the settling of new countries." Nonetheless, Stephen took an active interest in the Bryan children and freely offered advice about them to his sister. "Kiss all the children for me and be sure and make business men of them," he counseled, and "learn them some occupation or profession that will support them through life." Brown also had opinions about the children, and his advice to Emily was equally explicit: "Place your boys in some situation, severally, as they arrive at a proper age, whereby they may gain a correct knowledge of some kind of business." Emily tactfully agreed with her brother's sentiments regarding a business education, responding to Brown's observations, "I thank you my dear Brown for your advice respecting my sons, and be assured that they shall be raised men of business." Emily's pride in being an Austin showed through at this time with the publication of Henry Schoolcraft's *Journal*, dealing with his 1818 trip to Missouri. She wrote Stephen with satisfaction, noting, "I was much gratified not long since to see in a work of Schoolcraft a biographical sketch of our dear father; he speaks of every member of the family, and of father's early visit to this country."[17]

Emily styled herself in her letters to Brown and Stephen as "your truly attached sister and friend." The close bond between them as Austins did not apparently impinge on her situation as a wife, although history does not record James F. Perry's reaction to potentially giving up the Bryan children to Stephen F. Austin's care in Texas. This course of action was nevertheless an idea that Stephen continued to mention on several occasions, with the implicit assumption that the Perrys would have no objection to it. Each time, Emily demurred politely and put off discussion of the matter. In late 1825, Stephen informed them in a matter-of-fact way, "I should also like to have Austin with me—that is if I ever get finally settled and in a situation to benefit him. I am not in a situation to take any of them yet, and it is rather uncertain when I shall be." The vacillation that Stephen expressed about possible adoption of the Bryan children soon came to characterize his approach to the question about Emily's family moving to Texas, even after she married James Perry. At times he seemed almost melancholic about that taking place as soon as possible, while on later occasions he counseled delay until all proper arrangements were made for a trouble-free and expeditious move. Brown Austin sometimes shared in this ambivalence, although he often expressed to his sister a firm desire that she settle in the new colony. "I sincerely hope and flatter myself," Brown wrote Emily in early 1826, "that the period is not far distant when we shall all be reunited." In expressing this hope, he took some pride in telling her that Texas would be their family's memorial: "We have accomplished an enterprise that will perpetuate our name, and place it with honor on the page of history."[18]

Stephen understood that James Perry had good business prospects in Missouri, and he seemed sensitive to not forcing the family into a move that might disadvantage his brother-in-law financially. "It is not my wish that Mr. Perry should make any arrangements whatever to move here until he has first seen the country," Stephen wrote to Emily. "He positively must not move on my recommendation nor that of Brother's—perhaps he may not like it, but if he moves without first coming to see it, it will be too late to remedy it." In that regard, Stephen asked Emily to "tell my new brother-in-law that he must write me; let him inform me what his prospects are there, and I can better judge whether a removal would benefit or injure him and know better how to advise him." At the same time, he told his sister that he hoped for a family situation in which he and Brown would be settled on one side of his own homestead and "Mr. Perry and you on the other."[19]

In spite of the Austin brothers' hopes, the Perry family settled easily and happily into life at Potosi during the mid-1820s. It certainly appears that James and Emily were in no hurry to move to Texas, as they began to establish a solid family life for themselves in Missouri. By all accounts, Emily was an efficient mother and a popular member of Potosi's social elite. Starting in 1824, she helped arrange each year's Fourth of July gathering in Potosi, which was one of the gala civic celebrations in the town. She was also an active participant in her family network, which now included Austin and Perry relations. For example, in 1825, she helped a distant cousin, Mrs. Henry Elliott, open a school in Potosi. That same year, Emily attended the wedding of another cousin, and she assisted in setting up a house for the newlyweds in a former office building belonging to the Perry family. The next summer, she hosted a visit from an old friend from New Haven, who had come to recuperate in the Perry home "after a very long and severe illness."[20]

As the 1820s wore on, James Perry exhibited strong reservations about moving to Texas. Although Emily was more ambivalent about remaining in Missouri, she supported her husband while temporizing with Stephen about their joining him. "With respect to your sister and myself coming to that country," Perry wrote to his brother-in-law in Texas, "we have not yet come to any determination." Perry further explained his personal and financial situation in Missouri, pointing out, "I know we can make an independent living here," although he and Emily might never become wealthy in the process. He and his cousin Samuel Perry still operated the store, and he reported that "we have made some money." Perry estimated his net worth to be between eight and ten thousand dollars, a respectable sum of money for that time. This included his interest in the store, his land holdings, and several slaves that he owned, but it excluded any property previously belonging to Emily or to the estate of James Bryan. "I have not purchased a house yet," he told Stephen, as he was delaying that decision until they made up their minds about moving to Texas. In making these disclosures, James went so far as to agree to visit Stephen at some unnamed future date in order to learn about conditions in Texas and assess the possible benefits of moving. He was not, however, particularly encouraging. "I will visit your colony," he wrote his brother-in-law candidly in early 1825, "but unless I thought we could better our situation I would rather live here."[21]

Stephen appeared to accept this news from Perry, at least for the time. "Our brother seems to think," Brown Austin reported to his sister, "owing to the yet infant state of settlement that it would not be altogether advisable for Mr. P. to remove to this country at present—there is nothing that he could do to be advantageous to him for some years to come." Stephen apparently believed that Texas was too unsettled for them, but it was just as likely that Perry's earlier letter and the exposition of his assets convinced Stephen that there was no financial benefit to be gained from the Perrys leaving Missouri. Yet both of the Austin brothers still hoped that Emily and her family would decide to come to Texas. As Brown put it, "Indeed, my dear Emily, it certainly will be '*the most joyful period of our lives*' when we can embrace our sister, with 'peace and plenty' smiling around us after the many vicissitudes we have passed through the last six years." Meanwhile, in Missouri, the Perrys' lives went forward. Emily's domestic duties as wife and mother increased with the birth of a son, the first child of James F. Perry, on June 24, 1825. A healthy boy, they named him Stephen Samuel, honoring him with the first name of his uncle in Texas, while the middle name was that of both James' cousin and brother. "I am happy to hear," the new uncle wrote Emily from Texas, "that you have a fine son, and thank you and Mr. Perry for him giving him the name of Stephen after me." In a somewhat joshing tone, Stephen also reminded her that many years earlier, a fortuneteller in Philadelphia told Emily that she was destined to have nine children. This prognostication proved eventually to be inaccurate. Emily would give birth to four children during the time she lived at Potosi with James F. Perry. The second child, Emily Rosanna Perry, was born in September of 1826 but lived for only four months. Emily gave birth at Potosi to another daughter, Eliza Margaret Perry, on January 3, 1828. A son, James Elijah Brown Perry, was born two years later on May 17, 1830, and survived less than a year. Hence, only Stephen S. Perry and Eliza Perry lived into adulthood. During her lifetime, Emily would give birth to a total of eleven children, and six of them lived beyond childhood.[22]

Even with her considerable family duties in Missouri, Emily still hoped to be reunited with her brothers in Texas. She wished that Stephen might return to Missouri for a visit, writing to Brown, "I do hope you will exert yourself to try and persuade our Dear Brother to visit this Country." However, she realized that his financial situation would preclude such a trip, "for I well know that Stephen will never visit Missouri until he has it in his power to satisfy every claim against him." No sooner had Emily sent this letter to Texas than another one arrived at Potosi from Stephen, in which he again seemed to vacillate regarding Emily's move. "A new country would suit such a family," he wrote his sister about her prospects in Texas, "although I cannot take it upon myself to advise you to move to this—Mr. Perry must come when he has the leisure and look for himself." Two months later, Stephen expressed countervailing sentiments in a letter written at Christmastime of 1825. He appeared to be almost morose about the prospect of James Perry visiting Texas. "I am very well satisfied that you have not moved here," he wrote Emily, "the country is very new yet, and I think Mr. Perry can do better where he is for the present than he could do here—we have but little commerce as yet." Within the month, Stephen had changed his mind again. Soon after the new year of 1826, he wrote, "I wish Mr. Perry to come and pay me a visit, tell him to come next fall and take a good look at the country." Stephen advised Emily that Perry ought to plan a trip that would permit him to spend at least three months in Texas. Austin wanted him to come "without fail."[23]

A few weeks later, Brown wrote his sister from Texas to echo the opinion that they should consider a move within the year. By the end of that summer, however, Stephen had inexplicably cooled his ardor, and the reason he gave seemed curious at best. He reported to Emily that a constitution of government was in the process of being written for the state, and he worried that it might be a mistake for the family to come to Texas before its completion. It will "be finished shortly," he advised his sister, "and when I see it I can give Mr. Perry more certain advice as to the prospect of a removal here." Emily must have been disappointed to read that "until then I do not wish him to derange his business where by he is making any preparations for a removal." She most assuredly entertained hopes of moving to Texas, and she often worried about her brothers there. "I very often think of you," Emily wrote him, "and think of how much you must have suffered in that wilderness." Given the mixed opinions that she received from her brothers, almost two years of discussion and letter writing had not convinced James Perry to make the move. Perry had a well-deserved reputation as a man of determination, decisiveness, and practicality. Towards the end of 1826, he put the matter succinctly to Stephen in definite terms. Perry wrote, "Emily is anxious to remove to your country, but unless the prospects are very flattering I think it is very doubtful whether ever we remove there." This settled the matter for the time being.[24]

Of his own accord, Stephen ignored this rather frank refusal and petitioned the Mexican government to secure an eleven-league grant of land for the Perrys. He also suggested by letter to his brother-in-law that the small settlement at San Felipe would be a good location to open a profitable general store. By the late 1820s, the town had about thirty buildings, a small school, and a population of almost two hundred. James F. Perry responded in a somewhat noncommittal fashion in March of 1828, explaining, "I feel anxious to see the country but the situation of my business would not permit me to leave it, nor is my prospect any better at present." Such protestations had little influence on Stephen. By the late 1820s, he had found an additional inducement for the Perrys to come sooner rather than later: namely, the changing status of slavery in the colony. Elements in the Mexican government wanted to outlaw definitively the institution of slavery in Texas, although Austin and his associates had successfully opposed this development. All of that changed, however, when the Mexican state government at Saltillo authored a constitution that would end the importation of slaves into Texas from the United States. In particular, it stated that "from and after the promulgation of the Constitution in the capital of each district, after six months the introduction of slaves under any pretext shall not be permitted."[25]

Austin encouraged the Perrys to come to Texas before the provisions of this law took effect. He wrote Emily in May 1827 to recommend that "if there are any persons in your part of the country having slaves that wish to remove the year—Hurry them on before the expiration of time." Stephen realized that the slavery provisions in the new constitution had the potential to seriously curtail immigration into the colony from the United States. He therefore worked to influence the state government at Saltillo to grant him an exemption. It took him over two years to succeed, but by late 1829, he could write James Perry to report that "the difficulties as to slaves are all removed by a new exemption from the general colonization law." Nonetheless, Stephen advised the Perrys to go before a judge in the United States to "indenture their servants by right of contract," ensuring their status as slaves in Texas. This process took advantage of the legal technicality that Mexico had debt peonage laws. In effect, blacks brought from the United States were technically slaves as long as their owners had taken the protective measure of economically indenturing them with a contract at law.[26]

The right to bring slaves into Texas was important to the Perrys, and in that regard, they were typical of many families who contemplated a move from the United States to the colony. Austin understood that the great majority of immigrants would be arriving from slaveholding areas where cotton reigned as the fundamental underpinning of the agricultural economy. The decades after the War of 1812 were a time of marked westward migration of the elite southern planting class as planters and their families spread across the Gulf Coast and through the deep delta region of the Mississippi River Valley before spilling into Texas. As empresario, Austin believed that one of his functions was the guarding of slavery, as it was a viable institution for attracting settlers.

He wrote a series of legal procedures in 1824 as part of his Civil and Criminal Regulations for the colony, which constituted a "slave code" that was very similar to those found in the older southern states. He also worked with vigor during the 1820s to ensure that those officials in the Mexican government who wished to end slavery would not be able to do so in Texas. By 1826, it was clear that most of Austin's views about the importance of slaves had been accurate. During the first two years of settlement, sixty-nine of the Austin colonists came with slaves, and persons of bondage constituted approximately 25 percent of immigrants from the United States. These numbers continued to grow for the remainder of the decade. As historian Randolph B. Campbell noted of slavery during the Empresario era, Austin and his colonists "began to establish the institution just as it existed in the United States."[27]

Although the matter of slavery seemed resolved, the matter of the Perrys' move to Texas was still not settled. Emily stayed in touch by letter with Stephen and especially Brown, never abandoning the prospect. Throughout the years of this correspondence, she was tender in her letters to Brown. They had always been close as children, and now that he had gone to Texas, she eagerly followed his progress through life and took genuine pride in his accomplishments. Emily was particularly pleased when Brown married a Texas girl, Eliza Westall. Her father, Thomas Westall, had come to Texas in 1824. He established a very successful plantation on the lower reaches of the Brazos River and had business dealings with Stephen. Brown and Eliza had a son, born in 1828, who they named Stephen F. Austin Jr. in honor of his uncle. Emily warmed to the idea of being an aunt to this baby. Eliza also became involved in the effort to persuade Emily and her family to move to Texas, writing at one point to entreat her new sister-in-law to join them.[28]

By the time he became a father, Brown had taken up various business enterprises, one of which involved a foray into Texas coastal transportation. Emily was pleased about Brown's growing success in forging his own business operations, especially in following the footsteps of the New Haven relatives into maritime commerce. By the late 1820s, the Austin colony still lacked regular maritime communication that would link that region of Texas with New Orleans. Brown partnered with his cousin John Austin, and together they purchased the schooner *Eclipse* for the purpose of conducting such trade. Brown, along with several other men, traveled to New Orleans in August of 1829, where they were to make arrangements for establishing a shipping line between the Mississippi and the Brazos River. They arrived in the Crescent City to find that the area was experiencing a yellow fever epidemic. Brown was the first of his traveling party from Texas to take sick. During his first afternoon in New Orleans, he complained of a pain in his stomach and a mild headache. By the next day, his condition had worsened considerably. His host, John W. Collins, called for a physician to visit him, but the next morning, Brown succumbed to the disease. As was the custom during yellow fever epidemics, his friends and associates quickly buried him within two hours of his death. One of them shortly thereafter wrote to Stephen in Texas with the bad news.[29]

When news of her brother's death arrived, Emily reacted with predictable dismay and sadness. Brown's unexpected passing, however, devastated Stephen F. Austin to a much greater degree. He loved his brother very much, and as one biographer noted, he "had taken great pride in Brown's business success, and Brown had proved a valuable ally in everything from political lobbying to Indian fighting." This news so affected Stephen that he took to bed for nearly a month, most likely suffering from a recurrence of the malaria that routinely plagued him. He continued for a long period in an "extremely critical state" of health that at times made him appear to be "insensible and at the point of death." One associate noted that Austin remained "prostrate in bed, immobile and incapable of doing anything whatsoever." By the early fall, Stephen was able to resume some of his activities, although the unexpected loss of his brother remained a burden that he carried forever. Ever the practical businessman, the end of 1829 found Stephen arranging the affairs of Brown's estate on behalf of Eliza and his namesake nephew. As part of that process, Austin negotiated with the Mexican government and various settlers to secure title to the land holdings in which he and Brown had invested.[30]

Brown's untimely death and its debilitating impact on Stephen F. Austin caused the empresario to redouble his efforts to have the Perry family settle in Texas. Stephen felt very alone and wrote to Emily and James "not to delay any longer than is absolutely necessary to close all your affairs, or put them in training to be closed." He further noted, "I have never been as thoroughly convinced as I now am of the future rise of this country. In a year more this colony will be filled up. Now then is the time, if you remove soon you must make a fortune." Stephen followed this entreaty with a letter written on New Year's Day of 1830, in which he frankly told James, "You may be sure that I would not urge your removal in so positive a manner if I was not convinced that you will be greatly benefited. There is no time for hesitation or delay." Brown's widow joined in these requests, writing to her Missouri in-laws that "if Stephen were sure that you would move in the spring, he would fatten up and be a different man." Emily commiserated with her brother, and she professed to Stephen early in 1830 that she had long yearned to live in Texas. "You wish us to move," she wrote with a touch of melodrama, "and O! How joyfully I would commence preparing for such a journey." She indicated that her husband James was the reason they remained in Missouri. "I am fearful that there is nothing that I can say to persuade Mr. Perry even to go and look at the country," she wrote Stephen. "It has been my wish to move," she continued, "and I have every year urged my husband to visit you but cannot get him started; he is so completely bound to the mines and the mining business, that I believe he thinks he never can make money at anything else." However, economic conditions were changing for Perry in Missouri. By the start of 1830, he had become very discouraged about the continuing low price that lead commanded in the markets of the West. Indeed, Perry complained to his brother-in-law in Texas that the Missouri lead mining industry was "worth nothing."[31]

This news about the decline in lead prices prompted Austin to write numerous letters to James and Emily during early 1830, literally peppering them with requests to move. For many months, the Perrys chose not to respond. Their delay was no doubt occasioned by James' reticence. He and his family were surrounded by the extended circle of Perry in-laws. Nonetheless, Stephen's glowing reports regarding the potential for financial success in Texas seemed promising, if not beguiling. These prospects, coupled as they were with the death of Brown Austin, changed the situation in Missouri. Brown's passing had strengthened Emily's resolve to move, and James apparently agreed in order to satisfy her. The fact that Stephen had successfully secured an eleven-league grant for the Perrys was a further inducement for James to visit Texas. Under Mexican law, once the patent application for land had been approved, as had happened to this grant, the grantee had to complete the title process by personally claiming title to the land to be surveyed and settled. This meant that James Perry would have to personally appear in the province in order to prove the holding at law. He accordingly traveled to Texas during the spring of 1830, arriving at San Felipe in April to learn that Stephen was elsewhere in the colony surveying the land along the lower Brazos Valley. After finding lodging in the town, James struck out to locate his brother-in-law.[32]

THE MOVE TO TEXAS

James Perry found Stephen and the survey crew in an area east of the Brazos River near Galveston Bay. Austin was "most agreeably surprised" to see his brother-in-law. James stayed with him for about ten days as they tramped across the fifty-thousand-acre grant that Stephen intended for Emily's family and was then busily surveying. Perry liked the location and was particularly impressed with the rich agricultural prospects of the property. The two men talked much of Emily and the children. This prompted Stephen to write his sister, "I am really happy at the idea of your leaving that cold region. I look forward to many days of peace and enjoyment in this country. I hope in a few years to free myself from all my debts and to close my affairs here so I may have a quiet and relieved life in the society of my sister and her family." With the surveys essentially completed, Perry returned to San Felipe, where Stephen joined him several days later. Perry made ready to return to the United States and told Stephen that he and Emily would be moving to Texas the following year. It was Perry's intention to sell his business in Missouri, travel to the East Coast of the United States to procure goods to sell in the store he planned to open at San Felipe, and thereafter return with Emily and the rest of the family.[1]

The decision to move to Texas proved to be a somewhat atypical one for Emily and her family, at least within the larger parameters of westward migration by southern elite families on the antebellum frontier. Historical research has shown that men and women from the upper classes of the region frequently had different viewpoints about leaving the more established areas of settlement and moving to unsettled areas of the Southwest. For the most part, men, as the head of family, made such moves for reasons of potential economic betterment. They saw going to the new areas as an opportunity to gain greater wealth and personal prosperity. The women from these families characteristically did not favor migrating. They often disapproved of the move, equating it with an undesirable alteration in their lives. In the case of the Perry family, James and Emily did manifest different views about their move to Texas but with the gender roles reversed. In part, this might be explained by the fact that James was not culturally a southerner by birth or background. He had worked as a storekeeper and mine operator, as opposed to a planter. Emily's desire to migrate to Texas said much about her patrimonial identification as an Austin, since she clearly saw the move as reuniting her family rather than the departure of her husband, herself, and their children from the place where they had lived.[2]

Emily's move to Texas, however, did not progress as rapidly as James had promised Stephen F. Austin when he departed the province. Various problems soon appeared. One of them was a misunderstanding between James and Stephen regarding the grant of land that they had surveyed along the west end of Galveston Bay. Once Perry had returned to Missouri, he received a letter from Stephen and learned, to his surprise, that the title to this property had been jointly registered in the names of himself and Emily, also including the Bryan children. Perry had apparently assumed that the grant would be entirely in his name as the male head of household, which was standard legal practice during that era. Perry strongly took his brother-in-law to task for previously failing to mention how this grant would be legally registered with the Mexican government. He wrote a hotheaded letter, stating frankly, "Through the whole course of my life, I have ever acted candidly towards both relatives and friends and hope ever to do so and would wish them to act so towards me." He was "mortified" by the fact that Stephen had not mentioned this during his visit. Perry felt that his brother-in-law had not been forthcoming with him, and he told Stephen that he "did not expect you would have been reserved in anything that related to the sole object of my journey to that country." Emily's reaction to this dispute remains unknown, but James eventually calmed down and went forward with the move. The affair passed, and the grant remained registered jointly in the names of Emily and James Perry, along with the Bryan children—an unusual arrangement under Mexican law in which married women shared their community property with their husbands anyway.[3]

As plans accelerated in Potosi to close out the family's affairs, Emily made a decision that no doubt greatly pleased her brother. Stephen had long spoken of having one or more of the Bryan sons come to Texas for the purpose of being with him. Emily and James decided that thirteen-year-old Austin Bryan should leave as soon as possible to be with his uncle. It would be the young man's responsibility to help open a general store in San Felipe that would provide the family with an income. Ever the astute businessman, James Perry did not want to move to Texas until he had arranged for a steady source of money. He knew shopkeeping best, so that was the business he chose. Perry enlisted one of his Potosi business associates, William W. Hunter, and formed a partnership with him to establish the store at San Felipe as soon as possible and certainly before the family arrived. Emily knew Hunter well and approved of him taking Austin Bryan to Texas and reuniting him with his uncle Stephen. Young Austin would work in the store, thus gaining some of the business experience that his two uncles had advised over the years. This was to be the first time that any of Emily's children had been away from their mother.[4]

Austin Bryan kept in close touch with Emily once he left for Texas. She doted on his letters and always replied to them. He gave her detailed accounts of their stop at New Orleans and of seeing Texas for the first time. "On the second of January, 1831, we entered the Brazos River," young Austin wrote, "and I first put foot on Texas soil." Austin Bryan and Hunter continued up the river and landed at Brazoria. Hunter made contact with Josiah H. Bell, who agreed to warehouse some of the goods the two men had brought with them until they could find a location for the store at San Felipe. Hunter wrote several days later from San Felipe, informing James and Emily that he had rented a very small house that would serve as the location of the store. It was located near James Whiteside's boarding house, where Perry had stayed during his earlier visit. Hunter reported that Austin Bryan took his room and board there. Young Austin formed a closer relationship with Mr. and Mrs. Whiteside, calling them "Uncle Jimmy and Aunt Betsy." He also enjoyed the lively company of the other guests in the establishment, especially that of Colonel Ira R. Lewis, his wife, and two daughters, Cora and Stella. "It was there," an elderly Austin Bryan recalled fifty years later of the Whitesides', "that I used to dandle on my knee my present wife, Cora Lewis, who was then two and one-half years old."[5]

Back in Missouri, Emily was having a difficult time preparing for the move. Much needed to be done, including sorting through the accumulations of a lifetime, deciding what should go to Texas and what should be left with friends and relatives. The unusually cold and bitter winter months slowed these tasks. Two feet of snow covered the ground at Potosi for almost six weeks. Emily found it impossible to attend to any kind of business due to the harsh cold and bad weather, as she and the rest of the family were housebound. She wrote her son Austin in February, saying, "I hope that winter is over for I am truly tired of such extreme cold weather." Her letter also contained shocking news. The Perrys' small son James had died at only nine months of age. "Yes! My son, your darling brother is no more," Emily wrote. "He died on the

14th. He was taken with a vicious cold and sore throat which terminated his earthly career." She seemed philosophical about this: "I hope that my loss is his gain; he has in all probability escaped much pain and suffering, in this world. He was young, free from sin, and now is happy." Rather than dwell on this sadness, Emily characteristically used her letter to Austin as a means to encourage him to greater efforts. Emily was always a person of great moral rectitude, a champion of proper behavior, and an advocate of diligence. Application to duty was an important virtue that formed an integral part of her worldview. This she sought to pass on to her children. Even in reporting the sad loss of the infant James, she admonished Austin that he should work hard, learn, and persevere. She particularly encouraged him to keep good company and to avoid unsavory companions. She urged him to be steady, firm, and positive, doing only things that were upright. "You should apply yourself closely to business, be alert on all occasions," she told him, "and always have Mr. Perry's interest in view, he has been a good father to you." It was Austin's duty to repay him by being a success. Emily also told young Austin that the preparations for the permanent move to Texas were not progressing as quickly as she wished. "I am extremely anxious to commence our journey," she wrote. "Every day appears a month to me, there appear so many obstacles in the way, that at times I am quite low spirited." In perhaps an overbearing fashion, as only a mother could do, Emily admonished her son to "read this letter everyday, everyday, my dear Austin; by doing so, it will remind you of your promise to write often, and to prevent you from forgetting your friends in Missouri."[6]

In the meantime, the winter passed, and the warmer spring weather arrived at Potosi. Emily had regained her resolve after the death of baby James, and the Perrys began making their final plans to move to Texas. One of Emily's tasks in this regard fulfilled the wishes of Maria Brown Austin. She made arrangements to move the remains of her parents, Moses and Maria, to the cemetery in Potosi. This accomplished, Emily continued to pack the household goods. Perry traveled to New Orleans to purchase additional items to be shipped to the San Felipe store. He bought bolts of cloth, several reams of paper, an assortment of shoes, and cakes of gunpowder, along with two boxes of hats. James returned to Potosi by May, and he and Emily spent most of their time packing the household goods and arranging their personal effects. They had already sold their home in Potosi with the understanding that they would continue living in it until they moved to Texas, which they initially told the buyer would be in April. Since that time had come and gone, the new owner was presumably impatient for their departure.[7]

By June, they were ready to get underway for Texas. Emily's determination to leave seemed all the more remarkable because she had learned that she was pregnant, and estimates held that the baby would most likely be born after their arrival in Texas. She would thus make the trip as an expectant mother. Much about Emily's resolve and fortitude can be seen in the fact that she decided to go anyway. James' niece Lavinia Perry, who had been living with them in Potosi, would specifically care for Emily. The young girl had earlier come from Ohio to live with the Perrys in Missouri and was well on her way to becoming a permanent part of the family circle. Emily and Lavinia had forged a close relationship, almost as mother and daughter. The family decided to travel using the overland route through Arkansas, which was one of the three routes that immigrants usually employed in journeying to Texas. Another popular route involved traveling down the Mississippi to New Orleans, thereafter sailing to the mouth of the Brazos. A variant on this route gave travelers the option of disembarking at the point where the Red River flowed into the Mississippi and then traveling up to Natchitoches. Here, passengers and cargoes were loaded onto the carriages and ox carts by which they traveled to Texas overland. A third and oldest route followed the Southwest Trail through Arkansas to Fulton on the Red River and then turned southwards into Texas. Fulton had been founded by Emily's first husband, James Bryan, over a decade earlier. The Perrys favored the overland route through Arkansas since it would give them the ability to haul more of their possessions in heavy wagons. The caravan of almost twenty travelers departed Potosi on June 7, 1831. The family included James and Emily, the Bryan and Perry children, and Lavinia Perry. They brought nine slaves, presumably the ones who had come from the James Bryan estate along with several belonging to James F. Perry.[8]

Their household goods and the supplies needed for their new home filled two large wagons. Emily and Lavinia rode in a carriage that was driven by James or Joel, who was then sixteen years of age. The slaves herded several dozen horses and cattle, various chickens, and some geese. Ten-year-old Guy M. Bryan rode almost the entire way from Missouri on a mule, an animal that lived for a number of years thereafter in Texas as somewhat of a family pet. Emily and her family benefited from the very detailed instructions that Stephen F. Austin had given them regarding the items they should carry to their new home in Texas. "Bring all your books and bedding," he had written his sister. He cautioned her not to carry furniture and heavy articles, although in two instances, Emily ignored this particular admonition by transporting both her piano and an ornate bed frame. Stephen warned her "to start with provisions enough to last the whole journey, and try and bring a pair of geese or tame ducks." He told Emily to pack a supply of seeds for the garden, dried spices such as sage, summer savory, and horseradish, along with the pits from peach and crabapple trees to be used in replanting. "Try and bring some of the breed of English cattle," Stephen further advised. "Nature never made a better place for livestock." He also made a special request that his sister bring a copy of the laws of Missouri, as well as the state constitutions of Missouri and Illinois.[9]

Bedstead that Emily brought from Missouri to Texas.
Courtesy of the the Brazoria County Historical Museum.

The Perrys' arduous, slow journey overland took almost three months as they rolled through Arkansas and northeast Texas during the hottest part of the southern summer. Six months earlier, Emily had been living with two feet of snow; now the steamy temperatures daily approached the century mark. It is little wonder that most everybody on the trip took sick at some part of the journey. After they had arrived at their destination, James F. Perry tersely told a friend, "We had a long tedious journey getting here." This was especially the case for Emily, who was in the third trimester of her pregnancy. Lavinia did the best she could caring for her aunt, but the trip took a physical toll on Emily nonetheless. Emily believed that she would have to take to bed upon her arrival in Texas and leave the task of building their first home to James. As the Perrys neared San Felipe, Stephen and young Austin Bryan rode out on horseback to greet the travelers near the headwaters of the San Jacinto River. There Emily and her brother finally found themselves reunited for the first time in over a dozen years. It must have been a joyful occasion for all of them, although Austin Bryan would laconically refer to the event only by noting in his memoirs, "My mother arrived at San Felipe on August 5, 1831, after three months journey by land from Missouri."[10]

The small town of San Felipe that greeted Emily and her family did not present the new arrivals with a picture of much sophistication, even by the standards of Missouri's Ozark Plateau. The place seemed a bit rude and simple. Rosa von Roeder, another immigrant who came to Texas during the early 1830s, recorded in her diary an apt characterization of the place, noting that she found no church to attend. In addition, San Felipe had only "from two to four stores, besides a tavern and a saloon and from thirty to forty private houses. In the stores you could buy almost anything you wanted." The settlement, really a village of huts and other rude structures, contained about fifty buildings and houses, most of them small and constructed by amateurs. Only one wood-frame house existed in the entire town; everything else was made with logs. Emily and her husband never had any intention of settling at San Felipe, so they were not particularly concerned about what they saw. Nevertheless, all agreed that Emily could travel no further at that time because of her condition. James therefore secured lodging for her with "Aunt Betsy" Whiteside, and there she would await the birth of the baby along with Lavinia and the younger children. Emily left it to James to take possession of the tract of land he had proved the year before. James almost immediately struck out for the lower Brazos Valley to begin building the family a house on the property and plant the fall crops. Joel and the slaves went with him while Guy and the Perry children stayed at San Felipe, where Austin Bryan was working at the store. At this point, Emily and James received a rather surprising observation from Stephen, who was very free with his unsolicited advice regarding the Perrys' plans to start their plantation. Since James' visit to Texas the previous year, Stephen had apparently decided that he would prefer Emily and her family to settle at a new location several miles west of the area to which James and Joel were going. He mentioned this for the first time after their arrival at San Felipe. The new tract of land was located on the south side of the Brazos River and bordered a large, grassy prairie that filled most of the area from the river to the Gulf Coast several miles to the south. Locals called the area Gulf Prairie. It encompassed well-watered fields, rich pastureland, and timber stands. Stephen felt that its easy access to the Brazos would provide for convenient shipping and water transport to the small settlement of Velasco, which sat at the entrance of the river to the Gulf of Mexico. Importantly, Stephen knew that since the district was already well settled and populated, the Perrys would have neighbors and not be isolated. He called this tract of land Peach Point. In advancing this new location to Emily and her husband, Stephen clearly felt that their home was his as well, and somehow he felt entitled to participate in the Perrys' decisions about where and how they would establish their plantation. Emily remained neutral in this discussion between her husband and her brother, preoccupied as she was with the impending birth of a child.[11]

James F. Perry did not share Stephen's high opinion of Peach Point. He preferred the tract located on the west end of Galveston Bay near the place where he had met Stephen on his earlier trip to Texas. Perry found this location particularly picturesque and therefore decided on a parcel of land that fronted on Chocolate Bayou at the point where another stream, Pleasant Bayou, flowed into it. James went to the Chocolate Bayou location to commence the work of setting up the plantation. He, Joel Bryan, and the slaves cleared brush and began building a rude cabin to serve as a home place for his family. Perry had hopes that Emily and the children at San Felipe could soon join him. "If the sawmill goes any reasonable time," he wrote his wife, "I hope it will not be very long before we are prepared to move the family down." Meanwhile, Stephen was not convinced that Perry had made the best decision in choosing Chocolate Bayou instead of Peach Point. He wrote his brother-in-law again to observe that the Gulf Prairie area, where Peach Point was located, would prove to be a faster growing area, while Perry's chosen location would remain isolated. He warned that Emily "may complain that I sent you to Chocolate Bayou." Perry found this a hollow objection since Emily never complained about the matter, something that she would not have been reticent to do if she so desired. Moreover, James was impressed with the possibilities at Chocolate Bayou for cattle raising. "We have very good water, tolerable good land, and timber," he told Stephen, "but what is most valuable is for stock." He did, however, admit that the location had its drawbacks, especially that "mosquitoes are plenty there." Nevertheless, Perry continued to build his plantation, giving it the name Oak Grove.[12]

Emily followed events closely at Chocolate Bayou by staying in regular correspondence with her husband while she awaited the arrival of the baby. By mail, she gave James ample advice on the planning of a garden, how to store pork, and other matters related to setting up housekeeping there. As a portent of momentous events to come, Emily also reported on the political news she had heard at San Felipe. "There has been another revolution broken out in Mexico," she wrote James at Chocolate Bayou. "The whole country is in a state of warfare, I hope they will let us alone." Those concerns were swept aside when Emily gave birth to a son at San Felipe on December 1, 1831. She named him Henry Austin Perry in honor of her cousin. Unlike her other deliveries, Emily recovered and gained strength relatively quickly after Henry's birth. She remarked, "The baby is not two weeks old and I have been out into the eating room twice; as bad as the weather has been, we have the prospect of a pleasant day at last, the first for two weeks." It should be noted that Emily took the lead role in the care of all her newborns and young children although she had ready access to slave labor. The slave Milley, especially, had become close to her mistress. However, Emily never used a nanny or a wet nurse, nor did the Perrys ever hire a domestic for childcare. In that regard, Emily clearly subscribed to the traditional notions of childcare, despite the fact that many families from the elite classes increasingly brought women from outside the family into their nurseries. By early February, Emily had tired of being at San Felipe and desired to move to Chocolate Bayou to be with James. She wrote him only few a weeks after Henry's arrival that she was ready to make the move. In particular, she told her husband, "I wish to be with you to share your labor." She noted that "time hangs very heavy on my hands."[13]

News of the infant Henry's birth redoubled efforts by James Perry and his stepson Joel Bryan to make the Oak Grove Plantation ready for the arrival of the family. Emily, the new baby, Lavinia Perry, and the rest of the children made the trek sometime in the mid-spring of 1832. Austin Bryan, for the time, remained at San Felipe to help tend the store. Emily and her brood brought all of their remaining possessions and quickly settled into the new house James had built for them. Although no historical description of the home exists, circumstances dictate that it was probably little more that a hastily constructed two- or three-room log cabin designed in the then popular "dog run" style, in which an open corridor ran through the building from side to side, separating under a common roof the only two rooms contained in the structure. Both enclosed rooms likely served as sleeping areas at night, while one room had a fireplace for cooking and thus constituted the kitchen area by day. During warm weather, the "dog run" or "breeze way" between the two rooms provided shelter and served as the living area for the family, while in the colder months, the kitchen room functioned as the day area. This was hardly an opulent living arrangement. James Perry was proven correct in the summer and fall of 1832 when Chocolate Bayou showed itself to be an excellent location for the raising of livestock. His herd thrived. Yet as Stephen predicted, its isolated location was a disadvantage, and this now worried Emily, who felt cut off from the settled parts of the province.[14]

Although Stephen agreed that Oak Grove had good stock raising possibilities, he continued to urge the Perrys to reconsider Peach Point throughout the hot summer months as Emily and the children sweltered on the swampy land. Stephen particularly liked the fact that there were several plantations at Gulf Prairie near the proposed site at Peach Point. One of these was Ellerslie, the home of John G. McNeel. It was already one of the most prosperous plantations in the district. In fact, without Emily's concurrence, Stephen drew up elaborate plans for a plantation home that he hoped Emily and her husband would eventually construct at the Gulf Prairie location. His plans were clearly grandiose given both the family's economic circumstances and his longstanding desire that they present a modest appearance because of his role as the empresario of the colony. The home he planned at Peach Point would nonetheless have been the biggest and most opulent private residence in Texas. He drew for Emily's consideration a rough sketch of a house and outbuildings, guidelines for the planting of ornamental gardens, and the cultivation of fruit orchards. He also provided recommendations for the placement of the cultivated cropland on the property. Austin admitted to Emily that his plans called for a "very convenient, and pleasant house, although it is on a pretty large scale; but not too large, if you think your purse will allow you to venture so far." The blueprint for the house had a dozen rooms with long, open galleries on both sides. Many rooms would have a door to the outside, thereby affording privacy for people entering and leaving different parts of the house. There would be a center section with large wings at each end of the house, one of which would have a high garret providing a view of the Gulf of Mexico several miles to the south. Stephen viewed the home as being as much his residence as that of Emily and her family. To him, Emily's family was his family, and he saw himself as a part of it. In that regard, he designated one of the wings as his private area containing a bedroom and an office. He also gave detailed instructions for the kitchen and pantry, which he envisioned as a large space at least twenty feet in length. The pantry would be convenient to both the kitchen and dining room, the latter of which would be "large enough to entertain company in handsome style without being jammed to death for want of room, and it will make a very pleasant sitting room winter or summer."[15]

It may be that Stephen's plans for the garden began to win Emily over to the Peach Point land. He clearly understood her love of gardening. The area around Chocolate Bayou was very swampy and the home place not given to the plantings of trees and vegetables. Stephen touted the great possibilities for the location of the gardens he envisioned at Gulf Prairie. He indicated that trees and shrubs should be placed in the front yard to give it a pleasing appearance, while the backyard would be more utilitarian. As an adult, Guy M. Bryan recalled the beauties of the front gardens as they eventually existed at Peach Point. "It is pleasant for a sore eye to wander in the dead of winter through walks with roses and fragrant shrubs of every kind and color, to meet at every turn the orange, the vine, the fig, and pomegranate, all of which abound in my mother's yard, the products of our genial climate and mother's guardian care." From Chocolate Bayou, Emily tactfully reacted by complimenting her brother on the thoroughness of his plans but did not take a position on whether or not the family would relocate.[16]

During the summer of 1832, James and Emily increasingly looked with favor on the prospect of moving to Gulf Prairie and building a home at Peach Point. Chocolate Bayou was very isolated. Emily missed regular visits with neighbors, and although San Felipe was not a big town, she had never been lonely there while confined before Henry's birth. Moreover, it was hot at Chocolate Bayou in the summer because the inland location deprived it of cooling breezes from the Gulf, while the swampy land and sluggish water of the district made for a problem with mosquitoes. Emily and James discussed these drawbacks and considered the relative merits of Chocolate Bayou and Gulf Prairie. Stephen's arguments in favor of the latter, coupled with the muggy and isolated conditions Emily's family had been experiencing, won the day. The deciding factor may have been that the family would not be giving up ownership of the property along Chocolate Bayou, which provided the best grazing for livestock. James could continue to run cattle there whether they moved or not. Emily and James therefore decided in favor of Peach Point.

Construction on a home at the new location began during the late summer months of 1832. Rather than implement her brother's grand plans for a formal house of unusually large size, however, Emily wanted a smaller one-story building along the general lines of a regular farmhouse. Initially, what the Perrys built was made of raw logs, although several years later, much of the house was enclosed with milled lumber. It was situated along the top of a ridge several miles south of the Brazos River in such a way that the ocean breezes struck the rooms running across the south front of the home. By November 1832, construction of the log home was almost complete. While Emily superintended the finishing touches and the move into it, James Perry turned his attention to the planting of corn and potatoes. This ensured that the family would have basic foodstuffs for the coming spring. Corn, in particular, was a staple of their diet, and they produced nine hundred bushels that first year. The entire family finally moved to Peach Point in December 1832. The home that Emily and the family occupied was nothing more than

Main house at Peach Point Plantation

a recently finished log cabin that would, over the years, become the original part of a larger house. Yet it always remained a simple one-story home without any pretension. It never had the grandiose appearance of the great plantation homes that eventually became fixed as stereotypical images in the popular culture of the American South.[17]

As they settled into Peach Point, Emily's cousin Henry Austin moved to Texas as well. He settled several miles away at a plantation he named Bolivar. Henry Austin's family and the Perrys thus became neighbors and had frequent contact for decades thereafter. Emily no doubt found it reassuring that one of her favorite relatives and the person who had helped her so much when she was a schoolgirl at New Haven was now living nearby. Henry's sister, Mary Austin Holley, now a widow, visited her brother over the years, and Emily grew even closer to her cousin. The two women shared an identification with the concept of family as an essential part of their lives, and because of this, they would have much contact over the ensuing years, although it was sometimes tension filled when they disagreed on various family matters. The Perrys' move to Gulf Prairie also coincided with James' decision to sell his interest in the store at San Felipe and devote all of his efforts to establishing the new plantation. William Hunter had already given up his interest in the store because of ill health. Perry had taken on Alexander Somervell as his new partner in the San Felipe mercantile enterprise. Somervell was from Missouri and had known Perry there. Austin Bryan continued to reside at the store, where he assisted Somervell and studied Spanish. During that summer, the young man wrote his mother that "I am getting along as well as could be expected with my Spanish." By early 1833, Perry had sold the store, but Austin Bryan remained to work there.[18]

The satisfaction that Emily and her family felt in finally putting down a firm foundation for themselves at Peach Point soon faded in the face of a devastating cholera epidemic that swept across the southern reaches of the United States during their first year on the new place. This illness touched the family when one of James F. Perry's cousins from Missouri, also named James, decided to immigrate to Texas, perhaps on the recommendation of Emily and her husband. Cousin James Perry was among those claimed by the rapidly expanding contagion. He died at sea while traveling to the mouth of the Brazos River from New Orleans onboard the schooner *Elizabeth,* which may have been one of the plague ships that brought cholera to Texas. The full-scale epidemic hit the lower Brazos Valley approximately one month after the death of cousin James, in the summer of 1833. Every settlement along the Brazos had large numbers of sick residents, and the death toll grew throughout August. James Perry wrote his brother-in-law Stephen in Mexico City that many of the neighboring plantations had been decimated. The towns of Columbia, Matagorda, Brazoria, and San Felipe were all hard hit. The McNeel, Westall, and Munson families, neighbors of the Perrys in the Gulf Prairie area, lost family members to the disease. One of the dead, Henry William Munson, was among the most prominent residents of the lower Brazos Valley. Having befriended the Munson family, James and Emily felt his loss deeply.[19]

By mid-August, the epidemic had struck Peach Point. Emily was the first to be laid low by the cholera, perhaps because she had already been suffering from a bad cold. Soon sick himself, James later remarked that Emily had been "very low indeed. I scarcely thought she would recover." There were so many sick people in the area that the Perrys had difficulty finding a physician to visit Peach Point. Samuel T. Anger, a local doctor, responded to Perry's request for his services by sending word by messenger, "My health is not such as to permit me to visit you at the present." Dr. Anger did recommend to James that Emily "take 2 grams of jalap and a teaspoon of tarter combined and mixed with water, twice a day until the fever leaves her—and for yourself I would take it one hour preceding the Yorkshire pill if you have any more fever—and if it does not succeed the first time in removing the fever, repeat in the same manner." Both James and Emily thereafter began to improve. Emily's eleven-year-old daughter, Mary Elizabeth Bryan, was not as fortunate. She took sick early in the month. The cholera progressed rapidly in her case, and after only five days of fighting it unsuccessfully, she died. Her grieving parents laid her to rest a short distance from their house at Peach Point in a burial plot that would provide the nucleus of what became the Gulf Prairie Cemetery. Other victims of the cholera epidemic began to be buried in the cemetery, including members of the neighboring Munson family.[20]

The arrival of cooler fall weather slowed the contagion, and as fewer people became ill, the number of deaths began to decline. The Perrys, however, were not the only members of the Austin family to have grappled with the illness. It also struck the Henry Austin family at his plantation up the Brazos. Sadly, Henry's wife died at Bolivar several days before the passing of Mary Elizabeth Bryan. This loss devastated Henry, and he never fully recovered from his grief. John Austin, his wife, and children, all cousins of Emily, perished in the epidemic as well. John had traveled to Texas with James Perry on his visit several years earlier. "I am so much affected by the deaths by cholera in Texas that I can scarcely write anything," Stephen F. Austin wrote from Mexico City, where he was dealing with the Mexican government. By October, the cholera epidemic had passed through Texas. Perry could report at the end of that month that his family was "generally in tolerable good health." The epidemic continued its journey southward into Mexico, finally reaching the center of the country and devastating its capital city. There were a large number of deaths in the Central Valley of Mexico, where an even greater part of the population suffered at the hands of the illness than had been the case in Texas. Stephen F. Austin was among the sick, worrying for a time that he would not survive. He wrote home that he had availed himself of a special remedy, which he did not identify. Austin attributed his subsequent recovery to this unspecified treatment.[21]

The end of the cholera epidemic did not bring the peace and quiet to Texas that James and Emily had sought when they moved from Missouri. They arrived along the lower Brazos River at a time of growing tumult and difficulty for all of the Anglo-American settlers who had come to the Mexican province. As the decade of the 1830s progressed, Emily's family at Peach Point faced completely unanticipated trials and tribulations that she could never have imagined back in Missouri. The political events leading to the Anglo-American revolt in Texas against Mexico made the task of wresting a new life from the soil of Gulf Prairie even more difficult. Nonetheless, Emily and the family did their best to persevere through the hardships, difficulties, and sorrows that the Texas Revolution would bring to Peach Point.

Emily soon found her worries increased when news arrived that Stephen F. Austin had been arrested and imprisoned in Mexico City. He had been there for a number of months as part of his effort to gain greater political rights for Anglo-Americans in Texas. Stephen had not been successful. With some dejection, he left Mexico City in December of 1833 to return home. However, Stephen had earlier written a letter to the town council of San Antonio, suggesting that Texas become a separate Mexican state from Coahuila, to which it was linked. This was against the policy of the government, and when the council forwarded this "treasonable letter" to authorities in Mexico, they ordered Austin's arrest while he was on his return journey. This caused a good deal of consternation in Texas, especially at Peach Point. Stephen F. Austin languished in prison for months while the Perrys and others in the colony despaired for him. Emily was particularly worried because, by the spring of 1834, they had heard nothing from him for over four months.[22]

At Emily's urging, James took over Stephen's personal affairs in Texas during this imprisonment, while both of the Perrys worked very hard in an effort to secure his release. Stephen was eventually moved to better quarters in Mexico City where authorities permitted him pen and paper. He began a regular correspondence with Emily and James that continued for the rest of the time he remained there, from December of 1834 until the late summer of the following year. In one of these early letters, he reiterated his desire that Perry superintend his personal business in Texas. He wrote James, "I wish you to take charge of all my pecuniary interests and business in conformity with the power of attorney that I sent you in May and June last." He also sent Emily two miniature portraits of himself that had been painted in Mexico City, along with some seeds for Peach Point that he had collected there. With the family ever on his mind, Austin beseeched his brother-in-law to give his "love to Emily and all the children," along with the other family members, including Brown's widow, her son Stephen F. Austin Jr., and the Henry Austins. As for Emily's children, Stephen specifically advised "to keep them at school." An understandably gloomy tone found its way into some of these letters, and this probably provided little complacency for Emily or the others at Peach Point. "I know not when I shall be at liberty," Stephen wrote in October. "There is no more prospect now than there was nine months ago. I am of the opinion that you may look upon me as dead for a long time to come." In a letter to Samuel May Williams, Austin reiterated that James Perry would be in charge of all of his personal affairs in Texas during the remainder of his detention in Mexico. "I wish you to close and finish all my business and affairs in conjunction with my brother-in-law James Perry," Austin wrote Williams, "and give him all the aid you can in so doing—deliver to him all notes and accounts due me, my desk, trunks, papers, etc., also copies certified of all my land titles." Stephen was more candid with Williams than he had been with the Perrys in discussing his state of mind. "I expect to die in this prison," he told his associate. "I have no reason to make any other calculation. It is hard and unjust and cruel."[23]

Stephen's imprisonment, of course, took a toll on Emily, who had not recovered fully from the earlier ravages of cholera. "I am sorry to hear Emily is unwell," Henry Austin wrote to Perry. "She must not be anxious about Stephen; all is going well and will come out well, if we can keep him from starving, meantime, which I find it difficult to do." With this reality perhaps in mind, Stephen attempted to maintain a caring attitude about the family in his letters home to Peach Point. "Remember me to all the children," he told Emily and James in the late fall of 1834. "Tell them to mind their books and study hard and lose no time in idleness." He also was able to send small gifts by post from Mexico. "I send Eliza a small pair of scissors, as an emblem of industry and the domestic virtues," he noted, "which she will possess to a great degree if she will attend as she ought to do, the precepts and example of her parents." As had been a consistent theme of Stephen's correspondence with Emily since the birth of the Bryan sons, he again offered advice about their careers: "Joel must be a good *planter,* Austin a good *merchant,* and Guy a good *lawyer.*"[24]

Stephen's observations about the education of Emily's children echoed the similar concerns of their parents. Emily was a strong believer in the power of education and insisted that her children be well educated. Even during the darkest days of Stephen's imprisonment, schooling at Peach Point took place according to a regular schedule under the direction of a privately engaged teacher, Thomas J. Pilgrim. An itinerant Protestant minister, Pilgrim had been in Texas since the late 1820s. He first arrived at Matagorda, eventually making his way to the Brazos River country, where he settled at San Felipe. There he opened a small school in 1829 that offered a curriculum including Latin, Greek, and conversational Spanish. Stephen F. Austin served on the board of overseers for this tiny academy. Pilgrim, however, soon ran afoul of the Mexican authorities because he also began teaching a Protestant Sunday School in the town, and only Roman Catholic religious activities could be openly conducted under the law. This situation caused Pilgrim to depart San Felipe and move down the Brazos to the plantation belt near Peach Point, where he found Emily to be a committed supporter of education. He moved to the Gulf Prairie area and opened a school that had an expanded curriculum, while it offered room and board at the rate of $4 per month. This enterprise apparently did not prove successful, because Pilgrim entered into special contract with the Perry and Munson families in September of 1833, just as the cholera epidemic reached full force. The two neighboring families agreed that Pilgrim would teach the children on their respective plantations for the sum of $500 per year. They required Pilgrim to teach "in such a house as they shall construct for him on the Prairie between Thomas Westall and James F. Perry, obligating himself to teach every other week six days, the other five." No sooner was Pilgrim's "old field school" in operation than cholera claimed Munson, whose last words were reported to have been "Please educate my children." The Pilgrim school held classes without interruption during the crisis months of Austin's imprisonment. In May 1834, James wrote to his brother-in-law in Mexico City that "Mr. Pilgrim still continues with us, the children are very well. Stephen F. Austin [Brown's young son who was then living with the Perrys at Peach Point] is going to school with him and begins to learn very fast." Stephen responded, "Remember me to Mr. Pilgrim. I am greatly pleased with him as a teacher."[25]

By the summer of 1834, Emily and James had become very active in attempts to free Stephen from his confinement in Mexico City. They openly worked with Thomas McKinney and their neighbors, the

McNeels, to find a way to put pressure on the Mexican government for Austin's release. Their first tactic was asking the Ayuntamientos, or municipal councils, in the various Anglo-American towns to send memorials to Mexico City imploring that Austin be released. In turn, the Perrys and McKinney sought legal representation for Stephen, consulting with Peter W. Grayson and Spencer Jack about these two attorneys treating with the Mexican government on Stephen's behalf.[26]

Grayson and Jack traveled to Mexico City in late 1834 to present the various memorials asking for the release of Stephen F. Austin from prison. They also carried personal letters from Emily to her brother. Austin was particularly heartened to receive them, writing to Emily that "your letters by Messrs. Grayson and Jack were a great relief to me, and afforded me more gratification that I have experienced in a long time." With perhaps a small measure of self-pity, he wrote to his family, "How anxious I am to be with you, and settle myself along side of you on a farm free from troubles or other matters." By this time, Austin was relying heavily on James and Emily to conduct his affairs in Texas. In November of 1834, he wrote detailed instructions for his sister and brother-in-law to follow in various personal and political matters. Regarding his personal finances, he asked Perry to settle financial accounts with the Westall family, the estate of John Austin, and Samuel May Williams. He also asked Perry to meet with Williams to determine the status of the various land titles to property that he was reserving for himself. He cautioned them not to be harsh with Williams, in case they determined this had not been accomplished. "Emily must not be hasty in taking up prejudices against Williams," he wrote. "He has his fits and starts and faults, but I do not believe he is unfaithful to me." Stephen also gave Emily the task of attempting to improve relations with the Wharton family. In many ways, William Wharton had become the nemesis of Stephen F. Austin, emerging as his chief political adversary in Anglo-American Texas. Austin and the Perrys had solidly aligned with the peace party's viewpoint of moderation regarding the Mexican government, while Wharton had become the leader of the more bellicose war party. Perhaps looking to future days when it would be prudent to present a united front, Stephen requested that James and Emily find a way to soften relations with their adversaries should an opportunity present itself. "If Wharton wishes to be friendly and makes any motions towards a visiting state of matters between the families," he wrote to Peach Point, "meet it kindly and let there be harmony but make no undue advances—though I need not say that to Emily, for she courts no one, and wishes for harmony with all. Mrs. Wharton is an amiable and talented woman."[27]

While Emily maintained good relations with the Whartons, events in Mexico City improved for Stephen. On Christmas Day 1834, the authorities released him from prison. He was, however, required to remain in Mexico City and consider himself to be on parole rather than a free person. This positive change in circumstances was no doubt received with some satisfaction by Emily and James, who continued to superintend Stephen's affairs in Texas. Although his parole was less than they wanted, it did give them some hope for the future. So too did the unexpected arrival of Mary Austin Holley in Texas during the late spring of 1835. The death of Henry Austin's wife during the cholera epidemic had plunged him into a deep melancholy from which he found it difficult to recover. This made it almost impossible for him to care for his children, and the situation at Bolivar Plantation greatly distressed both Emily and her cousin Mary. Henry Austin had written his sister to request that Mary provide a home for his children in Lexington, where she lived following the death of her husband, and he offered to bring them to the United States. Mary responded generously by instead traveling to Texas in order to accompany them back to Kentucky herself. Emily approved of these plans since she could effectively do little from her home at Gulf Prairie to care for Henry's children. Bolivar Plantation was a bit too far away from Peach Point to permit daily contact.[28]

Due to the rather limited time Mary had planned for this visit to Texas, a trip to Peach Point was not in order. Thus, Emily went down to the mouth of the Brazos when Mary arrived aboard the *San Jacinto,* going out to meet the vessel as it waited to cross the bar. "Mrs. Perry came for us in a boat," Mary recorded in her diary, "and we all went ashore to see her." The two women spent the evening in delightful conversation during which Emily "talked about her brother and family, and other interesting topics." There was much to discuss, including the Perrys' recent move to Peach Point, their efforts to develop the plantation, the ravages of the cholera epidemic, and Stephen F. Austin's imprisonment. Following dinner, Emily and Mary took a long walk on the beach and then returned to the ship to spend the night. The next day, the *San Jacinto* crossed the bar into the main river channel. Emily returned to Peach Point while Mary continued up the river to Bolivar, where she took charge of Henry's children and departed with them for Lexington.[29]

In spite of this very satisfactory visit with her cousin, Emily could not contend that affairs at Peach Point were joyful or carefree. This was especially the case regarding her ongoing worries about her brother, who remained on parole in Mexico City. His letters continued to arrive at Peach Point. "I look forward with the most heartfelt anxiety to that period when I shall be restored to you all once more," Stephen wrote the family, "so that I can enjoy your society and that of my friends in a log cabin, or a camp—far, very far, from the intrigues and villainous entanglements of palaces and politics." Emily, James, and the older children cared little about the political intrigues that so troubled Stephen. They had more pressing concerns regarding their efforts to develop the new plantation. Stephen's imprisonment in Mexico coincided with the years that James and Emily finished the home at Peach Point, constructed many of the outbuildings, and opened up the fields to large plantings. Their first crops came in during 1833, and the Perrys hoped to begin turning a profit by the following year. That did not occur. Although some planters in the Anglo-American districts of Texas experienced a bumper crop, such was not the case along the lower Brazos. As James wrote his brother-in-law in Mexico during late 1834, "Crops throughout the colony have been very good this season, with the exception of this immediate neighborhood. Our crops here were about ruined with the worm and not more than a third made." This placed the Perrys in precarious financial circumstances at the very time that James and Emily were superintending Stephen's business affairs and working to secure his return to Texas. Perry was therefore forced to throw himself on the mercy of his commission agents in New Orleans. He wrote to them early in the New Year to explain his financial problems. "It was my intention to ship you what little I made," he told his agents, "but on inquiry I found unless the duties amounted to $200, the money would have to be paid to the collector." For that reason, he combined his small cotton crop for sale on shares with that of another planter, and even then he suffered a relatively large loss. Most other matters at Peach Point therefore became of secondary importance during the spring and early summer as the family turned to planting another cotton crop.[30]

At the same time, Emily and James increased the number of slaves on hand at Peach Point, anticipating eventual profits from their planting activities. For example, in March of 1833, Perry purchased a field hand named Turner, who had previously been at San Felipe. The Perrys bought additional slaves during the planting season of 1834, including two teenage girls and a young boy, all of whom went to work in the fields. John Rice Jones Jr., a neighbor and old friend who had moved to Texas from Missouri, also offered Perry several slaves in return for the cancellation of a debt. By the end of that year, at least two dozen slaves lived on the plantation, and the Perrys were well on their way to creating one of the largest slave populations found on any Texas plantation during the antebellum era. By the 1840s, there would be almost fifty slaves living at Peach Point. Even with this number, James and Emily sometimes had to hire additional slaves from neighboring plantations during peak periods. They had little trouble finding such individuals, because the locale quickly became the most heavily populated slave area in Texas, a situation that would remain true until the Civil War. From Bell's Landing on the Brazos to the north of Peach Point, down to its mouth at Quintana, the lower stretches of this river boasted some of the richest planting land of the coastal bend. Eventually, over forty plantations lined its banks, creating the highest concentration of slaves anywhere in Texas, with over one hundred slaveholding planters. By 1845, an estimated two thousand slaves lived in this district, and seven plantations in the Brazoria area served as home to fifty slaves or more. Peach Point was one of these plantations, although the ownership of its slaves was split between James and Emily.[31]

Given the amount of land under cultivation and the slave population needed to maintain the operation, business affairs were a crucial concern at Peach Point. As was the case for many antebellum plantation families, business management rested in the hands of the husband, although Emily maintained a keen interest in all these matters and James kept her informed about all aspects of the agricultural operation. Perry was very meticulous in keeping agricultural records, noting in his daybook the amount of work done by each hand. Plowing began about February 1 and continued for several months. Perry staggered the planting of the crop so that early fields were planted by the time the last ones had been plowed. This enabled a rolling harvest that used fewer pickers and made for a more efficient laying-away of the crop. Emily took part in these activities, supervising the house servants, planning and preparing the meals, and directing operations around the house and farmstead. By May of 1835, James could write Stephen in Mexico City that affairs on the plantation seemed to be running smoothly. Mr. Pilgrim was holding classes, and "all our children are going to school and improving well." He noted that Austin Bryan was still at San Felipe and busy studying Spanish. "Joel is attending to the farm," his stepfather also reported to Stephen, "and I think he will make a good farmer." The redoubled efforts to bring in a better crop proved successful, since by the end of the season, Austin Bryan could write from San Felipe to his parents, "I am rejoiced to hear that you are all in good health and getting along so well in the way of picking our cotton."[32]

It was just as well that the planting season had been successful at Peach Point, because the early fall of 1835 brought increasingly serious political disturbances to Texas that would alter the lives of Emily and her family. A friend of the Perrys, J. G. McNeel, wrote to them from San Felipe in June of 1835 that hotheads there were openly talking of revolt against Mexico. Henry Austin sent a letter a few days later from Columbia to report to the Perrys that "an attempt has been made here today to involve us in an immediate revolution." He noted that a meeting was to be held in that town the following week to prepare a public resolution. Henry beseeched James Perry to come to Columbia and participate in the meeting so that the peace party viewpoint could prevail. Breaking his longstanding practice of remaining neutral, James attended the meeting and became a member of the committee delegated to draft a memorial. This document, no doubt influenced by Perry's moderation, was conciliatory and expressed hope that Texas could continue in "union, moderation, organization, and a strict obedience to the laws and constitution of the land." This short foray into a revolutionary meeting was one of James Perry's few overt involvements in the crisis. Nonetheless, the coming of the Texas Revolution would touch the lives of Emily and her family in many explicit and tangible ways.[33]

CHAPTER 5 PEACH POINT AND
REVOLUTION

In the tension-filled political atmosphere of summer 1835, news arrived in Texas that greatly heartened most Anglo-Americans, especially Emily and James. Stephen F. Austin was to be freed from his parole restrictions and would be returning to Texas. In July, Stephen wrote to Peach Point, "I expect to leave here for home this week by way of Vera Cruz or Tampico, unless I meet with company going by land, in which event I would go that way." Austin received his passport from the Mexican government on July 11 and sailed later that month for Texas, taking a vessel from Vera Cruz to New Orleans. After arriving in the Crescent City, he stayed there for several days before sailing for Velasco. "I am," he wrote his cousin Mary Austin Holley, "once more in the land of my birth, and of *freedom*—a word I can well appreciate. I shall leave here in a day or two for Texas." He did avail himself of some of the urban opportunities available in New Orleans; for example, he visited the Hotchkiss Bookstore located on Charters Street. There he purchased the published letters of Robert Walpole, a volume by Sir Walter Scott, Washington Irving's book on the conquest of Granada, and Dr. Johnson's dictionary.[1]

Austin left New Orleans on August 25 onboard the *San Felipe*, bound for the mouth of the Brazos River, which he sighted on the first day of September. At this point, those on the *San Felipe* saw a small sloop, the *Laura,* sail over the bar and into the Gulf. This ship was coming to greet Stephen F. Austin. Emily's son Joel was one of the passengers on the *Laura* and hence the first of the family to be reunited with their now very famous relative. This was a moment of great pride for young Joel

Bryan, and the retelling of this reunion became one of the stories that he routinely related to his descendants for the rest of his life. Once on shore, Joel and his uncle made plans to continue to Emily's home. "He came to Peach Point, nine miles from the mouth of the Brazos," Joel's brother Austin Bryan later recalled, "where his sister, my mother, lived, and the news of his arrival spread over the country, his having been gone since April, 1833."[2]

Emily and Stephen enjoyed an emotional reunion, especially since she had manifested much concern about the fate of her brother during most of the previous two years. This meeting was all the more meaningful to both since Emily was also pregnant for the eleventh time in her life. It was an uneventful pregnancy, but at the same time, the tumult of affairs and the absence of her brother in Mexico were most certainly not reassuring situations for her. As well, she had only recently recovered fully from the cholera epidemic eighteen months before. She was still plagued by a series of colds, headaches, and intermittent malaise. Austin recounted to Emily and the family his adventures in Mexico, while he also began to discuss his views for the future of Texas. In that regard, his experiences in Mexico City had hardened him. Stephen was no longer the peace advocate that he had been previously, and he was bellicose in his opinion that the time for revolutionary action had at last arrived. As neighbors and supporters increasingly called at Peach Point in order to pay their respects, it became apparent to Emily that some sort of official celebration should mark her brother's return to Texas. This led rather quickly to her planning an elaborate banquet and ball that would be held in nearby Brazoria during the first week of September. It would prove to be one of most memorable social events of the year and, in retrospect, the last major social gala before Texas erupted into revolution. The festivities took place at Brazoria on September 8 with several hundred people in attendance. The grand event began with a sumptuous banquet at three o'clock in the afternoon, which only the men attended since this was seen as a political event and speeches would be made. Austin sat at the head table as guest of honor. All of the Bryan and Perry men were present, even the younger boys Stephen and Henry, along with a number of others from across the Anglo-American settlements. Stephen's nephew Austin Bryan recalled that "there was a general turnout of the whole lower country." Everyone sat down at long tables before steaming platters of turkey, venison, and a variety of vegetables, complete with side dishes. Much wine was also served, and a considerable amount of toasting spontaneously occurred, with cousin Henry Austin giving three toasts at various points in the proceedings. This saluting with wine glasses came to a crescendo after the dessert, at which time Stephen, as the guest of honor, gave a rousing toast that everyone interpreted as a condemnation of Mexico and a sanctioning of revolution. He thereupon issued a call for open defiance against the Mexican government. With dinner and politics done, a ball with the ladies and young women who had come to honor Austin immediately followed. The men pushed the tables back to clear the dance floor for the almost one hundred couples in attendance.[3]

In particular, the Bryan boys had a remarkably good time, since they were all of an impressionable age at which they found such entertainments to be very beguiling. Austin Bryan noted, "There were more ladies at the ball than I ever saw together in Texas." The dancing continued almost all the night. "The Oyster Creek girls," young Bryan further recalled about the dance, "would not have quit had not the room been wanted for breakfast." After this grand celebration, Stephen returned to Peach Point with Emily and her family for a few additional days of rest before departing for San Felipe, where he sought to resume his business interests and inform himself about the revolutionary fever that was then sweeping the Anglo-American settlements. Emily clearly worried that he was leaving Peach Point too soon after his return to Texas. She believed that he needed more time to gather his strength and that he should remain at her home until he had fully regained his constitution. Nonetheless, Stephen departed the lower Brazos for San Felipe against not only Emily's advice but also against that of some of his supporters' wives. "All the reasons given by my friends Mrs. McKinney, Mrs. Jack, and Mrs. Williams," he wrote James Perry after arriving at his destination, "and also by Emily, against my keeping bachelors hall, I have already taken into view and a thousand more—It is a dog's life to say the least of it—But I am not yet a free man." Stephen did, however, call upon Emily at Peach Point for some needed support, writing, "I must therefore have sheets and blankets and some other things—and beds—the house is not large enough to have a family—we must have private rooms to write in, far from noise and interruption."[4]

Stephen's days of living in his "bachelor's hall" at San Felipe lasted only a few weeks, because urgent events quickly overtook his affairs as Anglo-American Texans moved precipitously towards an open revolution. Fighting between Texian settlers and a troop of Mexican soldiers broke out at the small town of Gonzales on October 2, 1835, when a detachment sent from San Antonio de Béxar attempted unsuccessfully to take back a cannon previously given to the English-speaking local authorities for defense against Native American raiders. News of this skirmish at Gonzales instantaneously sent all of the Anglo-American settlements in Texas into consternation, resulting in the mobilization of an increasing number of men who were ready for a fight with Mexico. Stephen F. Austin quickly found himself the *de facto* head of government in Texas, as a general meeting of the colonists was scheduled to convene at San Felipe during the first week of November. This body quickly elected Stephen as the commander of the volunteers at Gonzales. Emily's two oldest sons wanted to be with their uncle, and she reluctantly gave them her approval to go. Austin Bryan thus traveled to Gonzales with his uncle, and Joel Bryan left Peach Point, riding furiously to join them. Emily and James obviously worried about Stephen and their two sons. After a few weeks, most likely at Emily's request, James finally wrote a rather plaintive letter to Stephen asking for family news. "We have heard nothing from you and the boys," he said. "Tell Austin and Joel to write us when they have an opportunity as mother is very anxious to hear directly from them." James did report that everyone at Peach Point was getting along well enough, although "Guy and Eliza have been very sick but are now both well." The two older Bryan brothers were not unmindful of their mother's concerns. At the same time that James was writing to Stephen about them, Austin had sent a letter to his mother from the banks of Salado Creek near San Antonio. He reported on the decision that the army would take San Antonio, hoping that "we will have Béxar in four or five days." He noted that Uncle Stephen had not been well but was attempting to provide inspired leadership. "Uncle in his short speech," Austin related about a recent talk with the troops, "told them that he would remain as long as 10 men would stick to him, because the salvation of Texas depends on the army being sustained and at the same time the meeting of the convention."[5]

It was at this point that Stephen received word that the consultation in San Felipe had appointed him commissioner to the United States. He would share this mission with his longtime enemy William H. Wharton, with whom he was determined to cooperate. This news infuriated Emily, who had a very low opinion of Wharton and did not appreciate the fact that her brother would have to cooperate with him. Emily told Stephen that she looked forward to the time when Wharton's "proud spirit is completely humbled." Austin counseled reconciliation and made preparations to leave the army at San Antonio, although he remained for several weeks until such time as a new commander could take charge.

While Stephen's preparations to travel to the United States went forward, Austin Bryan and his brother Joel stayed with their uncle at San Antonio during the early weeks of November. Austin Bryan wrote his parents that there were about six hundred men in the camp at San Antonio, and he still had high hopes that they would be able to take the Mexican garrison at Béxar. In spite of this optimistic intelligence, however, young Austin probably did not provide cheering news for Emily when he reported, "Uncle is better and tired enough of commanding militia." "My health has been very bad since I left the Cibolo," Stephen later wrote to Emily, "and I've been unable to attend personally to the duties of my station." He did observe that he was improving generally in his health and that he was looking forward to going to the United States very soon.[6]

Austin Bryan traveled with his uncle back to San Felipe, taking pains to write his mother, "I left Joel at camp in good health and determined to see the last of war." From San Felipe, young Austin went back to Peach Point for a short visit with the family. He arrived home dusty, dirty, and disheveled from being with the army. When the young man appeared, walking up the drive from the main road, Emily watched him approach the house without recognizing him as her son. Meanwhile, Joel remained at San Antonio and participated in the remainder of the siege against the Mexican garrison at Béxar. He took part in the December 5 attack on the town and was present to witness the surrender of the Mexican garrison several days later.[7]

At San Felipe, Stephen busily worked to close out his affairs in Texas before he left for the United States. Most of the work consisted of arranging and validating the various land titles that belonged to him, for which he had not finished proper legal filing procedures. Austin Bryan returned to San Felipe after the short visit home in order to assist him in these activities, serving as personal secretary to his uncle. In mid-December, Stephen wrote a long letter to the Perrys outlining various land transactions in which he had been engaged, giving his brother-in-law instructions on what should be done with them. While Stephen and his nephew Austin worked at San Felipe, Emily gave birth to a healthy girl at Peach Point. Born on December 10, 1835, the parents named her Cecilia Perry, the eleventh and last child born to Emily. News of this happy event quickly spread to Joel in San Antonio and to San Felipe, prompting Austin Bryan to write somewhat impishly, "I have heard that I have a fine sister that I have never seen."[8]

Emily was proud of the baby and eager to show her off. In a happy circumstance, Stephen F. Austin did get to see his infant niece shortly after her birth when he passed through Peach Point in mid-December on his way to New Orleans. He stayed at the plantation for several days surrounded by the Perry family circle. He undoubtedly enjoyed the company of young Guy M. Bryan, Stephen S. and Henry Perry, their sister Eliza, and the baby Cecilia. He discussed with James and Emily some of his business affairs, especially regarding his land holdings and the debts that he owed. He thereafter traveled to Velasco, where he spent some of Christmas day writing the Perrys detailed instructions about personal business matters that were still on his mind. He told James Perry, "My object now is to close all my own settled affairs, pay all my debts, and try to fix myself so as to be comfortable."[9]

The early months of 1836 after Stephen's departure proved uneventful at Peach Point. Emily was fully occupied caring for her young baby while James busied himself with the affairs of the plantation. By letter, the Perrys learned about Stephen's progress in the United States. Passing through Lexington, he enjoyed a short visit with Mary Austin Holley, no doubt relating to her all the family news from Peach Point. Importantly, he also broached a matter to cousin Mary that was of great importance to Emily: namely, the education of the older Peach Point children at boarding schools in the East. In conversations with Stephen before he left Texas, Emily told him that she had already decided that Guy M. Bryan, Eliza Perry, and Brown's son, Stephen F. Austin Jr., who was living at Peach Point, should eventually be sent to the United States for schooling. Stephen heartily approved of this plan and said that he would ask Mary Austin Holley's advice about appropriate schools for the Peach Point children. These conversations with Mary Austin Holley in Lexington did establish the groundwork for the children attending boarding schools in the United States.[10]

That, of course, lay well in the future, as developing news of the Texas Revolution continued to arrive at Peach Point. The appearance at San Antonio of a major army under the command of General Antonio López de Santa Anna early in 1836 drastically altered the military situation in Texas and placed the Anglo-American settlements on the defensive. The major body of Texan troops that had participated in the siege of Béxar was already withdrawn from San Antonio, mostly returning to Gonzales. Joel Bryan had gone with them. In late February, Santa Anna's main force arrived in San Antonio de Béxar and, for the next thirteen days, laid siege to the Alamo defenders, who were under the joint command of William B. Travis and James Bowie. Travis earned a measure of historical immortality by writing a now famous appeal for aid addressed to "The People of Texas and All Americans." A courier slipped out of the Alamo with this letter and carried it to Gonzales to be transcribed into several copies by a local judge, Andrew Ponton. Riders fanned out from Gonzales and carried Travis' grandiloquent missive to all the Anglo-American settlements. One of these dispatch riders hurried through the night towards Brazoria, where the letter came into the hands of fifteen-year-old Guy M. Bryan, Emily's son. Young Guy was then boarding with Josiah H. Bell at Bell's Landing, along with his cousin Stephen F. Austin Jr., so that they could attend school at nearby Brazoria. When the courier from Gonzales arrived there completely exhausted, Bell gave young Bryan the letter and dispatched him southwards to carry it to the garrison at Velasco. Guy rode as fast as he could, spreading the news as he went. He stopped at Peach Point to show his parents Travis' letter before continuing to Velasco on a fresh horse provided by the Perrys. When Guy returned to Brazoria several days after this excitement, he found that his school had been cancelled due to the general crisis, so he returned home to be with his family at Peach Point.[11]

The Perrys viewed the unfolding of the revolution with great concern, especially since Emily was nursing an infant and there were several other young children in the household. James and Emily talked about leaving Peach Point if the Mexican army should begin an eastward movement from San Antonio. On the day before the Alamo fell, Henry Austin wrote to them from Brazoria with the advice that "it would be judicious for you to send Emily and the younger children" away as soon as possible. Henry painted a horrific picture of potential disaster that, if Emily read her cousin's letter, must have given her great pause. "I fear our hardest fighting will be on the Colorado or upper Brazos," Henry predicted, "and the anxiety which Emily would feel at having the enemy so near, the apprehension of a possible rising of Negroes, and the danger that Indians may avail themselves of the opportunity for plunder, and make an inroad, will distress her much and probably impair her health."[12]

When Peach Point received news of the Goliad massacre (at which some 350 Texian prisoners commanded by James Fannin were put to the sword by the Mexican army on March 27), the Perrys made their decision. James and Emily packed a large wagon with supplies, loaded the children, and left, accompanied by their slaves. Emily rode on the front seat of the wagon with baby Cecilia on her lap. They headed east, crossing the Brazos and traveling towards the San Jacinto River. Guy M. Bryan would later recall, "We joined the throng of fleeing people. As far as the eye could see, extended backward and forward, was an indiscriminate mass of human beings, walking, riding, and every kind of vehicle." "I shall never forget that picture," Guy Bryan remarked, "of men, women, and children walking, riding on horseback, in carts, sleds, wagons, and every kind of transportation known to Texas." This exodus became known as the Runaway Scrape. By the time Emily and the family reached the ford at Cedar Bayou, hundreds of people were backed up waiting to cross. There they witnessed mass confusion. Much of the procession was bogged down because a hapless oxcart had become stuck in the middle of the bayou. As Guy later remembered, the oxen were "lying down in the water with their noses out to enable them to breathe; a woman and two little girls were sitting on a mound in the marsh waiting for someone who would help them out of the bog." Appraising the situation, Emily immediately took charge. She handed the baby away, climbed down from the wagon, and waded out into the water. She spoke tenderly but firmly to the woman and encouraged her to try once again to get the wagon unstuck, offering the help of the Perry oxen. Emily's swift action and determined encouragement spurred the woman to new effort as she rose up, cracked her whip, and began yelling at her oxen, "Up, Buck and Ball, do your best." With Emily's assistance, they freed the cart, and everyone made it to the other side. Emily got back onto her own wagon, and the Perry family continued on to their destination, the plantation of a friend that was located several miles south of Lynch's Ferry. Arriving there, they found temporary lodging. "Emily and the children are safe at Scott's," James wrote Stephen on April 8. "God knows, when or where we will meet again."[13]

With Emily and the younger children now secure, Perry decided to continue on to Galveston Island to assist in strengthening defenses there. He took most of the Peach Point slaves with him. Once there, he discovered that the influx of refugees on the island had created a critical lack of foodstuffs and provisions in the city, so he and several other men immediately devised a bold plan to bring these badly needed items to Galveston. They took the steamboat *Yellowstone,* then at anchor off Galveston, up the Brazos River through territory behind Mexican lines to Brazoria, where they would load cargo of food and supplies with which to relieve the island settlement. They made the trip without incident, landing at McNeel's plantation. Perry disembarked and took a wagon through the Gulf Prairie area, stopping at various plantations to load it with goods. After dropping him, the *Yellowston*e continued up the river to Brazoria, where, upon arrival, those onboard the riverboat spotted units of the Mexican army moving through. They hastily turned the boat downstream and rushed back to Galveston without any supplies. Perry, who was standing on the landing near Gulf Prairie, witnessed the vessel pass downriver without stopping for him and the supplies he had gathered. Assessing his options, he hurriedly drove his fully loaded wagon down the road to Velasco, made the crossing of the Brazos, and sped by night to San Luis Island on the west side of Galveston Bay. There, tenders from the city loaded his cargo and brought it to the waiting populace. He returned to Galveston very much the hero of the moment.[14]

Meanwhile, Emily and the children remained at their safe haven south of Lynch's Ferry, some six miles down the San Jacinto River below the point where Buffalo Bayou joined it. Joel Bryan found them there since, due to illness, he had received a parole from the army. His brother Austin Bryan, however, had left San Felipe with the Texian force when it passed through earlier. Young Austin was now a soldier in General Sam Houston's army, which was, at that time, moving eastward towards the San Jacinto River. Hearing that it was approaching the area, young Guy M. Bryan requested his mother's permission to ride north and join his brother Austin as a common soldier. This must have been a hard decision for Emily to make, but she reluctantly agreed. Upon reaching the area around Buffalo Bayou, Guy learned that the major part of the

Mexican army under General Santa Anna had just been seen in the vicinity. Unwilling to risk crossing the bayou and, in so doing, perhaps be spotted by Mexican soldiers, he turned back to warn his mother and siblings about Santa Anna's approach. Hearing this distressing news, Emily decided to pack up once again and move south to Galveston, but before she could depart, she met James Perry coming up the river road to rejoin them, his work completed on the island.[15]

It was at this moment that Sam Houston's army met Santa Anna on the battlefield at San Jacinto. Emily and her family heard the sounds of battle from their location down the river. Austin Bryan participated in that afternoon's fighting and witnessed much of the horrific slaughter of Mexican troops on the field and at Peggy's Lake. He saw General Houston wounded and observed Thomas J. Rusk take command of the victorious Texas troops on that fateful day of April 21, 1836. Young Austin also assisted for several days thereafter in the process of rounding up the scattered remnants of the Mexican army from the surrounding brush. In that capacity, he was present when the captured General Santa Anna was brought into the Texas camp, unrecognized by Houston's men because the Mexican commander wore a private's uniform. It was Austin Bryan, fluent in Spanish, who, among several others, understood the chatter of the Mexican captives and realized that the general had been made a prisoner of the Texans. General Houston drafted Austin as his interpreter and through him interrogated the defeated Mexican commander. Shortly after the battle, young Guy arrived to join his brother Austin in Houston's army, finally fulfilling his desire of several weeks earlier to become a common soldier. Not much happened thereafter, and after a month or so, Guy developed a case of the measles that forced him to rejoin his family.[16]

With the fighting over, like hundreds of other Anglo Texans, Emily and her family began their journey home the week after the battle at San

Jacinto. The roads all across the Brazos, Trinity, and San Jacinto river valleys experienced a constant flow of people now heading west rather than east. The return for many of them was just as arduous as it had been on the Runaway Scrape. One young woman, Dilue Rose Harris, later provided a graphic memoir of her experiences on the trip home. The Rose family visited the recent site of the San Jacinto battle on the same day as the Perrys and, indeed, it appears that her father, Dr. Pleasant W. Rose, talked with Emily and James during this excursion. Afterwards, Emily arrived home to find complete disarray at Peach Point. For weeks, there had been no one to care for the place, plant the seedlings for the vegetable garden, or watch the livestock. A number of plantation chickens had found their way into the main house and were roosting in all of the rooms. "The hens had taken possession of beds, closets, bureaus," Emily's cousin Mary Austin Holley later wrote. "Every place was a nest." One positive result of this messy situation was that the family had a "house full of eggs" that they ate for several days after their return. Emily and her family worked diligently during much of May and June in order to repair damage and restore their place to its former condition.[17]

As a good mother, Emily busied herself nursing Guy back to health, along with Joel, who was also sick. James turned to the croplands in an effort to salvage something from the 1836 cotton crop. It had suffered badly from neglect. Since the evacuation east had coincided with the main weeks of the planting season, everyone along the lower Brazos would be short on the cotton crop, and many of them would also lack adequate seed stock for the following year. James and the boys, as well as the slaves who had returned from Galveston, worked diligently to ready the crops and salvage what they could. By picking time at the end of the summer, the Perrys were able to produce twenty-two bales of cotton. This was a very poor yield, although under the circumstances, it was a respectable level of production. James shipped it off on a schooner down the Brazos to New Orleans, writing his merchant correspondents in Louisiana that this constituted "the whole amount of my crop, which I hope you will receive in good order and at a good price, for I need all I can get and more too." In dire financial straits, he realized that the sale of this crop would not be enough to pay expenses for the year, so in the same letter, Perry asked his New Orleans factors for a loan of $2,000 or $3,000 until the late spring of 1837. This would see them through the next planting cycle. The Perry family did take heart from the fact that the price of agricultural products had risen very high during mid-1836 because of the scarcity the Runaway Scrape created. Newspaper articles in the *Telegraph and Texas Register* took note of these higher prices and encouraged local planters to plant as much cotton and sugar as they could, in addition to increasing their livestock holdings in horses, mules, cattle, and hogs.[18]

In spite of such general optimism, conditions at Peach Point by June 1836 had not returned to normal. The Runaway Scrape, the illness of her sons, and the rigors of returning the plantation to an organized state took their toll on Emily. She had nursed the children, overseen all of the cleaning, replanted the garden, and was busily involved in the day-to-day chores of renewing the home for her family. Meanwhile, she continued to fight a bad cold. Emily also began to lay plans for a trip east in order to put several of the children in boarding school. This was a course of action that she and James had discussed the previous year and which Stephen had mentioned to Mrs. Holley during his visit to Lexington. Indeed, Mary Austin Holley wrote Stephen that she would welcome a long visit from Emily. "If your sister should come in view of placing her daughter at school, I should be glad to have her pass the summer with me and the family or any others of our Texas friends." In addition, Mary wrote her brother Henry at Bolivar, telling him to invite Emily to Lexington for the summer. Emily thus began making definitive plans for the trip in the late spring of 1836. Such a journey might improve her health, and taking the older Peach Point children with her, she would find good schools for them.[19]

It was at this point that Stephen F. Austin returned to Texas at the conclusion of his mission to Washington, D.C., an absence that had kept him away for almost six months. He arrived absolutely consumed by political matters. Stephen passed through New Orleans and entered the mouth of the Brazos on June 27. He spent several weeks meeting with various officials, including Interim president David G. Burnet, to resolve the fate of General Santa Anna, who still remained a captive. This initially left him very little time to think about Peach Point or make contact with Emily and the family. In fact, he did not see Emily personally for several weeks thereafter, during which time she and the children arrived at Velasco for the purpose of booking passage to New Orleans on their trip east. To Emily's astonishment, Stephen was adamantly opposed to her leaving Texas when he learned of these plans. In a rather stern letter, Stephen wrote his cousin Henry, who had apparently extended the invitation to Emily from Mary Austin Holley in Lexington. "My sister came down here the other day to embark for New Orleans," he wrote precipitously and with a bit of self-centered logic. "I will advise her to stay at home and abide the fate of Texas." The harshness of this view causes one to wonder if Stephen was aware that several weeks earlier, the infant Cecilia Perry had died on June 9, 1836. The rigors of the Runaway Scrape had been too much for the baby to bear, and although family correspondence fails to mention the exact nature of her illness, she suffered from some sort of feverish condition. The historical record does not note Emily's state of mind at the death of her youngest child, yet the passing of a six-month-old baby would have had a debilitating and depressing impact on any mother. Given that circumstance, Stephen appeared rather harsh and a bit presumptuous when he intoned to Emily, "I wish all of my name or connection to stay in Texas and abide by the issue what it may." He explained, "It was a panic caused by the flight of families last spring which came so near losing Texas, and if my sister goes, it will have its influence on many others."[20]

Stephen seemed, at least in historical retrospect, very insensitive at this time to Emily's desires in favor of his own. He clearly wanted his sister to stay in Texas so that he could maintain political appearances that were important to him. Given this view, it is interesting to observe that Stephen still did not have an accurate picture of his sister and her personality. The two had experienced only limited contact since Emily's marriage to James Bryan in 1813. In Stephen's mind, his sister was, to an extent, the carefree adolescent girl who had been taken to New Haven by a strong-willed mother driven by matronly desires for social pretension. Stephen had little understanding of, or appreciation for, the mature and independent person his sister had become. He apparently failed to consider that for almost twenty years, Emily's character had been steeled by frontier adversity and by a number of familial difficulties, including severe financial problems, the illness and death of family members, and the rigors of establishing a new life for herself and her family in Texas. To a degree, Stephen objectified Emily as a passive force in the affairs of his family. This was most certainly not the case. She was an active and involved figure in the family and at Peach Point Plantation. Whether or not Emily chafed under her brother's rejection of her travel plans, she decided not to press the issue and returned to Peach Point, albeit dejected. Stephen did eventually arrive there after concluding much of his business at Velasco, anxious to be within the bosom of the family after his months in Washington during the recent revolution. He and Emily, along with the rest of the family, had a short visit before he began his campaign for the presidency of the infant Republic of Texas that summer. His health had not been good since his return to Texas, and his single-minded fixation on political affairs only made his physical condition worse. Running for office that summer subjected him to a continuing series of stresses, including a constant barrage of personal accusations against him. The campaign for the presidency wore tremendously on his energy and became an even greater burden when General Sam Houston entered the race during its concluding weeks.[21]

In spite of his all-consuming interest in the presidential election, Stephen's thoughts never strayed completely from Peach Point. He advised the Perrys that he would like special lodgings built for him near the main house. "I wrote you the other day, requesting that you put up a cabin with two rooms for me," Stephen told them by letter from Victoria. "I need one room for an office sitting room, and one for a sleeping room." He offered to pay for this construction by selling some land. If he thought that this cabin might be useful to him as the new president of the Republic, those hopes ended when he lost the election several days later. His hurt feelings from this defeat weighed on him heavily, but his melancholy passed when the victorious Sam Houston appointed him secretary of state. Austin initially was not pleased by the offer and delayed accepting any position in the new administration. "I have been solicited to go into the new cabinet as Secretary of State," he wrote Emily, "or to go to the US as minister—I have declined." He ascribed his refusal of the offer to his weakened physical condition: "Besides all this, my health is gone, and I must have rest to nurse my constitution and try and restore my strength." Nonetheless, Houston persisted, and by late October, Stephen had accepted the position of secretary of state.[22]

All of Stephen's political activities seemed to have little impact on Emily and Peach Point, although she did follow the progress of the campaign through his letters and the newspaper reports, along with updates brought by friends. For the most part, Emily threw herself into gardening during the summer and fall months, the time when she had hoped to be in the United States. The garden at Peach Point had grown steadily over the years and reflected her deep interest in ornamental planting. Emily undertook a large landscaping project that fall on the drive that linked the Peach Point house to the main road. She had the slaves construct two sets of large, round entrance posterns to frame a semicircular carriageway that branched out from the main entrance in front of the house. Each of these imposing posterns resembled a small medieval turret some six feet across and undoubtedly presented a grand entrance for those approaching the house. Stephen, although increasingly consumed with governmental matters, did stay in close touch with Emily by letter, advising his sister on this and other improvements at Peach Point. He cautioned her, for example, about keeping the shrubbery well trimmed. He believed that shrubs added greatly to the value of a property, and any labor necessary to keep them well maintained was worth the effort. He also advised Emily on the kinds of perennials that ought to go into the garden, even to the point of noting particular plants that he thought would favor the location. He forwarded her some rose cuttings he had purchased, along with several black walnut saplings and instructions that the latter should be set out in January. "Do not neglect them, nor let children eat them," he directed. Stephen did not limit his advice about Peach Point to the garden only, but also shared his thoughts with James about pasture grass. He was particularly enamored of a strain called "crow foot" grass, of which he noted, "A small patch in Bell's yard has supported about a dozen horses and kept them fat." Stephen suggested, "Do not neglect this—set Austin and Joel with the children to gathering the seed."[23]

Even with all this interest in the garden and a stream of pleasant letters from Stephen in the summer and early fall of 1836, Emily still chafed about not being able to visit the United States and put the children in boarding school. On several occasions in his correspondence that fall, Stephen cautioned her not to dwell on her disappointment, but such observations apparently fell on deaf ears. This trip was important to her, not only for the proper education of the children, but also because she wanted to visit family and friends in the United States, especially Mary Austin Holley. This became obvious to everyone, eventually Stephen too. By late fall, he had relented and withdrew his objections of several months earlier. Emily and the children, he announced, should indeed make the trip. Although family correspondence on this matter does not hint at a reason for his change of heart, it should be noted that James had always favored Emily making the trip, as had her cousins Henry Austin and Mary Austin Holley. Stephen had been the stumbling block, and perhaps his recent political loss of the presidency in the election of 1836 had softened his view of the Perry family as a public model of patriotic rectitude that reflected directly on him. At any rate, sometime in late November, Stephen agreed to the trip and even sold some of his land holdings in order to help finance the costs of the boarding schools, since this too was a special concern of his. He wrote James Perry, "One of the main objects I had in selling land at so great a sacrifice was to furnish Emily with the means of going to the U.S. and taking the children to put them in school." He suggested that they go in March 1837 but understood that Emily might wish to leave earlier, since "she is always fretting on this subject, and it probably would be best for her to go in January or February." Stephen contributed over $500 in cash for the trip and anticipated within several months having an additional $3,000 to $4,000 for school expenses. In making this financial contribution to Emily, Stephen explicitly recognized that his opposition to her trip to the United States the previous June had been a source of great unhappiness to her. He hoped that his change of heart would elevate her spirits. The trip, he felt, "would restore her health and spirits, and correct the fretful habit which sickness and hardships have produced" in her. "I would sell all I have at any sacrifice rather than she should continue in the unhappy and fretful state she has been in ever since I returned home," he wrote to James at Peach Point. "She must spend next summer in the U.S."[24]

The arrival of the Christmas season of 1836 saw Emily, presumably now greatly elevated in spirit, preparing for her long-desired trip back to the United States, her first since marrying James Bryan some twenty-three years earlier. The longstanding delicate health that had characterized Stephen's physical constitution, however, continued to deteriorate with the rigors of his public duties. Sometime in the fall, he had moved to Columbia, where he took lodgings in the home belonging to Judge George B. McKinstry. Stephen's residence at Columbia would make it easier for him to exercise his duties as secretary of state, but the room he rented left much to be desired as a comfortable lodging. The house was a clapboard structure, and Stephen took a side room that contained no fireplace or stove. Already ill with a lingering respiratory condition, the arrival of a bitingly cold norther in December did little to improve his declining physical condition. Austin Bryan was with him in Columbia, serving as his uncle's secretary. By late December, young Austin was seriously concerned about his uncle's health. The young secretary summoned help, which arrived in the persons of cousin Henry Austin and George Hammeken, Stephen's business associate and longtime friend. They found him under the care of physician Branch Archer. By Christmas day, Stephen's condition had improved to the point that he was shaved, dressed, and carried into the main living room of the house to sit in front of the fireplace. Thereafter, he returned to his cold room, where his illness greatly worsened. Austin Bryan summoned his stepfather, James Perry, from Peach Point, who arrived to find his brother-in-law in a very grave state. Emily stayed at Peach Point with the children, anxious for news of her brother's condition. Stephen was weak and completely debilitated, although lucid. He sipped tea and seemed aware of his condition, but as the hours passed, he took a decided turn for the worse. Stephen F. Austin died sometime just before midnight on December 27, 1836, at forty-three years of age. James Perry, along with Austin Bryan and several others, including Dr. Archer and George Hammeken, stood at his bedside during his last moments.[25]

Perry immediately returned home to bring this sorrowful and unexpected news to a devastated Emily, and they both made plans for Stephen's funeral. Emily decided that her brother would be buried in the family plot at Gulf Prairie. The Perrys coordinated the funeral plans with Sam Houston, who would be attending the memorial service in his capacity as president of the Republic of Texas. Emily selected a quiet spot in the churchyard just a few steps away from where she had buried her daughter Mary Elizabeth Bryan thirteen years earlier. These arrangements made, several days later, family members, friends, slaves from the plantation, and several distinguished members of the government helped load Stephen's casket on the steamboat *Yellowstone* at Brazoria, from where the mourners traveled down the Brazos River to Crosby's Landing, a few miles from Peach Point. An honor guard met the cortege there and ceremoniously accompanied it to the burial ground. The funeral was bitterly cold as the mourners huddled against a blowing wind. Sam Houston bent at the concluding prayer, took a handful of soil, and threw the first clod of dirt on Stephen F. Austin's coffin. Emily was now the last surviving member of the Moses Austin family circle.[26]

Stephen's unexpected death understandably stopped all of Emily's plans for her visit to the United States. Arranging the funeral consumed much of her energy, and in the months thereafter, she and James had to busy themselves with probating her brother's estate, which was both large and very complicated. Stephen's relatively simple will had named James F. Perry as executor. All of the legal arrangements touching on the probate of the estate thus carried the name of James Perry, although Emily played a significant role in all decisions regarding disposition.

Austin's will split all of his assets into two different inheritances: one-half of the assets would go to Emily in her name as his only sister, while the other half went to his nephew, Brown's son, eight-year-old Stephen F. Austin Jr. In the event that the boy died without issue, that portion of the estate would revert to Emily as sole heir. Although this seemed a simple enough arrangement on the surface of things, James and Emily found that the estate was complicated by poor record keeping of personal assets, incomplete land records, and a general inattention to the specific details that would be needed for its probate. It did help that Austin Bryan had served for extended periods of time as his uncle's secretary. Young Bryan was therefore able at several critical junctures to assist his mother and stepfather in sorting through various complex matters, some of which had to be dealt with immediately. They soon learned, for example, that the Senate of the Republic of Texas had passed a resolution two months earlier requiring all of the colonial era empresarios or their legal representatives to make a long report on the fulfillment of their contracts, the number of families each agent had brought to Mexican Texas, and the amount of land that had been granted. In February of 1837, the Perrys began the tedious task of examining Austin's records and papers in order to produce this report. Probate became further complicated because Emily and James had to begin selling off parcels of land right away to pay the debts of the estate. In early 1836, they sold several town lots at Brazoria and San Felipe, along with property near Harrisburg, San Felipe, and Bastrop. In so doing, the Perrys engaged the services of the Allen brothers at the new town Houston and placed advertisements for the sales in the *Telegraph and Texas Register*. This also helped to raise some money for Emily's still-anticipated trip east.[27]

The greatest difficulty in settling Stephen F. Austin's estate and the one which would cause Emily the greatest anguish had to do with the one-half left to her nephew Stephen F. Austin Jr., the boy who had been living in her home at Peach Point. He had been born in 1828, the son of Emily's brother Brown and Eliza Westall. The Perrys knew the Westall family well since they were neighbors in the Gulf Prairie area. Eliza's father, Thomas Westall, was a native of Tennessee who came to Texas in 1824 as an early member of Stephen F. Austin's colony. The elder Westall had owned extensive property at San Felipe and lived on an impressive plantation in the Brazos River country near Peach Point. Westall died in the cholera epidemic of 1833. His daughter Eliza had married Brown Austin sometime in 1825, with the boy Stephen Jr. being the only child of that marriage. The baby lived with his mother, Eliza, for a time after the passing of his father but moved into the Perry household when Emily came to Texas, since everyone felt that he could be better cared for by her family. That may also have been because Eliza had remarried a man named Zeno Phillips. Thus, by the time of Stephen F. Austin's death, Emily and James looked upon Brown's son as part of the Peach Point family.[28]

There had come to exist, however, an increasingly strained relationship with the boy's mother, who became involved in a legal dispute with Stephen F. Austin before his death about the settlement of Brown's estate. The widow felt that some of the property claimed by her former brother-in-law Stephen actually belonged to her deceased husband Brown. Eliza engaged a lawyer in the hopes of settling this matter, which was still pending at the time of Stephen F. Austin's death. In spite of this tension between Eliza and Stephen, his young namesake apparently acclimated successfully to the Perry household, getting along well with his cousins. Stephen F. Austin Jr. attended classes taught by Thomas J. Pilgrim with Guy M. Bryan and later accompanied his cousin to a more advanced school at Brazoria. Emily looked forward to her nephew Stephen traveling with Guy and her daughter Eliza to be enrolled at boarding school in the United States. Through all of this, Brown's widow continued to agree to her son living permanently in Emily's household. Relations became increasingly strained when Eliza remarried for a second time in early 1836 after the death of Zeno Phillips. Her new husband was William G. Hill, her attorney in the suits against Stephen F. Austin. With the death of Stephen in December 1836, Eliza and William Hill told the Perrys that they wanted Stephen F. Austin Jr. to leave Peach Point and live with them. Although Emily's personal reaction to this development remains unknown, she was forced to accede since the Perrys never had legal custody of the young man; he had been living at Peach Point with Eliza's verbal permission. Emily thus had no legal recourse other than to let the eight-year-old boy take up residence with his mother and stepfather. Correspondence clearly indicates that Emily still expected that young Stephen Jr. might travel east to be placed in school, although Eliza Hill may not have approved. All of this, however, came to a tragic end when Stephen F. Austin Jr. died unexpectedly at the Hill home on February 2, 1837, only six weeks after the passing of his uncle. Now that the boy was deceased, Emily and James worried that the Hills would cause them continuing legal trouble over the pending probate of Stephen F. Austin's estate. In this they were proven correct. The Hills filed suit against the Perrys for part of the Stephen F. Austin estate, still contending that some of his property had really belonged to Brown. Emily engaged a longtime friend and attorney, William H. Jack, to represent her in a course of litigation that would take years to resolve. These complicated probate matters touching on the death of Stephen F. Austin Jr. and his uncle's estate further delayed Emily's departure for the East.[29]

Although the dispute with the Hills was not settled, Emily legally became, in early 1837, the sole heir of Stephen F. Austin. James Perry did not have any personal interest in the considerable amount of property that came into his wife's possession, though he would participate with her in its management. It was her property and hers alone, thus making her one of the wealthiest individuals in the Republic of Texas. Emily's status as sole heir in her own name had firm precedents in the common law concept of equity, despite the fact that the Texas legal system also manifested the community property provisions of law that flowed from its Spanish and Mexican heritage. "Under equity," one authority has noted, "a married woman could acquire a separate estate. This property was set aside for her benefit; over this property the husband was not allowed to exercise his usual common law rights." As a married couple, Emily and James jointly managed the Stephen F. Austin estate, always maintaining it apart from their community property holdings under the provisions of Texas law. Separate record keeping and careful management insured that monies from the Stephen F. Austin estate would never be intermixed with the financial accounts of Peach Point Plantation. Emily's main goal and purpose in administering this estate was to keep it intact for the Bryan and Perry children, using it to provide for their educations and as a source of capital investment that would benefit them as the ultimate adult heirs of their uncle Stephen. No money from the estate ever went to their regular expenses, since these were always paid out of profits from the operation of Peach Point Plantation.[30]

By late May 1837, Stephen's estate had been arranged as best it could be in the short run, so Emily undertook her long-anticipated trip to the United States. James Perry accompanied her as far as New Orleans, where they took lodgings for several days. The two youngest boys, Stephen S. and Henry Perry, stayed with family friends at Chocolate Bayou while Joel remained at Peach Point to manage affairs there. Austin Bryan, Guy M. Bryan, and Eliza Perry traveled with their parents. Austin Bryan, now twenty years of age, would be the accompanying male member of the family on the trip, since, given the sensibilities of the era, it would have been unseemly for a married woman like Emily to travel alone. One historian of southern families has noted, "White planter men traveled at will . . . planter women always had to travel with male escorts." Guy M. Bryan and Eliza Perry, of course, made the trip in order to be enrolled in boarding schools. While stopping at New Orleans, James made arrangements with the banking firm of Merle and Company to handle a letter of credit that would cover all of the expenses incurred by Emily and the children. Remaining in the city to transact plantation business after Emily's departure for Kentucky, James met an elderly man who had known Moses Austin back in the mining days of Virginia. "He recollects very well," James later wrote Emily, "the time your father first visited Missouri and relates all the difficulties of his journey." Regarding this conversation, James further mentioned that the old gentleman "is very anxious that the family name should be preserved and says we ought to have Austin Bryan and Stephen's [meaning Stephen S. Perry's] names changed by act of Congress to Moses Austin and Stephen F. Austin to preserve the name." This idea appealed very much to Emily, and she would mention it several times in the future.[31]

Having left James at New Orleans, Emily, Austin Bryan, and the children traveled by steamboat up the Mississippi and Ohio to Louisville, where they disembarked for an overland journey to Lexington to stay with Mary Austin Holley. En route, Austin Bryan wrote his father a long letter detailing their progress, noting that he had already engaged seats on the stagecoach for Frankfort, from where they would take the train to Lexington. Austin reported that they had visited some of the Perry relatives who were living in the area and that they had made a favorable impression. Showing his Texas roots, however, Austin told his stepfather that he was already tired of the United States because "it requires too much smartness, formality, politeness, and dress to be considered respectable to suit one who has lived in Texas as long as I have." This letter also noted that young Eliza had experienced some sort of illness consisting of a transient attack or fit. Austin reported that she "was taken the day before yesterday with a spasm and was quite sick all day; yesterday she was up again running about all day and today she appears perfectly well." Emily apparently attributed her daughter's spasm to having eaten too much fruit. In reality, the family was unknowingly seeing the first signs of Eliza developing a condition that would later be treated medically as an epileptic-like disorder by the physicians they consulted. This neurological condition would plague Eliza for the rest of her life. It would, however, take all of them a number of years to understand the full import of this development on their family circle.[32]

Emily handled Eliza's unexpected spasm successfully, and after

Eliza Perry

several days of further traveling, they arrived at the Holley home in Lexington, near Transylvania University, where Mary's late husband Horace had been president. Mary Austin Holley was well connected and respected in the town. She had been living with the children of Henry Austin in a large home on Constitution Street along with her son Horace. Emily and the children quickly settled into the family routine of the Holley household, with every indication that the Henry Austin and Peach Point children got along well. Cousins Guy M. Bryan and Edward Austin quickly struck up a firm friendship that made them inseparable as chums and daily companions. Sadly for Emily, Eliza's problems continued, and she initially interpreted them as her daughter's bad attitude. Emily wrote James, "She is so very rude and impolite, she keeps me in a fever all the time, and with all, is so very hard to manage." Emily decided to deal with this situation by finding a school in Lexington that her daughter could attend during the day. She settled on one conducted by a local Episcopal clergyman who had earlier taught in St. Louis. "He is," Emily noted, "well calculated to manage such a disposition as Eliza's." However, this did not work, and the young Perry girl was soon back in the Holley household after several additional attacks. Emily was forced to reconsider the plans for the remainder of her trip, because, as she wrote James, "I find that Eliza will require so much attention, for her head is not well." Emily was grateful to her cousin Mary for accommodating them in Lexington. "She is very kind," Emily noted about her cousin and observed of the Holley home that "it is very pleasantly situated." While in Lexington, Emily also received James' letter from New Orleans recounting the visit with the elderly man who had suggested changing her two sons' last names to Austin. Emily liked this idea. She reminded her husband in reply that she had already mentioned it after the death of her brother the previous year. "As for changing the names of our sons," she remarked, "you know that I spoke of it last winter, that I wish Austin to assume the name of his grandfather, and now that little Stephen F. Austin is dead, it would be the greatest pleasure in the world for our son [Stephen S. Perry] to take the name of his departed uncle, and I have the vanity to think that he will represent his uncle with much more credit than his poor little neglected namesake would have done." It was clear that Emily continued to see herself as an Austin.[33]

After almost a month in Lexington, Emily and the children moved on to Ohio, where they would stay with some of James F. Perry's relations. On leaving Lexington, Emily agreed that Mary Austin Holley and the Henry Austin children would visit Peach Point Plantation the following year. Once left to her own devices as a traveler on the road to Ohio, Emily became increasingly worried about nine-year-old Eliza. "She has acquired so many bad and ugly habits that it will be some time if she ever is broken of them," she wrote James. "You have no idea of the trouble and uneasiness I have had on Eliza's account." Given the unexpected context of Eliza's behavior, Emily felt badly that all of her children appeared to be unsophisticated in the company of their Kentucky and Ohio relatives. "You have no idea how awkward Austin appears in company," she noted somewhat ruefully. On the other hand, she had been impressed with the Henry Austin children during her recent stay in Lexington. "Henry's daughters are beautiful girls, and do great credit to their father in Texas. I hope in a few years our wild, rude little daughter will be as interesting as the Miss Austins." While in Lexington, Emily had chosen to enroll Guy at Kenyon College in Gambier, Ohio, a decision made with the cooperation of Mary Austin Holley. Mary's nephew Edward Austin accompanied Emily and Guy to Kenyon, where he would enroll at the same time. Kenyon College had attracted Emily's attention because it was an Episcopal institution, founded by Bishop Philander Chase in 1824. Emily and her son Guy M. Bryan were both active in the affairs of the Episcopal Church, having participated in its services at the parish located in Brazoria. The idea of young Guy attending an Episcopal college very much appealed to him and to his mother. By the time she departed Kenyon after leaving Guy and Edward Austin there, Emily was growing weary of having been on the road for well over a month. So too was Austin Bryan, who wrote his father that "I wish we were back in Texas; I for my part am heartily tired of traveling and I know that Ma is not fond of it."[34]

Emily, her son Austin, and Eliza traveled on to Ohio, where they arrived in late July. Emily had heard of several schools in that area that might be appropriate for Eliza to attend. At this point, neither Emily nor her son Austin realized the true nature of Eliza's condition. Austin Bryan wrote his stepfather, "Eliza had another fit the day we arrived here in the stage from Steubenville. She ate a hearty dinner, and two hours afterwards she was taken with a fit like that she had in Louisville, though not near so hard a one; in about three hours she was up and running about." They still wondered what was happening and why. "I cannot imagine what causes the convulsions," Austin wrote his stepfather back at Peach Point, "except it is from eating fruit—she looks fat and hearty." Emily decided to enroll Eliza at the Steubenville Female Academy, a boarding school for young ladies. It had been founded in 1829 by a Presbyterian minister, Charles A. Beatty, and his wife. As its catalog noted, "it was designed from the first to be based on Christian principles. The location of the seminary is peculiarly eligible. It is easily accessible from all directions, by river and railroad, and is in a region of the country remarkably healthful."[35]

Emily was especially impressed with the headmistress, Mrs. Beatty, who she saw as "an intelligent, smart lady and who conducts the institution with honor to herself and advantage to the scholars." The school's curriculum also met with Emily's approval since Eliza would be able to study music, art, and the French language. The Steubenville

Female Academy had the added benefit that it was located near James Perry's family. While in Ohio, Emily had visited the home of James Perry's eldest sister, meeting her family for the first time. "I love her because she looks so much like you," Emily told James. "I can see a very strong resemblance indeed, more so than any of your sisters that I have seen." She also noted of these in-laws, "Your sister is a handsome, fine looking old lady; they all appear much pleased at my making them a visit." Once the decision had been made to enroll Eliza at Steubenville, Emily took her daughter to Pittsburg on a shopping trip in order to buy clothes and school supplies. Difficulties continued between the two, and Emily ascribed her daughter's erratic behavior to irascibility. "Eliza has given me a great deal of trouble," she wrote to James. "She is so very rude and impolite, but I hope I shall soon have her at school." Austin wrote to Peach Point during the first week of September, "We left Eliza in excellent health four days ago at Steubenville with Mrs. Beatty. She appeared well satisfied to stay as there are so many playmates for her at the Seminary."[36]

Once Eliza had been placed at school, Emily and her son Austin began their journey back to Texas by a circuitous route that included stops at Louisville, Potosi, Herculaneum, St. Louis, and New Orleans. This also involved passing through Ohio again, where they visited with other Perry relatives and where Lavinia Perry joined them for the trip home. Lavinia, the daughter of James' deceased brother, had first lived with the Perrys as a girl in Missouri in the late 1820s and made the overland trip with them to Texas. She was the person who cared for Emily during the last stages of her pregnancy at San Felipe before Henry Perry was born. Lavinia continued living with the family at Chocolate Bayou and then at Peach Point. However, during the cholera epidemic of 1833, her Perry relations in Ohio had called for Lavinia's return to the United States. That danger long passed, Lavinia now wanted to move back to the Perry household at Peach Point. Emily's visit east gave her the opportunity to do so, and she joined her aunt and cousin Austin on the trip back to Texas. Making successful arrangements for the children's boarding schools obviously cheered Emily, who had apparently been suffering from a cold during much of the trip. She looked forward to returning home. Arriving at Louisville, Austin wrote James Perry with good news about Emily: "I am happy to inform you Mother's health has improved very much since we passed here going up—I think perhaps she will return home in better health than she has been in for years." This news must have greatly cheered James since Emily's malaise had been an important motivation for the trip.[37]

On her return journey, Emily received several letters from Mary Austin Holley that had been directed to her hotel at Louisville. Cousin Mary hoped that they could once again visit in Lexington on Emily's way back to Peach Point. This, however, was something that Emily now wished to avoid. Unknown to Mary, discussions between the two women several months earlier at Lexington had given Emily an uncharitable view of both Henry Austin and Mary Austin Holley. Emily minced no words in expressing her displeasure about Mary to her husband. "I think their friendship is nothing but a puff," she wrote James on receiving Mary's notes seeking a second visit at Lexington. Emily had come to the conclusion that her two cousins had designs on getting part of Stephen F. Austin's estate. In large part, this stemmed from Mary Austin Holley's contention that two hundred acres of Peach Point land might actually belong to her, something that Emily learned for the first time in Lexington several months earlier. "Austin received a long letter today from Mary Austin Holley," Emily wrote James from Louisville in September. "He has received several letters; in every one of them, she speaks of her claim on Peach Point. I am not at all pleased at the course she is taking, and hope that you will not involve yourself in any way with Captain Austin," meaning her cousin Henry. This soured relationship did not portend well for the future of family amity, since during their more cordial visit in June, the two cousins had agreed that Mary Austin Holley would visit Texas the following year. In that regard, Emily wrote to James that she would give a further explanation of this matter when she returned home. In the meantime, she cautioned, "Do not suffer yourself to be involved in any way with cousin Henry, for there is no end to the extravagance of his sister. She calls Peach Point land hers."[38]

It appears that while in casual conversation earlier in Lexington, Mary explained to Emily that Stephen F. Austin had promised her land that was now part of Peach Point. Years earlier, while the Perrys still lived in Missouri, Mary Austin Holley and her cousin Stephen had visited Gulf Prairie together, and he had shown her a fine plot of land that he pledged would be hers. However, little came of this, and when the Perrys moved onto the tract, nothing was ever done to prove any title in Mary Austin Holley's name. Nonetheless, although Stephen F. Austin had secured legal grants of land for her elsewhere in Texas, Mary believed that part of the Peach Point tract belonged to her, at least morally if not legally. Emily apparently did not mention her feelings to Mary, but she was particularly upset about this because the specific two hundred acres that Mary Austin Holley believed were hers had recently been deeded to Joel Bryan, who would eventually build a plantation he named Durazno on the tract. The Perry family considered this parcel of land to be one of the prettiest and most desirable locations on Peach Point. Emily thus sought to have no further contact with Mary Austin Holley on the return trip, although she knew that it could not be long postponed since Mary would be visiting Texas the following year.[39]

By the end of 1837, Emily was particularly anxious to be at Peach Point once again. She greatly missed both the plantation and her family. Texas had become home to her in a way that she had never experienced in Missouri. "Oh! How I long to be at home," she wrote James. "I long to be at home once more, there is no place like home." More specifically, she added, "There is no place like Texas that I have seen, and I shall return contented to spend the remainder of my days in that delightful climate." Always given to worry, she told her husband, "I often think of you, Joel, and our two dear little boys; if you should get sick, who will you have to nurse and take care of you all?" She also worried about Stephen and Henry, who had been spending the summer away from Peach Point at Chocolate Bayou. "I expect they will often think of their mother. I am sorry that Stephen is not in school. He will forget all that he has learned, and poor little Henry is left alone at Chocolate; I am fearful that he will be very much spoiled." She abjectly missed both young sons. "Oh! How much I want to see them, I hope that they will not go wild, and do they make improvement in their learning?" she wrote James, suggesting to him that "I hope that you will visit them as often as possible."[40]

ANTEBELLUM PEACH POINT

E mily kept in close touch with James during her entire 1837 trip east. Her letters provide a very clear indication of how she conceptualized her role as mistress of Peach Point Plantation and, in so doing, provide a window into understanding her life there. Emily's prolonged absence from Peach Point created an important opportunity for her to make an explicit catalogue of her daily duties on the plantation. She advised James in her correspondence about the wide range of chores that fell within her domestic routine in an obvious effort to ensure that they would take place as she wished during her absence. Most of these matters fell within the acknowledged sphere of the plantation mistress. "Even with the work created by their husbands' slave owning," Catherine Clinton reminds us, "the numerous tasks of antebellum housekeeping kept plantation mistresses busy; gardening, dairy activities, salting pork, preserving fruits and vegetables, mixing medicines, the making of candles, soap, rugs, pillows, linen, bedding, and so on." At Peach Point, Emily would no doubt have silently and efficiently dealt with many of these matters, but her absence required overt discussion of them. Her letters home prove absolutely the observations of historian Marli F. Wiener regarding the diligence and workload of the typical plantation mistress. "Although expected by their husbands and their society to appear refined," Wiener notes, "plantation mistresses in fact worked quite hard at fulfilling their domestic obligations."[1]

For that reason, much of Emily's correspondence during this trip had the tone of business communications rather than personal letters. She wrote in great detail about tending the gardens, food preparation, kitchen and household practices, clothing the family and slaves, cleaning the house, taking care of the yard areas and doorstep livestock, and many other similar concerns. Emily's status as an important person in the elite society of the lower Brazos area found its way into these letters. She gave James instructions about how to arrange the house for the entertaining of guests that would occur on her return. Management of the slave population was a chief concern of hers, as was the continuing construction of new buildings on the plantation as it continued to grow and prosper. After all, at the time of her trip east, the Perrys had lived on the place for only five years.[2]

Of Emily's many concerns at Peach Point, the gardens always remained foremost on her mind, both the ornamental plantings and the kitchen plots that provided foodstuffs for everyone on the plantation. Emily clearly had high standards for the garden and had delegated a particular slave at Peach Point named Simon to take care of it. Simon, it seems, was one of the most trusted and valuable slaves on the plantation. He originally belonged to Stephen F. Austin, who had purchased him in the early 1830s. Austin sent Simon to Peach Point before the Texas Revolution, where the slave soon assumed responsibilities that made of him of special significance to the Perrys. At times, James permitted Simon to drive the sale crops to market and collect the proceeds from the transaction. It is logical, therefore, that Emily entrusted Simon with garden care in her absence. "I wish the yard attended to, the grass kept cut down in the walks, and the rose bushes tied up," she instructed, "and oranges watered and mowed around." She wanted Simon to gather seeds from all the plants as they appeared on pods and save them for the following year's plantings. "Have some lettuce planted," she told James in November, and I "hope you have not neglected making a winter garden." She instructed that Simon fence the front yard. "I wish the division fence made," she noted, "so that the dogs and chickens can be kept out of the house." She desired that Simon build some new chicken coops that were tightly made in order to keep out rats.[3]

Emily also directed her attentions to housekeeping duties, and her tone often gave the impression that she might not have had full confidence that James and Joel, who remained at home, completely understood these chores. "Do not neglect having the beds and clothing that are in the drawers and trunks aired," she told them, "and you must get some gauze and have Stephen's portrait covered or the flies will ruin it." She instructed that "you must examine the drawers and see that the bugs do not cut everything to pieces." Emily likewise wanted them to check the trunks in the bedrooms to ensure that roaches had not infested there too. "Make sure the children clean and sweep under the house," she advised James. She wanted the house whitewashed inside and out. Emily's concern with putting up food items, in a similar vein to her housekeeping instructions, showed her equal attention to detail in that regard. "Tell Clarissa [one of the house slaves] to put up as many pickles as she can," Emily advised, and "to attend to them and scald them well." In addition, Emily wanted the pickle brine to be made only with rainwater. She instructed Clarissa to check regularly the cask of vinegar and not let any of it leak. Emily had concerns about the fowl in the house yard, instructing James to "tell Sarah [another slave] that she must attend to the chickens and turkeys, raise all that she can, for we shall have a very large family next winter." Indeed, a fully stocked larder remained one of her central concerns. "I hope you will have a supply of eatables, pickles and preserves," she wrote James, and "tell Clarissa to put up some butter; if possible have some hogs put up in a pen to fatten."[4]

Since Peach Point was still a relatively new plantation, the Perry family undertook various construction projects while Emily was away on her extended trip. Even while she was gone, however, she had many thoughts about the work that went forward at the plantation, especially regarding the main house. For example, Emily was a vocal proponent of closets, which had recently become popular in that era as a replacement for storing items in wardrobes and trunks. "They are so convenient," she noted, "and will do away with trunks." Accordingly, "if you should put up the addition to the house," she told James, "try and make as many closets as possible—have one made in our room behind the doors; I do not want it shelved but made into a kind of press to hang clothes in." She observed that "I think it would be more convenient to have the front door converted into a window and have a door opposite the kitchen door." Emily wanted the new construction to involve finishing both the front and back porch of the house, and she told her husband to "make a bedroom off one of the porches." She suggested that James build a storage cabinet in the hallway connecting their bedroom to the rest of the house. Thinking ahead to the impending visit of Mary Austin Holley and the Henry Austin children, Emily related additional practical instructions: "I wish you to have a necessary house built in the back yard in the corner of the fence by the lane, and on a line with the hen house; it can be set over the ditch, as these city dames will think it horrible to run into the woods."[5]

Emily's domestic sphere extended into the barn areas and to the horses on the plantation. "I hope that you will have my horses attended to," she cautioned James, "and also the two ponies, for they will all be wanted when I return home with the girls, and, if Mary Austin Holley visits Texas, she will want a horse to ride." Emily desired that James buy a new saddle for their young son Stephen S. Perry, and she worried about the rest of the riding saddles in the barn. "I want my old saddle taken care of," she advised, "and do not let the roaches eat it up, for it will do for Lavinia to ride." At times, her concerns reached beyond the house and barn to the agricultural operations of Peach Point, since this was the lifeblood of the family. "I hope you will have your gin up in time to gin all your first picking of cotton," she wrote James.[6]

The cotton crop, along with the maintenance of the household and smooth functioning of family life at Peach Point, was obviously dependent upon slave labor, as was the case for all Brazoria plantations of that era. Not surprisingly, Emily's thoughts often turned to matters dealing with the slave population. At most times after the mid-1830s, almost fifty slaves resided at Peach Point Plantation. Emily, of course, had specific concerns about those who worked in the house, around the homestead area, and in the gardens. Her numerous instructions to Simon, Clarissa, and Sarah regarding the household chores provide clear indications of her reliance on chattel servants. Nonetheless, Emily manifested a complicated attitude toward slaves that was typical of elite plantation women of her era. On the one hand, she viewed them as property, while on the other, she had explicit, strong personal feelings for them as individual members of the Peach Point community. This duality of viewpoint often crept into her letters regarding her notions about the good operation of the plantation. For example, she believed that slaves were good financial investments. "I think you had better buy all the Negroes you can," she wrote James from Pittsburgh in 1837. "If you can sell any of the land for Negroes, do so, for you cannot carry on your farm to any extent without more help." This attitude about the economic aspect of slavery placed Emily squarely within the values of her time and place. One historian has noted that "to southerners, slaves were property, valuable and substantial investments; women in plantation society were schooled from an early age to this view of the necessity and value of slave labor in southern agriculture."[7]

Emily did, however, manifest a sincere affection and concern about the slaves living on the plantation. As Catherine Clinton commented, "care of the slaves was the plantation mistress's constant chore." Emily worried about their clothing. If they "should want any overcoats," she wrote James, "there is plenty of Linsey in the box. Let Clarissa keep to sewing; she and Milley could make old Mary and Sarah dresses." Emily also had clear ideas about how the labor of individual slaves should be used on the plantation, at one point advising James, "I do not want Milley sent into the field; it will spoil her for the house, and as we shall have so much company next winter, I want her in the house. She is not very healthy and ought to be taken care of." In that regard, she also had worries about her house servant Clarissa, who performed many of the kitchen duties. Emily cautioned James, "If she is sick, she must be taken care of, for she is a good servant and must not be abused." Indeed, addressing the health of the slave population usually fell to the plantation mistress, and in these matters, Emily amply fulfilled her duties. "I hope the Negroes will keep healthy; tell old Mary and Sarah to take care of everything, also Clarissa," she instructed James. "If Milley should have the chills and fever, she must be attended to since if she is neglected it may be terminal." Emily's concerns for these slaves were very typical of southern plantation mistresses, especially regarding their house servants. "Mistresses did develop strong emotional ties to certain slaves," Laura F. Edwards has observed, "and often acted on these slaves' behalf." Emily's attention to the welfare of all the slaves on the place was no doubt motivated both by economic reality and the more laudable concerns of human compassion.[8]

James Perry shared his wife's views regarding the beneficent treatment of their slaves. Together they established a plantation that earned them a reputation as individuals who treated their slaves well and with consideration. By the late 1840s, their chattels were generally known throughout the lower Brazos River cotton lands as the "free slaves of Peach Point." Emily and James permitted slave families to flourish on the place, took special care in their diet and clothing, and afforded them the same medical treatment received by the Perry family. They also encouraged their slaves to develop special skills that gave them opportunities to earn extra money. In those capacities, the Perrys often permitted some of them to hire out to other planters and tradespeople. The hired-out slaves kept part of their earnings from these endeavors. Emily's letters over the entire time she lived on the plantation constantly manifested a concern for the slaves, and when traveling, she often asked after their welfare. The same later proved true for her children, who, after leaving Peach Point for boarding schools as young adults, routinely sent their written regards to particular slaves and inquired warmly about them.[9]

Indeed, Emily and James' treatment of slaves at Peach Point has subsequently informed a modern historical debate about the dehumanizing and exploitive nature of southern slavery as practiced by planters during the antebellum era. In the late 1970s, an historiographical discussion among historians of the Old South featured a group of scholars who contended that ill treatment and harsh exploitation was the norm for the stereotypical plantation slave. At the same time, other historians of southern slavery argued that life for slaves on the larger plantations of the Southwest, although morally reprehensible, was not as hard or cruel as their more critical colleagues contended. Among the most influential of the latter "well-treated" school of scholars was the distinguished historian Clement Eaton, who wrote a widely used collegiate southern history textbook. Using Peach Point as his example, Eaton stated that "the old idea that slaves were more harshly treated and harder worked on the plantations of the Southwest has been largely discredited." Whether or not Professor Eaton's claim had widespread typicality or not for the nature of plantation slavery generally, his observation about such affairs at Peach Point speaks to the way in which Emily and James Perry treated their slaves.[10]

Whatever the case in this regard at Peach Point, Emily clearly saw the slave-maintained household as an important unit of production, making her a stereotypical plantation mistress. Nonetheless, her status as the sole

heir of Stephen F. Austin forced Emily into various activities traditionally
reserved for men. This made her unique for her time and place. Emily
took an active role in the business management of the Stephen F. Austin
estate, although she acted through the legal participation of her husband
in these matters. This was most definitely the case in terms of land
management. Much of her brother's estate had come to her in the form
of land holdings, and the Perrys viewed land sales as a way to raise both
capital and disposable income. The sale of land had indeed underwritten
Emily's trip east, and for years thereafter, the family sold land whenever
they needed ready cash for the children's education. The Perrys began, in
the year after Stephen F. Austin's death, to engage in various development
schemes designed to make the inherited land desirable to potential buyers
and turn it to profitable uses. In particular, James and Emily sought to
develop the Austin land at the village of Quintana, located approximately
six miles southeast of Peach Point where the Brazos River entered the
Gulf of Mexico. Situated on the west side of the Brazos Channel across
from the port city of Velasco, Quintana had been the site of a Mexican
fort. Two of Stephen F. Austin's associates, Thomas F. McKinney and
Samuel May Williams, established their mercantile house there in hopes
that the village would become a major trading center. Hence, by early
1837, James and Emily had decided to develop some of the property she
had inherited there into town lots for public sale. Emily took an active
role in selling them. On her trip east, for example, Emily promoted this
venture to family and friends in hopes of making sales. She wrote James
from Lexington, "I hope you will have the town lots gone off; I wish very
much I had brought one [a land plat] with me, as Robert and Thomas
Baldwin would be very glad to see one." She suggested that one of James'
former business partners at San Felipe might be approached, noting that
"if Mr. Somervell should want lots in Quintana to commence business,
I wish you to let him have them." Hearing nothing from James about

these matters in his letters from home, she asked somewhat plaintively towards the end of July, "What have you done with Quintana? Have it surveyed and laid off the lots. Try to do something that will give the place a start." Emily remained hopeful that they would "realize some money from the sales of town lots." Such was not to be the case because of circumstances beyond their control. The firm of McKinney and Williams, the centerpiece of the village's economy, decided late in 1838 to leave Quintana and move its headquarters to Galveston, which it did the following year. Hence, the Quintana venture came to nothing, and thereafter the town never prospered.[11]

Although Emily's many letters home during the trip do provide a window into her activities at Peach Point, by the fall of 1837, she was clearly ready to return home. This journey involved Emily, her son Austin, and Lavinia Perry steaming down the Ohio and up the Mississippi River to Missouri, as Emily retraced the very trip she had taken as a young girl in the 1790s when she and her family moved to the lead belt country. On reaching Herculaneum, she must have delighted in showing Austin Bryan the place where he was born. They also traveled to Potosi, where she visited the graves of her parents in the small Presbyterian churchyard that was located only a few blocks from Durham Hall. Emily renewed her acquaintance with some of her childhood friends, while she visited her cousins from the Bates family who had come to Missouri with her and remained there. They also visited St. Louis before boarding the steamboat *Majestic,* which carried them south to New Orleans. Emily returned to Texas with several trunks of household goods and clothing that she had purchased on the trip, including tablecloths, sheets, towels, knives and forks, and a full set of formal tea china. She shipped home several armchairs, rocking chairs, and mattresses. In addition, since the vicinity of Steubenville was a premier area for the production of glassware, she had purchased almost $100 worth of these items and sent them directly to Peach Point. Emily planned to use some of these things in entertaining Mary Austin Holley during her cousin's upcoming visit, which turned out to be sooner than Emily expected. Surprisingly, she saw Mary Austin Holley and the Henry Austin daughters while en route to Peach Point. Shortly after their vessel, the *Majestic*, passed through the great confluence where the Mississippi and Ohio rivers joined, Emily and her party were on deck when their steamboat encountered another steamer coming south from Louisville. Looking across the water at the other vessel, Emily spied Mary Austin Holley and her nieces at its rail, furiously waving at her as they passed. Mary Austin Holley and the girls, Emily determined, were also on their way to New Orleans, from where they would take a coasting vessel to Galveston. After some discussion with Austin and Lavinia, Emily decided that she and the two young people would leave the *Majestic* at Natchez and take the land route to Peach Point. Although it was a harder journey, this would save them over a week of travel time and put them at home before Mary Austin Holley's arrival.[12]

Emily's return to Peach Point, although joyful, was thus tempered by the reality that she quickly had to make the place ready for Mary Austin Holley. Emily's soured relationship with her cousin at this point spoke significantly to the depths of her graciousness and hospitality as the mistress of Peach Point Plantation. Weeks earlier, she had been writing James about her uncharitable personal opinion of her cousins Mary and Henry. Yet, at the same time, as a hostess of good breeding and as a person steeped in the bonds among the Austins, Emily saw herself bound by family obligation and would be courteous to her guest. It is also clear that Emily enjoyed a typically southern relationship with her cousin Mary, which could be complicated at best. "The lives of women revolved around the family," one scholar notes," and if one group of kin visited more often than any other, it was probably the plantation mistress's female relatives." In this context, Emily welcomed Mary to

Peach Point. This was especially appropriate since Emily had been well received at the Holley home in Lexington.[13]

Nonetheless, Emily had silently convinced herself not to approve of her cousin's trip, since Mary Austin Holley's motives for visiting Texas were, in her view, not entirely guileless. In fact, Mary's trip was in large part self-serving. At base level, it revolved around money or, more precisely, Mrs. Holley's lack of it. Mary needed money and hoped to get some through her Texas lands, most of which had come to her in the form of grants Stephen F. Austin arranged in the late 1820s and early 1830s. Without doubt, Mary experienced profound sorrow over the passing of Stephen. They did have a special relationship, of which Emily did not necessarily approve since it appeared to have very explicit, yet sublimated, romantic overtones. It galled Emily that much of her cousin's piteous talk about the tragedy of Stephen's untimely passing was usually followed by talk of the land he had given her. Mary Austin Holley did not hesitate to point out to anyone who would listen that her trip to Texas was, in part, motivated by her desire to assess the financial value of her Texas lands. She also hoped these assets would ease the drain that caring for Henry Austin's children had placed on her finances in Lexington. Although she had treated them well and gave no indication of unhappiness with them, Mary wanted Henry to take his children back. Her recent contact with George Hammeken, Stephen F. Austin's longtime friend, proved to be another important motivation for the trip. By early 1838, Hammeken was involved in implementing a large land development speculation near Galveston, and he hoped to involve Henry Austin, the Perrys, and Mary Austin Holley in his plans. Hammeken advocated building a railroad from Galveston Bay to the Brazos River, with the eastern terminus at Dollar Point on lands that had been owned by Stephen F. Austin. Most of this land now belonged to Emily, but the proposed railroad site also contained one league that had been deeded to Mary Austin Holley before the empresario's death.[14]

Mary and her nieces arrived at Galveston aboard a vessel that had sailed from New Orleans. Befitting her ebullient personality and exuberant manner, Mrs. Holley had planned the trip more as a "grand progress" than as a quiet, private visit. She sought the limelight as much as her cousin Emily hoped to avoid it. Well known in all parts of the province as the author of the 1833 best-selling book *Texas,* Mary Austin Holley enjoyed celebrity status and eagerly accepted all attentions paid to her. "It was thought that 3,000 people were collected on the levee and steamboats to see us depart," she wrote her daughter about her departure from the Crescent City. "I assure you that Texas makes a sensation in New Orleans." Mary found, not surprisingly, given her penchant for music and gaiety, that the voyage to Galveston was delightful and entertaining. "We could not have enjoyed ourselves more," she recalled, since there were flutes, violins, and clarinets among the passengers. Many of the travelers sat at long tables below deck, engrossed "in conversation and very late at night with music." Mary and her nieces passed Christmas Day in the new town of Houston, where they stayed with the Allen family, the promoters of the settlement. Later, before Mary left for the Brazos River plantations, President Sam Houston paid her a courtesy visit.[15]

Leaving the capital city for Brazoria, Mary and her traveling party formed an entourage. She rented a barouche coach in which she traveled, while Henry's daughter Emily Austin (named for her aunt at Peach Point) rode alongside on a horse, accompanied by nine other outriders who were also going to the Brazos. By New Year's Eve, they had arrived at Brazoria. They lodged at the Andrews home and attended an end-of-the-year celebration. While at Brazoria, Mary talked with a number of people, including Mirabeau B. Lamar, who was also visiting the town. Lamar had a longstanding literary bent and had earlier agreed to write a biography of Stephen F. Austin. Indeed, he had discussed the biography with Stephen F. Austin himself while its subject-to-be was still alive.

Stephen had agreed that Lamar should write the book, and this met with Emily's full approval. In early 1837, after Austin's death, Lamar wrote to Gail Borden, "For some time past I have been collecting materials for the life of the late lamented Genl. Stephen F. Austin. The task was originally undertaken in conformity with the wishes of the deceased." Lamar observed that the Austin correspondence was large and, "if collected, will go a great way in explaining our political history." With the cooperation of the Perrys, Lamar issued a public call for people with letters and papers to deliver them to Peach Point. Emily had, at an earlier date, permitted Lamar to visit Peach Point in order to examine the various papers Stephen had left there. He now told Mary Austin Holley during their New Year's visit of 1838 at Brazoria that the press of other duties had forced him to abandon this biographical project. Lamar's news set Mary to thinking, and within a very short time in her own mind, she had made Lamar's study of Stephen F. Austin into her own. She would write the biography of Stephen F. Austin, determining to mention it to Emily at the earliest opportunity during her upcoming visit to Peach Point. Shortly after this talk with Lamar, Henry Austin arrived at Brazoria, taking his children to his home at Bolivar for a visit, while Mary went down the river to Peach Point. She rode on horseback from Brazoria and reached the Perrys' house at about sunset on January 5, 1838.[16]

Emily and James consummately played the role of hospitable and caring hosts to Mrs. Holley, anxious to cater to their guest's every whim. Early in the visit, Emily took Mary on a long walk over the plantation as she pointed out several of the improvements that had been recently made. Mary was completely enchanted by Peach Point. She found the weather to be charming; fig trees were blooming, and the temperature was so mild that they talked of gardening. They walked along Jones Creek, which formed part of the plantation's boundary. Mary noted that the stretch of several miles between the homestead and the beach was composed of verdant land. As they approached the high mound that ran through this area, she and Emily saw twenty to thirty deer ranging in the grasslands with their silhouettes framed against the sky. The women also enjoyed seeing "innumerable cranes, both white and brown, that were seated in long rows at intervals, or gamboling in the distance, filling the air with their discordant screams. Other birds, an immense flock of ducks, were flying or sitting in every direction." Mary later wrote in her diary, "How I wish this spot was mine with a fine house and garden on the top." She found the flatness of Gulf Prairie to be visually engaging, with a large tree here and there on the horizon that reminded her of "a vessel under sail." The distant sound of the surf and breaking of the waves on the Gulf beach several miles away also made an impression on Mary, who thought that it sounded like distant thunder. After several days, Henry Austin came down from Bolivar to deliver his children back to Mary. His appearance occasioned the only frank talk during her visit to Peach Point, since two pressing matters of Austin family business had to be resolved. The first concerned where Henry's children would reside. Mary had little faith in her brother's ability to care for them, so at least for the time being, everyone decided that they would go back to the Holley house in Lexington. The second, of course, had to do with the two hundred acres of prime Peach Point land that Mary Austin Holley believed might be hers, if not legally then at least in terms of Stephen F. Austin's desires. This was the matter that had occasioned Emily's ire the previous fall. Mary recounted again the story of her visit to Gulf Prairie in the company of Stephen F. Austin well before the Perrys had come to Texas. Emily listened politely but left the resolution of the matter to James, who was frank and firm in explaining that Stephen's will made absolutely no mention of any bequest of Peach Point property to his cousin Mary. In addition, the land in question had already been deeded to Joel Bryan. As far as James F. Perry was concerned, that settled the matter.

Emily tactfully agreed but wished to make amends with her cousin as a token of familial peace, so she offered Mary two town lots at Quintana. This gesture appeased Mary, especially because she had the impression that these lots would be of great value. "Business is brisk there," she wrote her daughter Harriet of this transaction, further explaining that "there is a great appearance of improvement" at Quintana.[17]

Several days later, Mary and Emily rode down to Quintana on horseback, visiting neighbors along the way. Mary, accustomed to riding primarily in carriages back in Kentucky, recalled that she did well enough on the horse but that she "would not be fond of ranging the whole country in that fashion." Once at Quintana, Emily and Mary stayed several days in the home of Mrs. Thomas McKinney, wife of one of the partners in the store there. "We had the finest oysters you ever saw," Mary wrote her daughter about the visit, "as long as your hand, some of them." She also enjoyed the fish dishes prepared in the village, noting that they had the best red fish she had ever tasted. "They live remarkably well there," she noted, "having everything they want from New Orleans—a brig and schooner came in while we were there and are constantly coming. London Porter and champagne were constant drinks." Emily and Mary spent a good bit of time walking around Quintana, which had its own hotel and several other small businesses. They climbed among the ruins of the old fort, ranged among the sand dunes, and crossed over the ferry to the mainland at sunset. "It was lovely," Mary wrote in her diary, as they saw "a schooner under full sail that was crossing the bar." Mary found the weather hot even though it was January. A high point of this leisurely walk through town came when Emily showed her cousin the two town lots that were being given to her. Mary fully approved of their location. She seemed particularly touched on this trip to Quintana because she rode a horse that had been Stephen F. Austin's favorite mount. She did allow herself a moment of some sadness when, riding back to Peach

Point, she saw the land Stephen had promised her. "We passed his chosen spot on this earth," she lamented, "where he and I were to have our paradise—beautiful indeed it is, diversified with copse and lawn, but how it is changed to me! This lovely tract now belongs to Joel Bryan, an excellent young man who was our cavalier."[18]

Another poignant moment for Mary came several days later when she and Emily visited the grave of Stephen F. Austin. While on her earlier trip east, Emily had written specific instructions that Simon should ready the grave for this visit. She instructed him to turn the soil around it, build a brick work above the grave, and whitewash it. The day chosen for Emily and Mary to visit the grave was a bitterly cold and windy one. A blustery norther had blown across Gulf Prairie, bringing with it bands of heavy rain. "There has been no getting about for storms," Mary recalled. "Everybody had to stop just where they were overtaken by them and use the best shelter they could." Nonetheless, that cold Sunday afternoon, the two women walked along the muddy trail from the plantation to the Gulf Prairie churchyard. Mary gazed upon the grave with respect, graced as it was with an inscription much like the one on the final resting place of Moses Austin at Potosi. Mary Austin Holley, standing in the wind, silently read the brief inscription: "Gen'l Stephen F. Austin—Departed this life on the 27th of Dec. a.d. 1836—Aged 43 years one month and 24 days." Mary said quietly, "My cousin sleeps in peace."[19]

Other than these few fleeting moments of emotion, most of Mrs. Holley's visit to Peach Point was a happy whirl of social activities and lighthearted entertainments, especially after she and Emily cordially resolved the question of her land claims. The presence of Emily's sons at Peach Point, particularly Austin Bryan and Stephen Perry, provided a welcome diversion for Henry's daughters, who were again with their aunt. One afternoon, for example, Austin Bryan took his two female cousins walking in the woods. Each of them picked wild bay leaves to keep as mementoes of this excursion. Although history fails to record what young Bryan did with his leaf, the two Austin girls carefully locked theirs away in their writing cases to become treasured family heirlooms for generations thereafter. Joel Bryan took his mother and Mary horseback riding several times along the beach. The women also went "circuit riding" through the neighboring plantations, visiting various other residents of the area. One day late in the month, for example, they rose early to visit the Jack home, passing on to the Calverts', and then visited Crosby's Landing. They arrived back home at Peach Point at dinnertime, having ridden almost twenty miles.[20]

The most memorable evening of Mary's visit came in late January when everyone at Peach Point attended a gala ball held at Velasco as part of the racing season. "All the world who can move, wind and weather permitting, are to be there," Mary wrote her daughter with clear excitement. The Perrys, all their sons, Lavinia Perry, and Mary Austin Holley, along with the Henry Austin nieces, rode down to Velasco in a covered wagon attended by several slaves. "Everything available for dresses in Texas has been brought up for the occasion," Mary crowed, "the clothes being all brought from New York ready made and of the newest fashion." A steamboat also traveled down the Brazos, picking up other revelers bound for the party. Mary was filled with anticipation for a good time as they rolled down the Velasco road to the dance. She happily exclaimed, "I expect it will be a great occasion." Even the beginnings of a drizzly rain before they reached Velasco did not dampen their spirits. "We danced until midnight," Mary later reported about the revel with satisfaction. "Those that did not have beds slept on the floor till daylight when the company went home."[21]

While at Peach Point, Holley had not forgotten her conversation several weeks earlier with Mirabeau B. Lamar at Brazoria, concerning his decision to forego writing a biography of Stephen F. Austin. Emily already knew of Lamar's decision, and she saw it as her personal duty to keep Stephen F. Austin's memory alive. On the first posthumous birthday after his passing, for example, Emily had hoped that prominent individuals might deliver public orations about him. During her trip east, she wrote James Perry, "I wish you to request W. H. Jack or Judge Burnet to deliver an oration on the third of November, in memory of my dear brother; you know that is his birthday, I think something of the kind ought to be done, for it appears that he is entirely forgotten in Texas." Emily had carefully saved many mementos of Stephen's life, including his tomahawk, knife, powder horn, and his branding iron. She kept many of his books as well, along with his papers and those of her father. These she housed in the room that had been Stephen's bedchamber at Peach Point. With Lamar withdrawn from the biography project, Emily had thought about approaching David G. Burnet as a possible replacement author. It was at this point that Mary appeared at Peach Point having already talked with Lamar. Mrs. Holley informed Cousin Emily of her idea to write Stephen's biography. Emily heartily approved, and for the rest of her visit, Mary spent many hours in Stephen's room at Peach Point reading his letters and papers. In particular, she filled several notebooks with information taken from the prison memoirs that chronicled his days in Mexico City during 1834 and 1835.[22]

"In the retirement of Lexington," she later wrote, "I shall have the leisure to undertake a work which has been much urged upon me, the memoir of our lamented Stephen. Strange as it may seem, it has become necessary to rescue his name from comparative oblivion even before the generation in which it shone has passed away." With an immodesty characteristic of her literary endeavors, she noted that "General Lamar and Captain Elliott urge me to do the work and even Houston is always preaching to me of Stephen." Emily and James cooperated with Mary's effort by issuing a second public call for individuals across Texas to donate any papers they might have to this literary project. Written in the name of James Perry as executor of the estate, this public notice explained that "the labors of Austin were expansive, and important: so intimately connected with all the interesting events of his times, that a faithful account of his life must necessarily embrace a large portion of the history of our country." For that reason, the Perrys sought any historical papers that might relate to Austin and the Anglo-American settlement of Texas. "What will be done with this material when collected?" they asked in the notice. "We reply that it will be placed with the material we have already obtained, and carefully preserved for the future by a historian of Austin and Texas." For several years, Mrs. Holley worked on the biography. For a variety of reasons, however, she was never able to complete it, and the papers remained for many decades thereafter in a large trunk in the main house at Peach Point.[23]

By the end of January 1838, Mary had decided to return to Henry's plantation at Bolivar. During her visit, she and Emily had restored the strong bond of kinship that they had experienced as cousins for almost a quarter century. Even the misunderstanding about the Peach Point land failed to make a permanent rift in their relationship. The town lots at Quintana, which Mary desired to sell as soon as possible in order to raise cash, helped to smooth her feelings toward the Perrys. By the late spring, Mrs. Holley was ready to return to Lexington, where she arrived in June of 1838. She did continue to follow events in Texas due to her continuing interest in writing Stephen's biography and because of her land holdings at Dollar Point, where George Hammeken was attempting to develop a town.[24]

Emily and James soon became involved with Hammeken in this development project as well. On May 24, 1838, the Republic of Texas chartered the Brazos and Galveston Railroad, which Hammeken had organized. James F. Perry served as the treasurer of this company and for good reason. Most of the land located at the eastern terminus of the proposed railroad had belonged to Stephen F. Austin and hence was now Emily's property. The new company proposed to build a railroad from the west shore of Galveston Bay to the Brazos River. The shipping of cotton from the Brazoria area to the major port facility at Galveston Island would provide the primary cargo for this line, thus freeing the planters from their risky reliance on maritime shipping between Velasco and the island port city. Harking back to a name first coined by Moses Austin in 1821, the new terminus town would be called Austinia. This must have been Emily's idea, since she was the only living person who would have known about that name. Besides, Austinia would perpetuate the family name of her father and brothers. Emily quickly became intimately involved in the land development scheme. In return for stock in the railroad company, she deeded approximately fifty-five town blocks to George Hammeken. She also gave a number of town lots to her son Joel. The development of Austinia was clearly a Perry family enterprise, and their involvement was further strengthened when Austin Bryan became secretary of the railroad company. Both Bryan sons routinely kept their mother informed of their activities regarding the development. Initially, the family and Hammeken had high hopes for the new town at Austinia. Emily even dreamed that it might become the capital of Texas. They also eagerly anticipated financial success. This was important to the Perrys because both James and Emily did not feel they had achieved economic independence. "As yet we cannot boast of wealth in this country," James wrote his friend John S. Brickey in Potosi during the spring of 1839. "We have had a hard struggling to get here. So far we have plenty of fine lands and hope, soon as they come into market, to be able to better ourselves more than we have."[25]

Success and wealth, however, were not to be found at Austinia. Hammeken determined by early 1839 that the proposed railroad right-of-way would be easier and cheaper to build if the terminus were moved south to San Luis Island, located on the coast directly to the west, across from Galveston Island. This change of terminus nonetheless proved very agreeable to Emily, because much of the land there had belonged to Stephen F. Austin and hence was her property. In August of 1840, she, James, Hammeken, and several other investors participated in the legal incorporation of the San Luis Company, which would oversee development of the town, also called San Luis. Austin Bryan and George Hammeken became the joint agents who would sell town lots on behalf of the company, in essence acting as realtors for Emily. The initial survey created 450 town lots to be sold to the public. The proceeds from some of these lots would be reinvested to build a bridge, a lighthouse, and make street improvements. The development scheme at San Luis had an additional benefit for Emily since it enabled her to help settle the longstanding legal dispute she had with Eliza Westall Hill, the widow of Brown Austin. Eliza and her husband, William Hill, still contested Stephen F. Austin's will, contending that some of the property that went to Emily Austin as sole heir should have been part of Brown Austin's estate. In 1837, the Hills had filed legal suit against Emily in an effort to recover the property. The development at San Luis gave Emily the opportunity to mollify them. In a complicated transaction, Emily sold much of the platted area of the new town to the railroad company in return for $80,000 cash. In turn, she promised to use this money to pay off the claims made by Eliza and her husband, should the Hills approve of the arrangements at San Luis and not contest the sale. This deal ultimately proved successful. Emily and her former sister-in-law, Eliza, participated thereafter in the joint development of San Luis.[26]

Emily had high hopes that the development would bring the family great prosperity. The town grew rapidly. In 1840, a man named John P. Follett established a shipyard that greatly enhanced the town's economic development. By the end of that year, San Luis had a weekly newspaper, a hotel, two general stores, and a cotton compress. The town received a boost in popular recognition when Mary Austin Holley visited it on a return trip to Texas in 1840. She had come back to in order to deal with family matters related to Henry Austin's continuing inability to manage his affairs. She also brought two of Henry's sons back to Texas. They had been living with her in Kentucky, and coming of age, they desired to return home. Arriving at Galveston in the fall of 1840, Mrs. Holley immediately met with George Hammeken, who was very excited about the development of San Luis. He drove her in a buggy westward from Galveston to the new town site. She liked it so much that she decided to stay at the hotel there, operated by Mr. and Mrs. Charles Bennett. Mary remained at San Luis for almost three months. Although she did not go to Peach Point on this trip to Texas, some of the family did visit her at San Luis. Joel and Austin Bryan both passed through the town on several occasions. Emily and her cousin Henry Austin rode down one Sunday in the Perry family carriage. They drove around looking at some of the land, and Henry showed Mary a piece of property that he had bought nearby. However, as the years passed, San Luis never prospered to the extent that Emily and its other investors had envisioned, and for several reasons. The most important of these related to the fact that George Hammeken became seriously ill and was eventually laid low by dementia. As Emily later wrote son Guy Bryan, "Poor Mr. Hammeken has gone completely mad." More importantly, the harbor at San Luis had begun to fill with silt by the mid-1840s, and over time, this made it difficult for ships to dock. In spite of the unprofitable investments at Austinia and San Luis, the Perrys were finding solid economic success at Peach Point. The plantation was starting to function as a profitable agricultural operation during the early 1840s, and the coming decade would see it achieve the full flower of its development.[27]

THE MATURE YEARS

The years of Emily's youthful adulthood had passed by 1840, and she was clearly becoming matronly. She had lived four-and-a-half decades, given birth to eleven children, married two husbands, and started a home life for herself on three different occasions in two different places. Peach Point was now her home in every way, although she had lived there less than a decade. It was there that she had finally put down roots. Emily would continue to work with her husband to build the plantation, which was entering its stride as an agricultural operation that would provide them with a substantial living. In every way, she had become a stalwart member of the Texas planter elite. The 1840s would also see all of Emily's surviving children grow into adults. Several of them would start families of their own. Her two oldest sons, Joel and Austin, were on the threshold of becoming independent and successful married men. For Emily Austin, the labors of a lifetime had come to fruition.

One of the first milestones of Emily's mature existence was the marriage of Joel Bryan to Lavinia Perry, which surprised no one in the Peach Point household. The two young people had known each other for many years. Lavinia was already a part of the extended family, although she was not related by blood to the Bryan sons since she was a Perry. By all accounts, she was a charming and pleasant young woman, and Emily's entire family liked her tremendously. A relative characterized Lavinia as "a woman of great character and determination," thereby giving her something in common with her mother-in-law, Emily. Family tradition holds that Lavinia was "handsome with strong features, dark hair, and an

Lavinia Perry Bryan. Courtesy of the Brazoria County Historical Museum.

erect carriage." She and Joel married on April 6, 1840. Joel had already decided that he wanted to follow in the footsteps of his stepfather and make a living from the land. Indeed, during 1837 and 1838, he had managed most of the planting at Peach Point while James had gone to New Orleans and Emily was in the East. Joel moved with his new bride to the property that his parents had given him and which earlier had been the plot desired by Mary Austin Holley. Only a short carriage ride from the main house at Peach Point, Joel named this plantation

Durazno, the Spanish word for peach. It was almost in easy walking distance of Emily's home, so there was constant contact between the two households. Joel planted a cotton crop at Durazno in 1840 and began raising cattle soon thereafter. He was a meticulous businessman, carefully planning every aspect of what happened on his new plantation. He purchased a large sheepskin-bound volume of blank pages in June 1840. In it he carefully recorded all of his business transactions over the next quarter century. Unlike at Peach Point, where cotton and sugar production were the major activities, Joel favored the raising of cattle. During his first summer and fall at Durazno, he bought a number of cows and horses. He also began building a grand home that, in the end, would be more opulent than his parents' house at Peach Point. By December 1840, he was buying large amounts of building supplies for its construction. Another milestone in Emily's life came on March 2, 1841, when Joel and Lavinia's first son, James Perry Bryan, was born. Emily was now a grandmother.[1]

Austin Bryan, like his older brother, was also establishing an independent life. After serving as his mother's companion on her long trip east in 1837, he returned to Texas and became involved in the various family activities developing Austinia and San Luis. As the secretary of the railroad company, he had numerous business duties that caused him to travel around the Republic. In addition, he supervised and kept track of the land that his mother had inherited from Stephen F. Austin, acting as her representative in its management. This seemed a logical arrangement for Emily, since young Austin had been the clerk who arranged many of the records pertaining to these lands during his uncle's lifetime. On several occasions, Austin traveled to locations around Texas where Stephen had owned land in order to check on their status. He spent a considerable amount of time, for example, in Bastrop, where he reviewed the land records and made sure that Emily's titles there were in order. He also supervised from time to time the sale of lands in order to raise money for his mother and stepfather. This proved to be a very hard job, as Bryan found that "there is a chance of our being robbed of what justly belongs to us by the lawyers and other avaricious people." It appears that at times, like his uncle and grandfather before him, he was beguiled by the notion that the Austin family had to defend itself against a hostile, ill-intending world. Austin Bryan's work as the chief land manager of his mother's inheritance was a most useful and valuable assistance to the family. In all of these activities, he kept his mother informed of what he was doing and sought her concurrence regarding the operation of the estate.[2]

Austin Bryan also helped superintend the land transactions at San Luis on Emily's behalf, while he pitched in to keep Peach Point running during those periods of time when James Perry was not in residence. A new, major opportunity for Austin Bryan came when he was offered a position as secretary to the Republic of Texas diplomatic legation in Washington, D.C. After consulting with his parents, Austin accepted this position and joined the mission to the United States. He updated his mother and stepfather about his many activities in the nation's capital by letter. Emily was filled with pride when she received news from Austin that he had been personally introduced to the president of the United States. Young Bryan also recounted to his mother much about the formal social life in which he participated, although he reported that it was much too grand for him. "We sat down to dinner at 6 pm, a fashionable hour to dine in those parts," he wrote, "and rose from the table about 9 p.m., and then went to a dancing party in Georgetown." His travels with the Texas diplomatic delegation at one point took him to Louisiana, and there he met a young woman named Adeline la Mothe, who came from an old Creole family. They married on February 20, 1840, at New Orleans. By that time, Austin had left the diplomatic mission, and the couple returned to Texas. He eventually settled a plantation he named Reterio, located to the east of Peach Point along Oyster Creek.[3]

With her two oldest sons starting families of their own, Emily turned much of her attention to the education of the younger children. The time and expense that Emily devoted to this effort continued to reflect her longstanding commitment to schools and learning. That can also be seen by the appearance of a visitor at Peach Point in March of 1840, one who would have an enduring impact on Texas education. In that month, a somberly clad horseback rider slowly made his solitary way up the drive of the plantation, past the flower garden, to be greeted on the front veranda by Emily and James. He was Reverend Daniel Baker, formerly the pastor of a Presbyterian church in Washington, D.C., the members of which had included both Andrew Jackson and John Quincy Adams. Reverend Baker left this prestigious pulpit several years earlier to evangelize the southern frontier. His widely acclaimed successes in these endeavors brought him to Texas in 1840 to help establish the Presbyterian Church in the young Republic. Daniel Baker arrived at Peach Point Plantation in search of financial support from Emily and her husband for a college he hoped to found in Texas. This was an adventurous plan for the relatively rude, rough-and-tumble frontier society that was the Republic of Texas in 1840. Nonetheless, Reverend Baker had persisted, and his fellow ministers at a recent meeting had approved his plan pending the securing of financial donations that would underwrite the new college. Reverend Baker knew that Emily and her husband had already established themselves as staunch supporters of religion in Texas. Although Emily thought of herself as an Episcopalian, James Perry was a devout Presbyterian. They listened as Baker enthusiastically outlined his ambitious proposal for the college. Such a school, he told them, would be a training ground for new Presbyterian ministers in the young Republic, while it would serve as a centerpiece for culture, refinement, and learning. Emily warmed to the idea immediately, and she promised a generous donation to the proposed college. In so doing, she made the first financial pledge to what would become Austin College, a school that Reverend Baker gratefully named in memory of her deceased brother. Emily transferred to the college legal title to fifteen hundred acres of land near Peach Point that she had inherited from Stephen F. Austin.[4]

In spite of her support for furthering the cause of education in Texas, Emily had a marked preference for eastern schools for her own children. This may have stemmed from her own experiences as a young girl when she attended school in Lexington and New York City. In addition, during her 1837 trip to the East, she had come to the conclusion that her own children appeared provincial. For that reason, she insisted that her younger children attend school in the United States. Joel and Austin, of course, were too old for much formal education, and moreover, they had grown up in times before the family was able to afford such expenses. An eastern education had proven very successful for Guy M. Bryan, who flourished at Kenyon as he easily settled into college life. He wrote his mother, "This is, I believe, a good place to study, and all the students will admit that." The young man's positive view of Kenyon College was typical. "Most students who went to church colleges not only remained in place," historian Robert F. Pace has noted of southern college men during that era, "but expressed positive enthusiasm about their educational activities." Guy was a faithful and loquacious correspondent, especially with his mother. He filled his letters to her with news of the college, his thoughts on the various events that had affected him, and much philosophizing about the nature of existence. At times, his long and somewhat rambling letters might have appeared sophomoric in their tone, but they never seemed so to his mother, who greatly enjoyed reading them. She was proud of her son's erudition. Sometimes, in fact, these letters were filled with puffery that might have been specially calculated to impress Emily. In one such letter, Guy began by telling her that "I have nothing of consequence to write until I receive a letter from you, which I look for everyday." Nonetheless, he was able to fill several pages that followed with rhapsodically crafted verbiage that may have indicated he was homesick or perhaps just a bit nostalgic. "I think that I could almost give up my desire of making a learned man," he wrote, "if I could only see Texas and its enjoyments again, for I long to tread the extensive prairies of Texas and give free scope to my strange disposition and look with delight upon the various attractions of this, my Beloved Country, exceeded by none in its natural advantages and beauty."[5]

Guy, however, had a less prosaic side to his personality as well. He made friends easily, joined a literary society, and within the year progressed from the preparatory department to college level work. He clearly had his mother's social grace and hospitable personality. He also thought much about his younger siblings. It was Guy who, in a letter to Emily, apparently first suggested that his half brother Stephen S. Perry join him at Kenyon. Stephen was twelve years of age when Guy left for college, and he continued to attend school at Brazoria. Stephen's age made him a candidate to attend boarding school, since many youngsters from the plantation belt routinely went away for school at even younger ages. Eliza Perry, for example, had enrolled at the Steubenville Female Academy at age ten, an occurrence that no one in the Perrys' circle thought unusual. After some consideration, however, Emily decided that she preferred Stephen to attend preparatory school in Steubenville rather than at Kenyon, as Guy desired. The Perrys thus decided on Steubenville's Grove Academy, where young Stephen Perry would be very near the female institute Eliza attended. This would place both children close to some of the Perry family relations in nearby Ohio, while there was the obvious logistical benefit of having them at school in the same town. Accordingly, in late 1838, Emily made another trip east, this time for the purpose of delivering her son Stephen to the Grove Academy, which, like Eliza's school, was a Presbyterian institution. Both the Grove Academy and the Steubenville Female Academy enjoyed excellent reputations. The trip also gave Emily the opportunity to visit with Eliza.[6]

For about a year thereafter, all went well for both of the Perry children in school at Steubenville. This situation, however, did not last because Eliza's medical condition eventually reappeared. Given this development, James and Emily decided that the young woman should attend a school closer to home and near the relatives in Kentucky. James wrote Reverend Beatty that "we have decided to take Eliza further south." The Perrys selected the Nazareth Academy located at Bardstown, Kentucky. This school had been founded by the Sisters of Charity, a Roman Catholic order known for its concerns regarding education, the poor, and the indigent. Sister Catherine Spalding served as the headmistress of the school, which was establishing a reputation for high-quality instruction. The decision to move Eliza to Nazareth coincided with the Perrys' decision to enroll Stephen with his brother Guy at Kenyon. Stephen supported this decision because he had never really liked the Grove Academy. "This Academy has fallen since I have been here," he wrote his parents after the first year, "and I believe that it will break up in another session." Accordingly, James and Emily traveled east in the spring of 1840 in order to transfer Stephen to Kenyon and take Eliza to the Nazareth Academy. They again visited family along the way, seeing relatives in Kentucky and Ohio. While they were gone, they left affairs at Peach Point under the joint care of Joel and Austin, both of whom were newlyweds. By the late fall, Stephen and Eliza had been enrolled in their new schools, and the Perrys returned to Peach Point.[7]

Having been back only a few weeks, Emily began to receive letters from Eliza that caused her a great deal of concern. Eliza did not like

Nazareth Academy and claimed to be miserable there. She was clearly homesick. "I am very sorry to tell you that I do not like Nazareth as much as I thought I would," she wrote her mother. "It seems that I have been here two years," Eliza added, at that point having been there two weeks. "The girls are not half so clever as they were at Mr. Beatty's." Young Eliza professed great loneliness and, missing her companions at Steubenville, told her mother that "I feel the want of such a friend now, that would take my part, but here I am poor without a friend. I try to please and gratify them as much as possible, but no, it is all in vain." Eliza reported that she had stomach pains from time to time because "they have such victuals I believe that make me sick." Indeed, Eliza found much lacking in the school's cuisine. "I'll declare sometimes I do not believe the hogs would not eat what we have to eat and starve," she observed. "I am nearly dead for something good to eat; we have very plain fair bread, potatoes, and boiled cabbage without vinegar." The sleeping accommodations were no better to Eliza's liking, as she noted that "they have two rooms that they keep us in while out of school hours that are just as hot as they can be; it gives me such violent headaches now I can hardly write, and a very bad cold." Eliza found some satisfaction in her studies, especially French. "I am studying all of the common branches such as reading, writing, arithmetic, grammar, geography," she wrote Emily, "and you wish to know whether I liked French any better than I did. Yes, I do." She also enjoyed dancing class but found the male teacher unusual. "I do not like to take from him much because he scolds so," she observed. "His name is Mr. Malloy; he is an old man, I expect, because he wears a wig, the girls told me so."[8]

This correspondence caused Emily to write a "candid and open" letter to Sister Catherine Spalding in the hopes of sorting through the various complaints. "I think that Eliza is just as happy as you could expect her to be so far from home," Sister Catherine replied. "She is always cheerful and seems to enjoy herself with her companions." The headmistress counseled Emily to have patience with Eliza, noting that Nazareth Academy was very well qualified to deal with young women of her age and disposition. "I sincerely hope you will never have reason to regret the preference you have given to our institution," she told Emily. Additional information about Eliza in this letter, however, was not encouraging. Sister Catherine noted, "I am sorry to say she has had two spasms since she is here—each time at night. I have since put her to sleep in the Infirmary where we can watch over her more closely. I am inclined to think she caused it each time by imprudence in eating apples." Emily and James decided to leave Eliza at Nazareth. As time passed, the young girl did settle in, made friends, and prospered in her studies. Happily, the attacks she had been suffering had also gone away. The following year, Sister Catherine wrote the Perrys that Eliza was doing very well. Emily responded, "We are truly grateful that Eliza's deportment and industry and improvement have been deserving of your approbation, and our anxiety about her health has been much relieved since we received your letter." James, as well, offered profuse congratulations and encouragement to his daughter. "I cannot express the pleasure it gave us yesterday," he wrote, "on the receipt of Miss Spalding's report on your improvement and deportment last session."[9]

Such equanimity did not last as Eliza's health began to decline during the following year. Her spasms began anew, causing both the Perrys and her teachers a good deal of worry. Interestingly, everyone still blamed her malady on eating too much fruit. "I am sorry to say she overindulged too freely in the use of fruits," Sister Catherine wrote Emily, "notwithstanding our vigilance." The consequence of this was, according to the headmistress, that Eliza had experienced two spasms within ten days. As well, her deportment had become problematic. Just as Emily had observed several years earlier on the first trip to Steubenville with

Eliza, the girl sometimes became moody, uncooperative, disrespectful, and surly, but her changing mood would thereafter appear happy and cheerful. Sister Catherine explained to Emily, "Sometimes she may be docile and attentive," and at other times not. Sister Catherine secured the services of a Bardstown physician, a Dr. Harrison, to treat Eliza. Although initially optimistic about a cure, Harrison gave up his treatments after only a month and recommended to Sister Catherine that Eliza be sent home to Texas in order to be with her parents.[10]

To their credit, the Sisters of Charity were very reluctant to do this. Their order, which had been founded in Kentucky in the early 1800s, followed the Rule of St. Vincent de Paul, thus giving them a special empathy for the distressed, the sick, and the needy. In that regard, the Sisters also operated an infirmary in Louisville, located about sixty miles from the Academy. Sister Catherine Spalding believed that it would best for Eliza to be treated there rather than to have the young girl return to Texas, where the medical facilities might not be of the same caliber as in Louisville. She presented Emily with a new plan to move Eliza to the Sisters of Charity infirmary. If Emily gave permission, Eliza could be treated by a Dr. Wantyn, who "has been for many years a practitioner in Louisville, and he stands foremost in his profession. He is well known by us, and deservedly possesses our confidence as a physician." The headmistress also advised Emily that Dr. Wantyn had ruled out the eating of fruit as the cause of her daughter's condition. "He wishes particularly to know whether she received at any time an injury on her head by a fall or otherwise," Sister Catherine asked. "Unless this has been the case, he thinks he can remove it as the cause of her fits." There had been no fall that anyone could remember.[11]

After a good deal of discussion and soul-searching, Emily decided that Eliza should indeed go to Louisville for treatment by Dr. Wantyn at the Sisters of Charity infirmary. The Perry family viewed Louisville as a sophisticated place. It was also near members of the family, including the Robert Baldwins, who were cousins to James Perry. Emily therefore gave Sister Catherine her consent. "I am glad to tell you," Sister Catherine wrote in February 1842, "that Eliza's health is again much better; she has not had but two slight fits within the last eight or nine weeks, and one of them was caused by her imprudently eating some pickles she met with." Eliza spent about two months in the infirmary in Louisville, where she had "the latest and most approved course of treatment." Sister Catherine brought her back to the Academy at Bardstown in April, only to find that Dr. Wantyn's treatments had no permanent curative effect. She wrote Emily that month from Bardstown, "I am sorry to say that yesterday she had another spasm. I cannot account for it, as I do think she now has tried to be prudent in her diet." For that reason, the headmistress reported that she was taking Eliza back to Louisville in the near future so "that the doctors may see her again and perhaps they might think proper to change her course of treatment." She further wrote Emily at Peach Point, "My own candid and disinterested opinion is that it is very probable her recovery and permanent restoration may be promoted by her spending next winter in Texas." Thereafter, Eliza could return to Kentucky if her condition improved. With this news, the Perrys decided that the time had come for Eliza to travel home for a rest from school. In reality, Eliza Perry would be coming home for good.[12]

The decision to bring Eliza home coincided with Guy Bryan's leaving Kenyon after six years of study in the preparatory and collegiate divisions. Guy had been a good student who made high marks. He was also engaging personally and formed lifelong friendships at Kenyon. A future president of the United States, Rutherford B. Hayes, became one of his closest school chums, and they remained in touch for the rest of their lives. Unlike Guy, Stephen was not a strong student while at Kenyon. His lack of scholarly application concerned Emily, and she routinely wrote Stephen letters of encouragement. "My dear son," she told him, "we wish you to acquire an education that will fit you for anything which you may wish to pursue." She further observed that "a good education never disqualified a person from any occupation, but without it, it very often happens that persons are placed in situations where they feel the want of it. I sincerely hope that you will embrace it with energy and perseverance." By the summer of 1842, Guy's time at Kenyon had come to an end. In early October, he accompanied Eliza back to Texas. Stephen remained at Kenyon, where he continued his studies without the sobering influence of his older half brother. Once her two children had arrived home from Ohio, Emily and Eliza spent much of the winter staying at Matagorda, where they sought the services of a local physician to treat the young girl, apparently without much success. James, Guy, and Henry Perry, the youngest son, rode over from Peach Point to visit them whenever possible.[13]

Even with the distractions of Eliza's illness, Emily did not confine her interests and attentions only to the needs of the children. She was first and foremost the mistress of Peach Point Plantation. As historian Catherine Clinton has observed, the concerns of such women extended across "the entire spectrum of domestic operations throughout estate, from food and clothing to the physical and spiritual care of both her white family and her husband's slaves." Like her husband James, Emily had worked long and hard to make Peach Point an economic success. Her sphere of interest and activity on the plantation permeated the entire household, and it extended through the gardens to the shops and barns of the homestead area, as evidenced in her letters home to James in 1837. She thus took an active interest in all facets of Peach Point's operation. This included monitoring the activities of slaves, keeping cognizance of the agricultural operations, and making sure that the finances ran in a well-organized manner, responsibilities that patently fell to James but in which she shared. Unlike some plantation mistresses, Emily kept herself fully apprised of all events occurring at Peach Point and maintained a holistic view of the plantation's operation. She clearly would have been competent to operate the plantation by herself, although the events of her life never demanded that.[14]

Emily remained intimately involved in all of the activities at Peach Point during the cycle of the agricultural year, because it was her responsibility to keep all of its residents healthy, fed, clothed, and able to work. Health concerns were vitally important to Emily, both for her own family members and for the slaves on the place. A visitor to Peach Point noted, "Mrs. Perry, instead of having the care of one family, is the nurse, physician and spiritual advisor to a whole settlement. She feels it her duty to see to their comfort when sick or hurt." Most of Emily's letters across the entire span of her life regularly mention health. As one historian has noted of southern life in general for elite planting women, "Life on the plantation necessarily brought the mistress into intimate acquaintance with the unhealthy features of the southern climate," and this generated "a preoccupation, almost obsessive for some plantation mistresses, with health." This constant concern served as a measure of the relatively poor medical conditions of the era. This proved especially true for minor illnesses. In that regard, the Perrys were typical of almost all literate people in antebellum Texas, as they incessantly wrote about how they felt physically in their correspondence to friends and family. "Health was essential to family survival," historian Sally G. McMillen has noted, "and no southerner's health was assured in the antebellum period."[15]

Plantation life at Peach Point often presented serious medical problems with which Emily had to deal as the mistress of the place. Mishaps and accidents constituted an ever-present reality. On one occasion, lightning struck the cotton compress, injuring several slaves.

Emily nursed them back to health. A slave named Turner died in a later accident at the compress house when the main traveling arm collapsed on him. Emily sometimes found herself treating the entire plantation for various kinds of contagions. In 1844, James observed that "our family, white and black, have been sick with the grip or bad colds, but they are now in better health." A malady the Perrys called "brain fever" swept through the plantation the following year, taking one of the slave children. Emily also presided over the birth of babies among the slave population at Peach Point, although there was a slave midwife resident as well. One year, 1843, there were four babies born among the female slaves. The Perrys were fortunate in having the resources to bring a doctor to the plantation when medical problems exceeded Emily's ability to deal with them. Emily often called upon Dr. Johnson Calhoun Hunter whenever the situation demanded that a physician be consulted. He treated family members and the slave population alike. In that regard, Emily and her husband were unusual in the region, because they demanded that their slaves receive the same level of medical care as did the Perry family. In a notable case, Milley, a slave who had come with Emily from Missouri, developed breast cancer. After local treatments failed, Stephen Perry (then back from school in Ohio) took her to New Orleans, where she was treated at the Circus Street Hospital affiliated with the Medical College of Louisiana, one of the few facilities in the South that admitted slaves as patients. Doctors there performed breast surgery on her, and Milley later returned to Peach Point, although the historical record does not document the ultimate success of her treatment.[16]

Emily also paid close attention to the preparation of meals at Peach Point. In terms of food for the slaves, many cotton plantations in Texas followed the advice offered by a well-respected planter named Charles William Tait, who drew up an extensive list of rules for the management of slaves. One of "Tait's Rules" called for giving each slave, or slave family, an entire week's worth of rations and having them cook it for their meals. This had the potential to save the planter money, but it sometimes created situations in which the slaves did not eat as well as they should. Emily rejected Tait's rules. Instead, during most of the year, she operated a communal kitchen at Peach Point that fixed three meals a day for everyone on the place; the same food was served to her family and the slave population alike. That was a very unusual practice on Texas plantations. By the early 1840s, the kitchen at Peach Point was located in a separate building from the main house, about twenty feet away. James and Emily did this in order to protect the house from fire, and indeed, on several occasions the kitchen building did burn down.[17]

Emily's system of communal meals, except for special occasions and other times when the Perry family entertained guests, meant that her family and the slaves shared the same diet for considerable periods of the year. The Perrys, however, usually ate in the dining room of the main house instead of eating with the hands. Nonetheless, everyone enjoyed a rich larder. Since the Perrys attempted in the 1840s to make Peach Point as self-sufficient as possible, Emily supervised the planting of rather large vegetable gardens, while the plantation raised a considerable number of cows, hogs, and chickens for consumption. A smokehouse stood near the kitchen, and there, during appropriate seasons of the year, Emily would prepare meat for storage. Mostly, the Perrys slaughtered hogs in the cold winter months, killed cows for beef in the spring season after calving, and ate chickens regularly. The Perry boys and some of the slave men also hunted on a regular basis, and venison or wild fowl often found their way to the Peach Point kitchen, along with fish from the nearby Gulf of Mexico. Sometimes there was a surplus in the larder and Emily sold excess foodstuffs to other planters in the neighborhood. Plantation records document her regular sale of eggs, chickens, ducks, turkeys, geese, butter, pecans, tallow, hominy, and soap.

Potatoes and corn also proved to be favorites in Emily's kitchen, if not the culinary mainstays. Peach Point routinely produced an abundance of corn, which provided sustenance for both the people and the livestock on the place. It appears that a considerable acreage had corn planted on it each year, because from 1838 onwards, the plantation sold excess corn on the open market. In 1845, the year of a bumper crop, Emily also sold two hundred bushels of sweet potatoes and eighteen bushels of white potatoes to local buyers. In essence, she was running a very profitable vegetable operation at Peach Point for the local market economy. This was not unusual, for as Catherine Clinton has noted, "southern society remained rural, provincial, and dependent upon staple crop production. The household, not the marketplace, was the central force of the southern economy." This led to what Clinton has observed as a fundamental misunderstanding that slaves did much of the work on a plantation. Such was not the case since the mistress often worked alongside the slaves while supervising. This was certainly true for Emily. Like the wife on many a typical plantation, she "administered food production, purchase, and distribution not only in the planter home but for the whole plantation." She also "managed the dairy, the garden, and the smokehouse." In short, as Clinton has noted, "The plantation mistress held the keys as the symbol of her domain," and Emily proved to be no exception in this regard.[18]

As Peach Point continued to prosper, the Perrys also diversified into raising cattle and planting sugarcane. By the late 1830s, James had a respectable-sized herd of cattle on the plantation and at Chocolate Bayou. He sold, for example, approximately forty to fifty head of cattle to Gail Borden, another early settler in the region, to help him start his own herd. Because of the fertility of the agricultural land at Peach Point as arable acreage, James converted the property at Chocolate Bayou entirely into a stock-raising farm for cattle. It was there that the Perrys had first settled after arriving in Texas and where the youngsters Stephen and Henry Perry had lived when their mother traveled east in 1837. Emily always had an interest in the Chocolate Bayou operation and often visited there. Her son Stephen, in particular, liked the stock farm and would eventually take delight in managing it once his schooling was completed. Until that time, the Perrys had settled one of Henry Austin's sons, Edward, who had earlier attended Kenyon with Guy, on the property to manage it during the 1840s. It became customary each spring to drive the cattle from the junction of Chocolate Bayou and Pleasant Bayou down to Dollar Point on Galveston Bay, where they would be on loaded on barges for shipment to market, thus making for one of the earliest trail drives in Anglo-American Texas. By the mid-1840s, Peach Point had also turned to sugar production. The first large planting of sugar occurred in the early 1840s, and by 1850, the Perrys had constructed a sugar mill on the property. In that year, the plantation produced 165 barrels of molasses, four of which were reserved for use at Peach Point by Emily, two for Joel Bryan's Durazno household, and one barrel for Austin Bryan. Because of variations in weather, especially in rainfall amounts, sugar seemed more adaptable than cotton to the temperature and moisture extremes of the lower Brazos Valley. Hence, this new crop gradually replaced cotton in many parts of the coastal Texas plantation belt during the course of the decade.[19]

As Peach Point prospered during the 1840s, it became the gathering place for the various Bryan and Perry children and grandchildren, with Emily at its center. Joel and Austin Bryan, each with their own growing families, lived nearby and frequently saw their mother. Emily took great delight in their company and enjoyed the succession of grandchildren they began producing. Both of the married Bryan sons participated on a regular basis in many of the business transactions at Peach Point and also helped with the management of the Stephen F. Austin estate. In the

Stephen Samuel Perry

latter activities, of course, Emily remained heavily involved and played a significant role in decisions having to do with investments and land management, many of which occurred legally through her husband or grown sons. For example, in the mid-1840s, she and Guy traveled to Little Rock in an unsuccessful attempt to untangle the complicated business and land claims that stemmed from the residence of James Bryan and her brother Stephen in Arkansas twenty-five years earlier. Sometimes the activities of her children, even her adult sons, brought her apprehension. Austin Bryan caused Emily some motherly concern in 1842 when he joined a military force commanded by Alexander Somervell, the man who had been his father-in-law's partner in the San

Felipe store. Sam Houston asked Somervell to organize an expedition of militiamen in response to Mexican troops that had recently crossed into Texas on several occasions. Hundreds of volunteers signed up to fight with Somervell, including Austin Bryan. He joined approximately seven hundred men that November as they marched to Laredo. Nothing happened, however, and Somervell ordered his expedition disbanded. Some of these men, disgruntled at not having had a fight, continued south into Mexico, where several were killed and others captured at the Mexican town of Mier. Austin Bryan was not one of them since he returned home when Somervell canceled the expedition.[20]

By the mid-1840s, Emily had four children still living at home: Guy, Eliza, Stephen, and Henry. Shortly after returning from Kenyon, Guy decided to read law, although bad eyesight eventually hampered this effort. He apprenticed himself to William H. Jack, the attorney who practiced at Brazoria and routinely represented the Perry family in their legal affairs. The Perrys had known the Jack family since James and Emily's first days in Texas. W. H. Jack was considered to be one of the most accomplished, honest, and successful attorneys in Texas. Guy studied with him until Jack's untimely passing in a yellow fever epidemic during 1844. That illness swept Peach Point as well, where some of the family and slaves became ill. James and Emily survived the epidemic, but it took a toll on both of them. Austin Bryan checked on them at its height and wrote, "I found my poor old mother in miserable health. She has had an attack of fever which has reduced her so much that she has been confined to her bed and is still most of the time. She looks worse than she ever has in my recollection and I fear is not long for this world." Austin went on to note that "Mr. Perry is very thin in flesh; you would scarcely know him. He has lost at least fifty pounds." Happily, everyone at Peach Point recovered from the yellow fever except for one of the slaves. William Jack's death, however, deprived Guy of his law study, although he probably would have quit anyway due to continued difficulty with his eyes. For the next several years, he remained at Peach Point, living with Emily and James while he nursed his eyesight, which did later recover. He often traveled and handled family business. Eliza, like her older brother Guy, also stayed at Peach Point after her return from Ohio, and it would be her permanent home for the rest of her parents' lives. Emily never ceased in her continuing efforts to find a cure for Eliza's affliction. Mother and daughter regularly traveled to the cities of Austin and Houston seeking a successful treatment. Emily and the girl customarily spent much time during the hot summer months at Quintana, where the beachfront location and its sea breezes made the heat more tolerable. Henry attended school in the area, most years going to Brazoria to take classes in the academy there. Stephen, however, continued his studies at Kenyon College. Unlike Guy, he returned home on several occasions during school vacations. This was likely a result of more affluent family finances and the Perrys' willingness to pay for these trips.[21]

In 1843, Emily permitted Stephen to return to college in Ohio by himself without an escort, the first time she had ever allowed one of the children to do that. This became a great adventure for him, and he kept his mother apprised of his travels in a series of letters sent en route. Leaving New Orleans, Stephen traveled alone by steamboat up the rivers to Louisville and visited with family there. He did note to his mother that he had attended an Episcopal church service and that there "was not much except for some young ladies who attracted my attention more than the preacher." He seemed to find that experience better than the Presbyterian church he attended later in the journey. "While I was there," Stephen related of the service, "I slept all the time . . . and before long I got to snoring and grunting. It is not natural to go to a Presbyterian Church and not go to sleep." Stephen eventually arrived back at Kenyan College, where he continued to enjoy his extracurricular activities as much as his academic studies. Apparently, being there without Guy motivated him to write more letters home to his mother than he had done formerly. This greatly pleased Emily, and Eliza replied to one of these by saying, "I was surprised to see it so long as you always had such an aversion to writing letters." Stephen, however, soon decided that additional collegiate education was not for him. "I have concluded that it is decidedly best that I should leave Kenyon," he wrote Emily. "I have become dissatisfied and almost discouraged. I would prefer any place to Kenyon now." He felt that he was not progressing as rapidly as the rest of his class, and he worried that the college was too expensive. He seemed adamant about this decision, but James, Emily, and Guy all expressed their opinion that this was the wrong course of action for the young man. Strong letters passed from Peach Point to Ohio that admonished him to finish his education. "I can say no more to you," Guy wrote him, "than has been said by your father in a letter he wrote you a few weeks ago." Nonetheless, Stephen remained obstinate. In the end, the Perrys relented, and Stephen came home to Texas.[22]

 This created a new problem for the Perrys as they considered whether Stephen should continue his education back in Texas and if so, where. Again, Emily's Episcopal background showed through in answering this concern. Both Stephen and his younger brother Henry, she decided, would attend the new Episcopal school that had opened several years earlier at Matagorda. The first Episcopal priest to come to Texas, Caleb S. Ives, had arrived at Matagorda in the fall of 1838, founding Christ Church there. Shortly thereafter, Reverend Ives and his wife established a school for boys that soon earned a reputation as one of the best in Texas. Emily had regularly attended services at Christ Church, especially when she took Eliza to Matagorda for medical treatments. In 1843, Reverend Ives paid a visit to Peach Point, holding an Episcopal Eucharist in the church at Gulf Prairie. Eliza wrote to her brother Stephen,

"The Reverend Mr. Ives of Matagorda came to us for a visit about a week ago; he preached on the Sabbath and all of the neighbors attended." Emily apparently liked Reverend Ives, deciding that his school would be appropriate for both Stephen and Henry. The school operated from Mondays to Saturdays, so it was possible for the boys to return home on Sundays. This also kept Emily and the Bryan sons in touch with the Episcopal Church. Louisiana Bishop Leonidas Polk, who would later be a general in the Confederate Army, made an official visit to Texas at this time. Emily met him and made a generous donation to help underwrite his trip. Later, in February of 1848, Episcopal Bishop George Washington Freeman of Arkansas visited Peach Point for the purpose of seeking Emily's support in organizing a missionary Episcopal diocese in Texas. Guy and Austin Bryan, who considered themselves to be Episcopalians, also met with Bishop Freeman on this visit to Texas. Bishop Freeman received a donation from Emily and held a Eucharist at the Gulf Prairie Church, assisted by three priests. There attended "a congregation of thirteen gentlemen, six ladies, and five children," including Emily. James Perry, who considered himself to be a Presbyterian, seemingly tolerated this with goodwill. It turned out that as adults, Stephen and Eliza Perry would join their father in that denomination rather than the Episcopal Church, to which the Bryan sons belonged.[23]

While Emily had a very serious side to her nature, manifested in her religious beliefs and her desire that each of her children get the best education possible, she also enjoyed having a well-rounded social life. Although the main house at Peach Point was not opulent even by the standards of Texas plantation country, she routinely entertained there and happily participated in the society of the district. One historian has noted that entertainments on most southern plantations were always "extravagant and grand," further observing that "parties and balls, like other public displays, were planned to demonstrate a planter's wealth and liberality." As Emily's granddaughter later recalled, "the social life of Peach Point was typical of the whole South, and while entertainments were necessarily far spaced, any possible occasion was utilized as the excuse for a party." Emily enjoyed serving gala meals of special dishes on these occasions, some of which became family traditions over the generations of her descendants. "The dish which remained in my mind, particularly, as unusual," a granddaughter remembered, "was boned young turkey served cold and sliced on the table." Emily served dinners on a fine lace tablecloth with elegant glassware. She also used for special occasions a set of silver spoons that her father, Moses Austin, had purchased in Lexington when she was a schoolgirl there in 1811. Records of the plantation also indicate that from time to time Emily bought additional sterling silver items for use in formal entertaining. For example, in 1848, she purchased a selection of coffee and teapots, a silver cup, and flatware. She ordered the following year a silver soup ladle, a set of butter knives, and some sugar tongs from a jewelry store in New Orleans. George Hammeken, the old family friend recently recovered from his illnesses, was then living at New Orleans and supervised these purchases for Emily, including arranging for their shipment to Texas aboard the vessel *Sultana*. Emily had inherited from her mother a silver service that Maria received at the time of her marriage in 1785. Each piece had been engraved with the letter "A." By the late 1840s, this service was small and outdated, but rather than buy a new and larger one, Emily sent it to New Orleans, where the firm of Hyde and Goodrich melted it down. Additional sterling silver metal that had been ordered from New York City especially for this purpose was added, and an entirely new, more modern set was struck from it. Emily had this new silver service engraved with the letter "A," continuing the Austin motif, rather than the "P" for Perry, presumably because it contained the original metal from her mother's set. Often, there would be dancing at

Peach Point after the gala dinners that Emily served. There was a large cabin near the main house which, when cleared of its contents, served as a makeshift ballroom. Guests frequently danced most of the night and enjoyed breakfast before they went home.[24]

The greatest moment in the history of entertaining at Peach Point came just after Christmas in 1848, when an old friend from Guy M. Bryan's student days at Kenyon College arrived for a visit. He was Guy's schoolmate Rutherford B. Hayes, who was traveling with his uncle, Sardis Burchard. Hayes' father had died when he was a boy, and Burchard (his mother's brother) had stepped in to fill that role. Burchard was reputed to be one of the wealthiest men in Ohio, owning a tremendous amount of real estate and the largest store in Cleveland. During their student days, Guy M. Bryan had visited his friend "Rud" at the Burchard home in Ohio. Thereafter, the two young men remained in touch with one another, maintaining a regular and lively correspondence. Guy had been elected to the Texas legislature the previous year, in 1847, so he still had much in common with Hayes, who was also interested in politics. Guy had been anxious to reciprocate for his earlier visit to the Burchard home, and as a result, Emily graciously extended an invitation for Hayes and his uncle to visit Peach Point. Although no one in the Perry household knew at the time that they were entertaining a future president of the United States, Emily fully realized that her guests came from one of the richest families in Ohio, if not the whole country. Hayes was an inveterate diarist and recorded his impressions of Peach Point, the Perry family, and each of its individual members in great detail, thus giving a fairly complete version of Emily's hospitality.[25]

Hayes and his uncle traveled down the Mississippi to New Orleans, where they made their way to Galveston. From there they took the steamer *Samuel May Williams* over the bar of the Brazos at Velasco and up the river to the landing just north of Peach Point. Since the

Perrys did not know exactly when they would arrive, no one was there to greet them. The two men thus borrowed horses and rode the two miles south down the road to Peach Point, where they found James Perry and introduced themselves. Hayes was pleased with the pastoral scene that initially greeted him. "The home is delightfully situated in the edge of timber," he observed, "looking out upon a plain on the south extending five or eight miles to the gulf." He was particularly struck by the beauty of the plantation and the fact that everything seemed green and lush. He found the shrubbery to be very rich, with "roses blooming and birds singing as if it were the first of June instead of January." Furthermore, he admired the "large and beautiful flower-garden in front, trimmed and cultivated under the guardian eye of Mrs. Perry." Hayes took stock of the family as he was introduced. A careful observer, he noted details about each of them: "The family consists of Mr. Perry, a sensible matter-of-fact sort of man, full of jokes and laughter, and of course a great friend to Uncle; Mrs. Perry, an excellent motherly sort of woman, whose happiness consists in making others happy; Eliza Perry, a young lady of twenty, a fine girl, free from silly notions, and agreeable company as all such girls are; Stephen, the business man of the establishment; Henry, a fine romantic boy of seventeen who is at home from school to spend the holidays with one of his chums of fewer years—both spend their time visiting the girls and hunting."[26]

Emily and her son Guy planned a full and elaborate round of social events for their guests. On Hayes' first Friday night at Peach Point, Guy hosted a "great soiree and dancing party," no doubt held in the large cabin that served as the impromptu ballroom. The following day, Eliza took Hayes to visit the neighboring plantations on an outing that involved "a fine gallop over the prairie, with an occasional adventure, crossing a swale or a mud hole." Hayes seemed particularly taken with the rich larders and abundance of food that was served at mealtime, which he saw as impressive evidence of Emily's efficiency in running the kitchen. He enjoyed the "seven or eight kinds of meat, sweet potatoes in two or three shapes, half a dozen kinds of preserves, and pastry in any quantity." Guy and Stephen took Hayes and his uncle hunting on several occasions. At one point, they all simultaneously shot at a crane flying overhead, and when it fell, they cut it open to determine who had actually killed the bird by gauging the size of the shot inside. Hayes was also very impressed with the nearness of the Gulf of Mexico. "The roar of the Gulf is heard for miles like the roar of Niagara," he noted. One day, he and Guy rode over to the San Bernard River to eat fish and oysters, a true delicacy back in Ohio. Hayes' uncle Sardis likewise had a good time during the visit, forming a strong bond of friendship with James. "Mr. Perry and uncle are constantly together telling anecdotes, talking politics, playing backgammon, and attending to the business of the plantation," Hayes recorded. In early February, Hayes, his uncle, and Guy left Peach Point for a month's tour around Texas before the visitors returned to Ohio.

One of the Perrys who particularly impressed Hayes during his stay on the plantation was young Henry Perry, with whom he had gone hunting and stayed up late into the night playing chess. By the time of Hayes' visit, Henry had left the Reverend Caleb Ives' Christ Church school at Matagorda and begun his collegiate education at Trinity College in Hartford, Connecticut. An Episcopal school, it was the alma mater of the Reverend Ives of Matagorda, who had been Henry's teacher for several years. Undoubtedly, Ives must have had a hand in encouraging young Henry to study there, and Emily presumably approved as well because of its Episcopal affiliation. Once enrolled, Henry enjoyed his studies at Trinity, especially mathematics, although he did not care for Latin and Greek. He found the relatively more urban nature of Connecticut to be very different from rural Texas. "There are so many people here," he wrote his mother. "Wherever it is possible for a man to live, some

Yankee has settled, and there is scarcely a place to be found but what is under cultivation." In an almost poetic manner, Henry observed, "I love the wilds of Texas, where one can roam far from the haunts of man and view the works of nature in all their natural beauty." Henry had also developed an interest in the history of his family, so Emily sent him a long letter explaining the personal histories of Moses and Stephen, enclosing a copy of Mary Austin Holley's book *Texas*.[27]

During the fall of 1850, Henry began to receive disturbing news in letters sent from family members at Peach Point. Two distressing health problems had developed in the Perry household: Eliza's condition had worsened, and Emily had become chronically ill. By the time cold weather arrived that autumn, Emily often felt weak, listless, and had to spend long periods of time in bed to conserve her strength. Henry Austin, in several letters to his mother, lamented that she was bedridden for long periods of time. "From sister's letter I hear that the health of my dear mother was no better," he wrote his father in March. "That makes me unhappy when I think how unwell she was when I left home," he added, "what a weak constitution she has to bear up against disease." This presented James with a problem, since Emily was too ill to care for Eliza. James and Emily accordingly made the decision to send their daughter to Galveston, which was already beginning to establish a reputation as a burgeoning medical center. A local physician there, Dr. Frank Godin, seemed specially qualified to treat conditions such as the one that plagued Eliza. Moreover, it would not be necessary for Emily to be in Galveston with her daughter, as a family friend, Hugh J. McLeod, had volunteered to monitor Eliza's treatment so that her mother could remain at Peach Point. The girl thus went to Galveston alone for a prolonged series of treatments. Unfortunately, her condition deteriorated badly once she began her course of therapy there. McLeod became concerned about the number of her seizures, writing letters to James that detailed each occurrence. Eliza suffered several severe episodes that Dr. Godin had been unable to control, and this greatly worried the physician. He had attempted every remedy he knew without success, including blistering, packing her in ice, and putting ointment on her. McLeod deemed this news so discouraging that he cautioned Perry not to share it with Emily due to her own illness. The girl's condition worsened to the point that McLeod even reconsidered the wisdom of bringing her to Galveston. "I now regret that I persuaded her to make the trial of Dr. Godin's skill," he wrote James, "not because I think his remedies have injured her, for in many respects she is better, but because it may confirm the despondency of Eliza and the fears of us all—this is a very great affliction to all the family, and being a parent, I know how to sympathize with you." After discussion with the Galveston physician, McLeod reported to Peach Point that both of them favored Eliza traveling to Philadelphia. There was an accomplished doctor in practice at the College of Physicians in that city who might be able to help her. They also thought that the change of climate and latitude would be beneficial for Eliza.[28]

James discussed Eliza's worsened condition with Emily because something had to be decided about the girl's future care. Moreover, James was also very concerned about his wife's health. It was clear that Emily suffered from a chronic respiratory problem, although surviving correspondence does not indicate its exact nature. Emily's condition apparently had not improved, so by the spring of 1851, she too was in need of medical treatment beyond the capabilities of physicians in Texas. For that reason, as Emily and James considered the news about Eliza from Galveston, they decided that both mother and daughter should travel to Philadelphia, where they could secure treatment together. Stephen S. Perry, who had been busily engaged operating the stock farm at Chocolate Bayou, would travel with them as their companion. Before she left, Emily discussed with James the fact that she should make a formal last will and testament, although there would not be enough time to complete it before her departure. James assured her that this would be done during her absence and set to work on the process. This seemed important to both of them because of her independently held property. Due to this unusual arrangement, which was not legally typical in that era regarding a married woman's possessions, James agreed with Emily that making a will was imperative. "As I told you," he wrote while he worked on getting one written during the trip, "it was principally on my account that you wished to make a will. This will make it unnecessary that the law will have to determine what interest I have in the property." The writing of this will caused James some anguish as he contemplated the probability of his wife's passing. Shortly after Emily left Peach Point, he worked for a number of days writing her a tortured and grief-stricken letter that he never mailed in its entirety. A full draft nonetheless remained in his papers. It speaks, in retrospect, to some of the conflicting emotions and issues with which he was dealing. One of them was the move to Texas that he and Emily had made twenty years earlier. "All I regret," he wrote, "is that I ever left Missouri." He worried that he had not worked hard enough in Texas and assured Emily that all he had ever done was for his own benefit and that of his family. James told Emily that he wanted nothing from her. He had not come to Texas to share in the Austin estate. James excised these paragraphs from the final version he eventually sent. The deleted sentiments constituted one of the very few times in his life that James Perry ever expressed, even privately, any frustrations. The circumstances of his doing so in this instance were understandable.[29]

By early May, while James was working on his letter, Emily and Stephen were in Galveston, where they prepared Eliza for the trip. This journey presented daunting prospects to Emily. "I am kept in a state of constant excitement," she wrote James about Eliza, "for fear that she will have a spasm. It would be intolerable for such a thing to happen while we are with strangers." Emily made arrangements for them to take an express steam packet, the *Winfield Scott,* on a nonstop voyage directly to New York City. Although this was much more expensive than taking a ship that made stops along the way, Emily felt that the circumstances justified the additional price of the tickets. They arrived in New York, where Emily had to rest. She reported that she felt "tired and low spirited." After a few days at a Manhattan hotel, the three of them traveled by train to Hartford for a quick visit with Henry at Trinity College before moving on to Philadelphia. "Ma has a fire in her head," Eliza reported back to James while they were there, further noting that "she has caught cold in her head, which has been the cause of her feeling so unwell." After several days with Henry, the three travelers departed for Philadelphia, where Emily and Eliza both placed themselves under the care of Dr. Samuel Jackson, one of the nation's most eminent physicians. A member of the College of Physicians at Philadelphia, Jackson had been a leader of the Pennsylvania medical community for many years and was a founder of the Academy of Natural Sciences. He routinely lectured at the medical school there. Importantly, he had a national reputation as a physician who had achieved great success in treating female disorders. Jackson's treatment of women's medical conditions had been favorably reviewed by Dr. Oliver Wendell Holmes in the influential 1843 essay "The Contagiousness of Puerperal Fever," published in the *New England Quarterly Journal of Medicine.*[30]

After several weeks of consultation and examination, Dr. Jackson came to the conclusion that there was nothing he could do for Emily. He therefore discussed with her the idea of going back to Texas and leaving Eliza alone in Philadelphia for a further course of treatment. "Dr. Jackson thinks the heat will be too oppressive for Ma here," Eliza wrote home, and "she has determined to return with Stephen to Texas, and leave me under Dr. J. in this place." Emily and Stephen again decided to travel from New York to Galveston on the *Winfield Scott*, thus making for the shortest possible trip. Although correspondence between James and his wife that month fails to mention the last will and testament that they had previously discussed, Emily no doubt realized that it had been prepared in Texas during her absence and that she needed to sign it. Eliza, who did not want to stay alone in Philadelphia, reluctantly saw her brother and mother off on their journey back to Peach Point. Emily's state of health greatly worried Eliza. "She was so weak when I bid her goodbye that I was doubtful that she would stand the voyage," Eliza later admitted.[31]

The historical record fails to record Emily's exact illness beyond mentioning her symptoms, but she suffered from an unspecified lung ailment, a fact noted explicitly in her newspaper obituary. This poses for the historian questions regarding the possible exposure of Emily and the Moses Austin family to environmental pollutants over forty years earlier, during the time of her childhood when they had lived in the lead smelting districts of Virginia and Missouri. Obviously, there was potential for lead poisoning at Austinville, Potosi, and Herculaneum. A lead smelter in Potosi, for example, routinely operated less than a modern city block from Durham Hall during the entire time Emily and the family resided there. Nevertheless, almost five decades of their correspondence thereafter make no mention of symptoms related to lead poisoning among family members. No evidence exists supporting the possibility that any of them suffered from it. However, beginning in the 1810s, their letters provide numerous reports of respiratory-related complaints experienced over the ensuing decades by Moses, Maria, Stephen, and Emily. Their symptoms included congestion, malaise, headaches, flu-like conditions, and muscle aches, all of which can be caused by diminished pulmonary capacity of a non-acute level. Only Brown Austin, who lived in the lead country for the shortest period of time, seems to have escaped these medical conditions, at least to the extent that family correspondence never comments about them in his case.

In addition to the obvious potential for lead poisoning, from which the Moses Austin family apparently did not suffer, the industrial process of unfiltered lead refining (undertaken without consideration for hazardous environmental pollutants) can also produce a wide variety of particulate-related maladies. Such are caused by aerosol ingestion of dust, fibrous materials, trace metals, and other inorganic elements. The ingestion of airborne contaminants over time by people in the neighborhood of an unfiltered refining process can cause both silicosis and chronic obstructive pulmonary disease, among other conditions, which are not directly related to lead poisoning but can be just as dangerous. In addition to a possible ingestion of silica in the smoke coming from lead smelters, thereby causing silicosis, there was an opportunity for the Austins to have ingested trace metals in aerosol form that could have permanently injured their health as well. For example, the smoke from unfiltered lead smelting also releases airborne trace particles of cadmium in amounts that generate toxicity in humans at chronic, rather than acute levels. "Chronic exposure to cadmium dust and fumes," one modern occupational study of the metal refining suggests, "has been suspected as a cause of emphysema, obstructive lung disease, pulmonary fibrosis, and lung cancers." Their years of residence in the lead mining districts of Missouri thus provided the Austins with ample opportunities to experience permanent injury to their health.[32]

During the last decades of his life, Moses Austin noticeably suffered from medical problems that most likely indicated a long-term pulmonary malady. It was characterized by regular congestion, the production of phlegm, difficulty breathing, exhaustion, and intermittent muscle pain of unspecified origin. Stephen F. Austin also experienced recurring medical episodes across his adult years that spoke to a possible pulmonary debility of a chronic nature, including his final illness of 1836. Although the cause of Maria Austin's death remains unspecified, she too battled health problems during the latter years of her life, especially what family letters described as rheumatism. Cadmium toxicity of a chronic, rather than acute, nature can produce over time in some individuals a diminishing of bone mass, increased muscle weakness, and joint pain, all symptoms consistent with Maria Austin's medical complaints as an older woman. Generally, acute cadmium exposure can cause various combinations of "fluid in the lungs, irritation of the nose and throat, coughing, dizziness, weakness, chills, fever, chest pains, and labored breathing." Although milder in form, chronic toxicity from cadmium exposure results in "chronic obstructive pulmonary disease, emphysema, and kidney disease. It may also result in adverse affects to the cardiovascular system and the skeleton." There is a probability that Moses, Maria, Stephen, and Emily all suffered in different degrees from cadmium poisoning, because this heavy metal can be "a byproduct of the mining and smelting of lead." Emily's letters across her adult life intermittently complained of headaches, general respiratory problems, colds, and a recurring lack of energy—often described as malaise—from the 1820s to the early 1850s, especially during her last ten years. The illness that resulted in her return to Peach Point from Philadelphia in the summer of 1851 fits within this etiology. By themselves and in isolated occurrences, such medical complaints in a single individual at a specific point in time might not be considered unusual when viewed in historical retrospect. However, an observable, consistent pattern clearly formed for the Moses Austin family of Potosi starting in the mid-1810s. That Moses Austin, his wife, and their two eldest children suffered from some sort of chronic syndrome caused by particulate aerosols such as cadmium is, in retrospect, a very real possibility, although such a contention exists by circumstantial inference alone and lies absolutely beyond the ability of the historical method to prove.[33]

Whatever the exact nature of her illness, Emily arrived back at Peach Point in early July exhausted and spent. She could not walk unassisted. James had the last will and testament ready for her to sign, and she did so on July 5 from her sick bed in the main house at Peach Point. Few letters went out from the plantation over the next month, as everyone presumably found themselves fully occupied with her deteriorating medical condition. Eliza and Henry did not return home but wrote anxious letters inquiring about their mother's condition. These went unanswered. The Joel and Austin Bryan families often appeared at Peach Point as July turned into August. Lavinia Perry, who lived only a short distance away at Durazno, most likely participated in running the household at Peach Point, no doubt assisted by the faithful slave Clarissa, who had long been Emily's hardworking and competent house servant. Emily Margaret Austin Bryan Perry died quietly and peacefully on August 15, 1851. The family buried her several days later in the small cemetery next to the Gulf Prairie Church, just a few steps from the graves of her brother Stephen F. Austin and her daughter Mary Elizabeth Bryan.[34]

The life that had begun in the foothills of the Appalachians, within living memory of those who had fought the American Revolution, ended fifty-six years later on the windswept coastal plain of antebellum Texas. Hers had been a lifetime filled with movement. It carried Emily to the Ozark Plateau of Spanish Louisiana as a young girl, and it later gave her a role in territorial and statehood Missouri as a vivacious adolescent, a married woman, and then a widow. These treks made Emily very typical for her era, especially as a woman living within the context of a family that migrated through the westward-moving frontiers of an expanding United States. In so doing, it was always within the parameters of family that Emily Austin dwelt; family was truly at the center point of her existence. She was fundamentally a daughter, a sister, a cousin, a wife, a mother, a sister-in-law, an aunt, a mother-in-law, and a grandmother. She remained absolutely an Austin during her entire lifetime, although marriage made her a Bryan and a Perry, too. All of these were her identities, and taken together as a whole, they formed the personal foundation upon which she rested her being as a complete person. No part of her could exist without any of the others or otherwise function outside the touchstone of her family. That was how she lived, and that was how Emily Austin died.

EPILOGUE

Within a few days of Emily's passing, James began the process of probating her estate. Guy M. Bryan assisted him in these efforts since he had legal training and, as an elected official, knew personally many of the individuals who would be involved

(Left to right) Moses Austin Bryan, Guy M. Bryan, and
William Joel Bryan as Adults. Courtesy of the the Brazoria County Historical Museum.

in the settlement of his mother's estate. By the end of September, all of her property had been inventoried according to law, and the division of the estate in probate went forward. Under the community property laws operative in Texas, Emily also owned one-half of all assets and property that came into her marriage with James F. Perry from the moment of their legal union. This community property passed directly to James, who became the sole owner of Peach Point Plantation, the stock farm at Chocolate Bayou, and other assets they had jointly accumulated. The property that Emily had from her previous marriage to James Bryan, along with Stephen F. Austin's estate, remained separate from community property with its own particular disposition. Her last will and testament took great care to make an equitable distribution of the Stephen F. Austin estate to all of the Perry and Bryan children. James Perry was excluded from the division of these assets. Emily's will meticulously explained on a plot-by-plot basis how the land holdings that had belonged to Stephen F. Austin would be distributed to his nieces and nephews as her beneficiaries. However, since Stephen, Eliza, and Henry Perry would also eventually be the heirs of James F. Perry and while the three Bryan sons would not share in the inheritance of Peach Point since the family considered it Perry land, Emily thus made greater provision for Joel, Austin, and Guy from the Stephen F. Austin inheritance in a successful effort to be fair.[1]

The wealth of her probated estate was belied by the fact that Emily had never lived in opulent fashion, nor did she engage in the sort of conspicuous consumption that was sometimes seen elsewhere in the plantation society of the antebellum South. Peach Point was always a modest place. In fact, there were grander and more luxurious homes belonging to many planters all along the lower Brazos River. The Perrys did own almost fifty slaves, placing them by numbers in the highest echelon of Texas slave owners. At the same time, the Perrys lived most of their lives short of cash and could thus be counted as members of that category of planters who were "land poor," meaning that most of their property and other assets of value existed in the form of real property. Emily and James seldom had much, if any, disposable cash income. Nonetheless, the probate of Emily's estate clearly indicated that she was the wealthiest woman in Texas at the time of her death, this status being specifically due to her sole ownership of all of Stephen F. Austin's assets.[2]

James Perry continued to live at Peach Point after Emily's passing. Within a short time after her mother's death, Eliza returned home from Pennsylvania to make her home with the family. Henry Perry continued at school in Connecticut, graduating from Trinity College in the late spring of 1853. It was at that time that tragedy again struck the family. In April of that year, James took his daughter, Eliza, to Biloxi, Mississippi, for additional medical treatment of her condition. They remained there into the summer, when Henry joined them on his way back to Texas from Connecticut, just as yellow fever broke out along the Gulf Coast. James and Henry both died in the contagion, leaving Eliza in Biloxi in the company of Lavinia Perry Bryan, who had accompanied them on the trip. Eliza returned to live at Peach Point, where Stephen S. Perry had already taken on the significant responsibility of running the plantation after his mother's passing two years earlier. Stephen S. Perry had previously married a cousin from Ohio, Sarah Brown. They would live at Peach Point together until 1874, the year of his death. Eliza Perry never married, and she divided her time for the remainder of her life between the households of her brothers. She died in Austin, Texas, in January 1862. Joel Bryan lived all of his life at Durazno Plantation. He served the Confederacy during the Civil War and afterwards became involved in railroad development. The town of Bryan, Texas, bears his name. He died on March 3, 1903. Austin Bryan also participated in the Civil War on the Confederate side. After the war, he helped organize the

Texas Veterans Association, an organization in which he was active for the remainder of his life. He died on March 16, 1895. Guy M. Bryan, the youngest of the three Bryan brothers, had a distinguished career in public service. He was elected to several terms in the state legislature, both in the House and Senate. After Confederate service, he was a member of the United States House of Representatives for two terms. He died on June 4, 1901, and is buried in the Texas State Cemetery at Austin near the remains of his uncle Stephen. The passing of her children's generation, however, did not end the story of Emily's family in Texas. Over the last century and a half, hundreds of Emily Austin Bryan Perry's descendants have played a variety of roles, both large and small, in the continuing historical development of Texas and the nation.

ACKNOWLEDGMENTS

A number of individuals greatly assisted my research and writing. I remain much indebted to all of them. Gregg Cantrell provided constant encouragement, patiently answered all of my questions, and currycombed pages of manuscript in its final stages of production. His sophisticated knowledge as the modern biographer of Stephen F. Austin along with his accomplishments as an expert in Texas history are surpassed only by his graciousness and professionalism as an historian. David Gracy II unselfishly shared much of his knowledge, along with important historical materials gleaned from his writing of the biography of Moses Austin. Marie Beth Jones, a native of Brazoria County, Texas, and a longtime journalist who wrote a history of Peach Point Plantation, discussed with me many intricacies regarding the history of the lower Brazos River region and the historical contributions of the Austin/Bryan/Perry family to that area.

Several descendants of Emily Austin Bryan Perry have given me particular encouragement and assistance. It has been my pleasure to have known Annadele "Ann" Holm Ross for most of my career as a member of the Austin College faculty. She is an alumnus of the college and a descendant of Emily's son Stephen S. Perry. Ann Ross not only provided me with encouragement but also donated to the Austin College Archives a small collection of family papers never before seen by historians. These had been in the private possession of family members. It has been a distinct pleasure to use those papers in this biography. Stephen S. Perry, the current occupant of Peach Point Plantation, extended exuberant hospitality during one of my visits to Brazoria County. His engaging personality and infectious enthusiasm for the history of his family, along with the extended tour he gave me of the area, greatly added to my understanding. J. P. Bryan encouraged this study and gave me cogent advice about his ancestor Emily. Beyond that, it must be noted that J. P. Bryan remains one of the staunchest friends of Texas history. His longtime support of the Texas State Historical Association, of which I am a member, has enriched the work of every historian who writes on any aspect of this region's history. I have also enjoyed talking with a number of Emily's other descendants. In acknowledging the kindnesses of the Austin/Bryan/Perry family, I hasten to note that none of them has ever sought to influence the nature or character of my historical viewpoints about their ancestors. Instead, they stressed that I should freely come to my own conclusions as a scholar and express my historical opinions in an unfettered manner. That I have done, and all of the opinions and errors in this volume are mine.

I wish to thank several individuals in Missouri who greatly assisted my research in the lead belt region of the Ozark Plateau, where Emily and her family resided prior to coming to Texas. Esther M. Ziock Carroll and her husband, Gene Carroll, served as considerate, hospitable hosts during my visit to Potosi. In particular, Esther Carroll's impressive knowledge of Washington County served as a useful resource. Jerry Sansegraw of Mineral Point gave me a fascinating tour of many local historical sites while opening to me the resources of the Mine Au Breton Historical Society. William O. Saffell of Bonne Terre took an entire day out of his schedule to give me an extensive tour of the Hazel Run area where Emily resided with her first husband, James Bryan. James Baker, the director of the Felix Valle State Historic Site at Ste. Genevieve, helped me understand much about that historic town. He selflessly provided his index to the court records of Ste. Genevieve County, ensuring that my research in those materials would be most efficient. In Texas, I wish to thank Watson Arnold, MD/PhD, and

Anne LeMaistre, MD, for reading and commenting on the section of the manuscript dealing with Austin family medical problems that may have been related to environmental pollution.

A number of libraries and archives extended every courtesy to me. The Center for American History at the University of Texas at Austin served as the essential center of my efforts, as it contains almost all of the extant Austin, Bryan, and Perry family papers. I am indebted to Don E. Carleton, director of the center, along with his entire staff, especially Patrick Cox, Brenda Gunn, Lynne Bell, Alison M. Beck, Margaret Schlankey, Stephanie Malmros, John Wheat, Evan Hocker, Linda Peterson, and Kathryn Kenefick. I also wish to thank John West, director of the Abell Library at Austin College, along with Justin Banks, the college archivist, for securing a complete microfilm set of the James F. and Stephen S. Perry Papers, thereby permitting me to do much research on my home campus. The staff of the Lois Brock Adriance Library at the Brazoria County Historical Museum, one of the finest smaller archives in Texas, made me feel at home during my research there. I especially thank its curator, Michael Bailey, along with Jamie Murray, information services coordinator, and Bettye Snell, curatorial assistant. I also extend my appreciation to Lynn Foster of the William H. Bowen School of Law, University of Arkansas at Little Rock; Peggy S. Lloyd of the Southwest Regional Archives, Washington, Arkansas; Terry Ann Hall of the public library, Farmington, Missouri; Seth Smith and Lauren Leeman of the State Historical Society of Missouri, Columbia; Cary Cox at the Butler Center for Arkansas Studies, Central Arkansas Library System, Little Rock; David Gregg and Donna Schwent, Clerk of Courts Office, Ste. Genevieve, Missouri; Mary Beth Brown of the Western Historical Manuscripts Collection, University of Missouri; and Dorothy Lore, librarian, Washington Country Library, Potosi, Missouri. I also wish to thank Russell Martin, director, and the staff of the DeGolyer Library at Southern Methodist University, along with the staffs of the Bridwell Library at SMU, the Texas State Library in Austin, the Perry-Castañeda Library of the University of Texas at Austin, and the Albert and Ethel Herzstein Library of the San Jacinto Museum of History. I am sorry that my lack of success in gaining access to the special collections and archives of the J. Douglas Gay Jr.-Frances Carrick Thomas Library at Transylvania University in Lexington, Kentucky, prevented me from developing the relationship that the Austin family had with that historic institution.

Colleagues at Austin College have been consistently supportive of this project. Michael Imhoff, dean of the faculty, and Bernice Melvin, dean of humanities, arranged for a semester's leave of absence during which I wrote much of the manuscript. A history department colleague, Jacqueline Moore, kindly read the entire manuscript and made many insightful suggestions. I am appreciative that one of my former students, Robin Henry, who currently teaches the history of women at Wichita State University, also read the manuscript and greatly improved it with her observations. I am indebted to the Sid Richardson Foundation and the faculty development fund at Austin College for financial assistance that supported several research trips. I also wish to thank Steven M. Mobley for his establishment of the Andrew Pickett Mobley Scholars Fund in memory of his son, who was an Austin College student. I am grateful to Heidi Rushing and Elena Muñiz for their dependable office and typing skills. I also express my appreciation to Julie Schoelles at TCU Press for her diligence in editing this book. Finally, I wish to express my profound gratitude to my wife and departmental colleague, Victoria Hennessy Cummins, who took much time away from her own historical and scholarly pursuits to assist me at every turn. Like Emily Austin a century and a half earlier, my wife moved to Texas after growing up elsewhere and, in similar fashion, became a true Texan thereafter. I therefore dedicate this book to Victoria H. Cummins and our two daughters.

A NOTE ON NAMES AND QUOTATIONS

There are two stylistic conventions that I have adopted in this volume. The first concerns Emily Austin's name and the way I have chosen to render it. She was born Emily Margaret Brown Austin and many individuals in her family called her "Emily Margaret." After her marriage to James Bryan, she most often styled herself "Emily Austin Bryan." Following Bryan's death, she married James F. Perry and, during most of her years in Texas, officially rendered her name "Emily Margaret Austin Perry." The *New Handbook of Texas* denotes her formal name in that latter fashion. On the other hand, many publications and biographical entries (along with the extended Austin/Bryan/Perry family) often call her "Emily Austin Bryan Perry," showing no favoritism to either of the two present-day family lines of Bryans and Perrys that descend from her. I have opted for a simpler approach, calling her "Emily Austin." Such a rendering of her name makes for a more uncluttered narrative and a uniformity of nomenclature. In addition, I sometimes simply call her by her first name alone, as "Emily." This convention is employed only for reasons of stylistic variety in the flow of the narrative. It implies no condescension whatsoever, nor does it represent a diminution of any sort. For similar reasons of style and uniformity, in the case of her children, I employ the names they were called in the family instead of the more formal names by which they are known to history.

The second convention involves my use of quotations from the personal letters of the Austin family, some of whom were extensive correspondents. In spite of their relatively prolific production of letters to one another, none of them paid much attention to grammar, punctuation,

223

or spelling. In attempting to give Emily and her family a voice in my narrative, I reluctantly decided to edit many quotations to make the language, punctuation, and vocabulary sensible to the modern reader, in each case taking great care not to change the meaning.

NOTES

[1] Elizabeth Fox-Genovese, "Family and Female Identity in the Antebellum South: Sarah Gayle and Her Family," in *In Joy and in Sorrow: Women, Family, and Marriage in the Victorian South,* ed. Carol Bleser (New York: Oxford University Press, 1991), 19; Rebecca Sharpless, *Fertile Ground, Narrow Choices, 1900–1940* (Chapel Hill: University of North Carolina Press, 1999), 36; Margaret Ripley Wolfe, *Daughters of Canaan: A Sage of Southern Women* (Lexington: University of Kentucky Press, 1995); Elizabeth Fox-Genovese, "Texas Women and the Writing of Women's History," in *Women and Texas History: Selected Essay,* ed. Fane Downs and Nancy Baker Jones (Austin: Texas State Historical Association, 1993), 3–14.

[2] Anne Firor Scott, *The Southern Lady: From Pedestal to Politics, 1830–1930* (Chicago: University of Chicago Press, 1970), 17; Anya Jabour, *Scarlett's Sisters: Young Women in the Old South* (Chapel Hill: University of North Carolina Press, 2007), 10. For a full discussion of the value structures that permeated the antebellum South, see Bertram Wyatt-Brown, *Southern Honor: Ethics and Behavior in the Old South* (New York: Oxford University Press, 1982). A highly reasoned discussion about the nature of elite southern women can be found in the chapters dealing with the antebellum era in Laura F. Edwards, *Scarlett Doesn't Live Here Anymore: Southern Women in the Civil War Era* (Champaign: University of Illinois Press, 2000), 10–64. Moreover, as Cynthia Kierner observed, "Although virtually all articulate southerners idealized women as domestic beings, by the 1820s some were beginning to redefine domesticity in the context of a growing regional consciousness." In the antebellum mind, domesticity had, to an extent, become bound up with being southern. Cynthia A. Kierner, *Beyond the Household: Women's Place in the Early South, 1700–1835* (Ithaca, NY: Cornell University Press, 1998), 203.

[3] Patriarchy is a complex topic that embodies gendered social conventions, discussion of which lies well beyond the focus of this biography. For a foundational analysis of patriarchy as an historical concept, see Paul Conner, "Patriarchy: Old World and New," *American Quarterly* 17, no. 1 (Spring 1965): 48–62. Many historians of the South observe that patriarchy in the antebellum era was often manifested in a pervasive male-defined viewpoint that relegated proper women to existing within the parameters of a "cult of true womanhood," a widespread definition of southern women as virtuous, pious, obedient, pure, and fully focused on the domestic arena. Anne Firor Scott, "Women's Perspective on Patriarchy in the 1850s," in *Half Sisters of History: Southern Women and the American Past,* ed. Catherine Clinton (Durham, NC: Duke University Press, 1994), 76–92. For more on the "cult of true womanhood," see Barbara Welter, "The Cult of True Womanhood: 1820–1860," *American Quarterly* 18 (Summer 1966):

151–74. A number of historians have recently questioned many of Welter's assumptions about women whose lives were circumscribed by this construct. A consideration of Emily Austin's life supports these criticisms. For a powerful critique, see Mary Kelley, "Beyond the Boundaries," *Journal of the Early Republic* 21 (Spring 2001): 73–78. One study focusing on South Carolina concluded that few elite southern planters actually achieved the full implementation of a true patriarchy within their families; instead they only approached it. Michael P. Johnson, "Planters and Patriarchy: Charleston, 1800–1860," *Journal of Southern History* 46, no. 1 (February 1980): 46. Other recent studies of patriarchy in the South have found that domesticity actually empowered antebellum women and made them anything but submissive. See Kelley, "Beyond the Boundaries," 76. Jeanne Boydston has noted, "Domestic ideology thus offered one rationale for expanding woman's sphere and increasing female influence. Domesticity may have been an empowering motivation in this process." Jeanne Boydston, Mary Kelley, and Anne Margolis, *The Limits of Sisterhood: The Beecher Sisters on Women's Rights and Woman's Sphere* (Chapel Hill: University of North Carolina Press, 1988), 5. See also the discussion of paternalism in Victoria E. Bynum, *Unruly Women: The Politics of Social Control in the Old South* (Chapel Hill: University of North Carolina Press, 1992), 59–87.

[4] A study of southern widows during the antebellum era has informed the discussion of the period when Emily Austin kept her family together after the death of her first husband: Kirsten E. Wood, *Masterful Women: Slaveholding Widows from the American Revolution through the Civil War* (Chapel Hill: University of North Carolina Press, 2004). Many points relevant to understanding Emily's independent spirit, such as the discussion of companionate marriage, are made about elite women living in urban Petersburg during the mid-nineteenth century in Suzanne Lebsock, *The Free Women of Petersburg: Status and Culture in an Antebellum Southern Town, 1784–1860* (New York: W. W. Norton, 1984). Angela Boswell's study of women in Colorado County, Texas, during the mid-nineteenth century has shown that many of them played important roles, as noted in the public records. They had an impact on the legal, governmental, and business affairs of their era. See Angela Boswell, *Her Act and Deed: Women's Lives in a Rural Southern County, 1837–1873* (College Station: Texas A&M University Press, 2001).

[5] It is ironic that there exists today no manuscript or archival collection of letters cataloged under Emily Austin's name. Instead, the major collection of her personal letters and documents carries the names of her husband and son in its cataloging designation. This collection, known as the James F. and Stephen S. Perry Papers, is housed at the Center for American History at the University of Texas at Austin. It is composed as much of Emily's letters, documents, and papers as those of her husband and son. However, the archival naming of the collection occurred in the 1930s; had these papers been accessioned by modern archivists, they would probably be cataloged as "The James and Emily Austin Perry Papers."

[6] Cathy N. Davidson and Jessamyn Hatchers, eds., *No More Separate Spheres!: A*

Next Wave American Studies Reader (Durham, NC: Duke University Press, 2002), 7. For a discussion of the evolution of the separate spheres as an interpretive historical model, see page 10. The phrase "intimately intertwined and mutually constitutive," which characterizes the nature of Emily's existence, is taken from page 8. Kierner, *Beyond the Household*, 140; Nancy F. Cott, *The Bonds of Womanhood: "Woman's Sphere" in New England, 1780–1835* (New Haven, CT: Yale University Press, 1978). Linda K. Kerber notes, "The metaphor remains resonant because it retains some superficial vitality. For all our vaunted modernity, for all that men's 'spheres' and women's 'spheres' now overlap, vast areas of our experience and our consciousness do not overlap." Linda K. Kerber, "Separate Spheres, Female Worlds, Woman's Place: The Rhetoric of Women's History," *Journal of American History* 75 (June 1988): 39. In addition to the volume edited by Davidson and Hatcher, the idea of "separate spheres" has been questioned in recent years by other historians writing on women. See especially Nancy Grey Osterud, *Bonds of Community: The Lives of Farm Women in Nineteenth-Century New York* (Ithaca, NY: Cornell University Press, 1991), 1–15. For additional studies that have modified the "separate spheres" perspective, see Boydston, Kelly, and Margolis, *Limits of Sisterhood*; Carroll Smith-Rosenberg, *Disorderly Conduct: Visions of Gender in Victorian America* (New York: Oxford University Press, 1986); Anne Goodwyn Jones and Susan Van D'Elden Donaldson, *Haunted Bodies: Gender and Southern Tests* (Charlottesville: University of Virginia Press, 1997). Laura F. Edwards expansively argues to end binary frames of reference in considering the antebellum South. Laura F. Edwards, "The People's Sovereignty and the Law: Defining Gender, Race, and Class Differences in the Antebellum South," in *Beyond Black and White: Race, Ethnicity, and Gender in the U.S. South and Southwest,* ed. Stephanie Cole and Alison M. Parker (College Station: Texas A&M University Press for the University of Texas at Arlington, 2004), 3–34.

[7] For a characterization of the male southern planter's relationship to his family and household, see Robert L. Griswold, *Fatherhood in America: A History* (New York: Basic Books, 1993), 17. See also Craig Thompson Friend and Lorri Glover, eds., *Southern Manhood: Perspectives on Masculinity in the Old South* (Athens: University of Georgia Press, 2004); and Steven M. Stowe, *Intimacy and Power in the Old South: Ritual in the Lives of Planters* (Baltimore: Johns Hopkins University Press, 1987). Joan E. Cashin's essay "Culture of Resignation" makes a powerful argument for the existence of a broad-based, diverse women's culture in the Old South that coexisted with an equally broad-based and diverse male culture. These interrelated cultures had numerous points of intersection, an interpretive viewpoint different from that of separate and atomized spheres of existence. Joan E. Cashin, "Culture of Resignation," introduction to *Our Common Affair: Texts from Women in the Old South*, ed. Joan E. Cashin (Baltimore: Johns Hopkins University Press, 1996), 1–41.

[8] Edwards, *Scarlett Doesn't Live Here Anymore,* 1–2. Any study of southern women must begin with a classic analysis: Julia Cherry Spruill, *Women's Life and Work*

in the Southern Colonies (1938; repr., New York: W. W. Norton, 1972). This pioneering examination of southern women in the generations before Emily Austin provides a basic starting place for understanding the roles that women traditionally played in both the private and public spheres. Spruill catalogues and analyzes many of the domestic contributions that women made to the development of southern culture. Although understandably dated in comparison to modern scholarship, Spruill's analysis informs almost every study of southern women that has since been published. So does Anne Firor Scott's groundbreaking book *The Southern Lady.* Also important is Anne Firor Scott, *Making the Invisible Woman Visible* (Champaign: University of Illinois Press, 1984). A useful study of domestic duties proves valuable in understanding antebellum plantation mistresses: Glenna Matthews, *"Just a Housewife": The Rise and Fall of Domesticity in America* (New York: Oxford University Press, 1987).

[9] Catherine Clinton, *The Plantation Mistress: Woman's World in the Old South* (New York: Pantheon Books, 1982); Elizabeth Fox-Genovese, *Within the Plantation Household: Black and White Women of the Old South* (Chapel Hill: University of North Carolina Press, 1988). As Fox-Genovese noted twenty years ago and which still proves true today, "Southern historians have, by and large, paid less attention to the role of households than have historians of the northern colonies and states, notably those who study colonial and rural America" (ibid., 83). Fox-Genovese and Clinton are not in complete agreement about all aspects of life for women on the plantation. For example, Fox-Genovese holds that white women and slave women did not have common bonds, while Clinton contends that there was less of a gulf between them. Nonetheless, both studies provide a solid framework for understanding Emily Austin. For additional elucidation on southern elite plantation women, see Drew Gilpin Faust, *Mothers of Invention: Women of the Slaveholding South in the American Civil War* (Chapel Hill: University of North Carolina Press, 1996).

[10] Elizabeth Fox-Genovese, "Scarlett O'Hara: The Southern Lady as a New Woman," *American Quarterly* 33, no. 4 (Autumn 1981): 398–99. The work of historians Julie Roy Jeffrey and Adrienne Caughfield regarding women on the westward-moving frontier also speaks to various aspects of Emily's life. Julie Roy Jeffrey, *Frontier Women: The Trans-Mississippi West, 1840–1880* (New York: Hill and Wang, 1979), 25–50; and Adrienne Caughfield, *True Women and Westward Expansion* (College Station: Texas A&M University Press, 2005).

Chapter One: Frontier Beginnings

[1] The only book-length study dealing with Emily Austin, concentrating especially on her years in Texas as mistress of Peach Point Plantation, is Marie Beth Jones, *Peach Point Plantation: The First 150 Years* (Waco, TX: Texian Press, 1982).

² The Texas descendants of Emily Austin have organized themselves into a group known as the Austin/Bryan/Perry Family Association. On the national scale, the modern descendants of the extended Austin family in the United States have organized themselves into two genealogical associations: the Austin Families Genealogical Society (AFGS), an international organization composed of members from many countries, and the Austin Families Association of America. In the latter case, members are primarily descended from Richard Austin of the Massachusetts Bay Colony. Both hold annual conventions that attract hundreds of descendants. The two groups also maintain a genealogical database of over ninety thousand persons from thirty-eight Austin family lines. The Austin Families Genealogical Society sponsors the "Austin Slaves Data Project," which seeks to compile genealogical and historical information on all slaves once owned by Austin households. It also sponsors the publication of a multivolume series of articles about the family history entitled *Austins of America,* currently projected at three volumes. This association maintains the online AFGS library, containing an array of digitized documents and links to hundreds of genealogical publications dealing with the Austins. The Austin Family Association of America also has a large genealogical database on its Internet website, in addition to sponsoring a reference book of Richard Austin's descendants: Jim Carlin and Liz Austin Carlin, *Some Descendants of Richard Austin of Charlestown, Massachusetts, 1638* (Green River, WY: Gateway Press for the Austin Families Association of America, 1998). For the websites of these two organizations as they existed in the spring of 2007, see www.austins.org and www.afaoa.org.

³ The definitive biography of Moses Austin is David B. Gracy II, *Moses Austin: His Life* (San Antonio, TX: Trinity University Press, 1987). For the birth of Emily at Austinville, see 52. Two additional historical studies make seminal contributions to assessing Moses Austin and his family, especially his son Stephen F. Austin: Eugene C. Barker, *The Life of Stephen F. Austin, Founder of Texas, 1793–1836: A Chapter in the Westward Movement of the Anglo-American People,* rev. ed. (1925; repr., Austin: University of Texas Press, 1949); and Gregg Cantrell, *Stephen F. Austin: Empresario of Texas* (New Haven, CT: Yale University Press, 1999). A biography by James Alexander Gardner examines Moses Austin and his family during the years they lived in Missouri: James Alexander Gardner, *Lead King: Moses Austin* (St. Louis, MO: Sunrise Publishing, 1980).

⁴ David B. Gracy visited Anthony Austin's home as part of his research on Moses Austin. He observed, "The modern visitor to the two-storey, English gambrel Anthony Austin House on old Feather Street, whose construction dates back to 1691, perhaps earlier, can see the head of a black flint arrow point recovered not many years ago from the back wall of the house. Thought to have been shot during Queen Anne's War, the flint penetrated two layers of chestnut clapboard siding, each one inch thick, and buried itself in the interior pine wallboard." Gracy, *Moses Austin,* 8–9; Art Sikes, "Who is Anthony Austin?" (paper delivered to the Austin Convention, Pittsfield, MA, 2001).

[5] The author has observed a tombstone in the Suffield Cemetery with the following inscription: "I'm proud to lie next to my 6th generation grandfather Anthony Austin (1632–1708) and his wife Esther (1642–1698) who fostered 4 sons and 19 grandsons. Those lines sired 50 Austins who served in Connecticut and Massachusetts regiments to gain our independence 1775–1783. To the left of my feet lie Richard (1666–1733) and Anthony (1668–1733) two of my seventh generation uncles. Elsewhere in this cemetery lie others of that ilk." Grave of Harris Munro Austin, November 2, 1920–January 20, 1999, Suffolk Cemetery, Suffolk, Connecticut. A recent discovery in the Elias Austin house in Durham has brought to light a portent of things that were to come for Moses, whose life was characterized by a degree of wanderlust and restlessness. During a restoration of the property in the late 1990s, workers discovered a chalk drawing on an original wall of an upstairs bedroom, which had remained covered for generations. It was the image of a sailing ship under full sail scrawled in a childish hand, above which appeared the letters 'M-O-S-E-S-A-U-S-T-I-N." John Christie, "Living with History," *Middletown Press* (Middletown, CT), February 19, 2004.

[6] Moses and Stephen F. Austin Papers, 1676, 1765–1889, Center for American History, University of Texas at Austin; Moses Austin to Maria Brown, January 25, 1785, Moses and Stephen F. Austin Papers; Hallie Bryan Perry, "Family Notes by Request," typescript, Texas State Library, Austin; Gracy, *Moses Austin,* 22–23.

[7] Gardner, *Lead King,* 26; William A. Christian, *Richmond: Her Past and Present* (1911; repr., Spartanburg, SC: Reprint Company, 1972), 31; Eugene C. Barker, ed., *The Austin Papers,* vols. 1 and 2 (Washington, DC: American Historical Association, 1919–1922), vol. 3 (Austin: University of Texas, 1927); "Genealogical Notes," *Austin Papers,* 1:1–6; H. A. Buehler, "The Wythe Lead Mines," 1917, typescript, Western Historical Manuscripts Collection, Missouri University of Science and Technology; Gracy, *Moses Austin,* 26.

[8] Maria Austin to Moses Austin, August 24, 1789, *Austin Papers,* 1:19. Maria was obviously reticent about moving away from her established home. This was a common reaction for many women of that era. Historian Joan E. Cashin examined this trend in her study: Joan E. Cashin, *A Family Venture: Men and Women on the Southern Frontier* (New York: Oxford University Press, 1991), 32.

[9] Lewis P. Summers, *History of Southwestern Virginia, 1746–1786* (Richmond, VA: J. L. Hill, 1903), 435–39. On November 3, 1997, the town of Austinville dedicated a park near the location of the Austin home, which no longer stands. Representatives of the Austin family, along with residents of Brazoria County, Texas, attended. *News* (Carol, VA), November 3, 1997.

[10] Stephen F. Austin to Mary Austin Holley, December 29, 1831, *Austin Papers,* 1:727; Cantrell, *Stephen F. Austin,* 22; Gertrud R. Rath, "The Life and Times of Moses Austin in Missouri" (master's thesis, Hollins College, 1934), 20–22.

Moses' relationship with Maria in the area of child rearing was typical of the era. Historian Sarah Woolfolk Wiggins observed that some fathers saw "the family patriarch as 'source, provider, protector, example, and judge.'" This accurately categorizes the view of Moses Austin. Sarah Woolfolk Wiggins, "A Victorian Father: Josiah Gorgas and His Family," in *In Joy and in Sorrow,* 234. Gracy, *Moses Austin,* 73. For child rearing and the nature of the relationship between husbands and wives during this era, see Ann Douglas, *The Feminization of American Culture* (New York: Alfred A. Knopf, 1977); and Hendrik Hartog, *Man and Wife in America: A History* (Cambridge, MA: Harvard University Press, 2000).

[11] The Norfolk and Western Railroad Historical Photography Collection in the Digital Library and Archives of Virginia Tech University, Blacksburg, Virginia, contains numerous images of the Wytheville area. All of them are from the early nineteenth century or later.

[12] Cantrell, *Stephen F. Austin,* 23.

[13] This eventually became Spanish grant number 430, as filed in the Washington County Circuit Court Records, Potosi, Missouri. The grant was never fully legitimized under Spanish law. It also conflicted with some of the land holdings of the French inhabitants who had earlier staked land claims granted by France. The land plat for this grant is reproduced in Walter A. Schroeder, *Opening the Ozarks: A Historical Geography of Missouri's Ste. Genevieve District, 1760–1830* (Columbia: University of Missouri Press, 2002), 290. For the development of this region, see also Carl J. Ekberg, *Colonial Ste. Genevieve* (Tucson, AZ: Patrice Press, 1996), 153; Gracy, *Moses Austin,* 65; John Francis McDermott, ed., "The Diary of Charles de Hault de Lassus," *Louisiana Historical Quarterly* 30 (1947): 359–438. Carl J. Ekberg, *French Roots in the Illinois Country: The Mississippi Frontier in Colonial Times* (Champaign: University of Illinois Press, 1998); George P. Garrison, ed., "A Memorandum of M. Austin's Journey from the Lead Mines in the County of Wythe in the State of Virginia to the Lead Mines in the Province of Louisiana West of the Mississippi, 1796–1797," *American Historical Review* 5, no. 3 (April 1900): 518–23.

[14] Gracy, *Moses Austin,* 68–69. The route that the Austins followed was first blazed for settlers in 1780 by the American revolutionary general George Rogers Clark. He sponsored and escorted an initial group of migrants from Virginia and Pennsylvania to new settlements located in the region where the Ohio River met the Mississippi. See Light Townsend Cummins, "Her Weary Pilgrimage: The Remarkable Mississippi River Adventures of Anne McMeans," *Louisiana History* 47 (Fall 2006): 389–415; and Stephen Aron, *American Confluence: The Missouri Frontier from Borderland to Border State* (Bloomington: University of Indiana Press, 2006).

[15] "Genealogical Notes," *Austin Papers,* 1:1–6. The incubation period for malaria is from ten to thirty-five days, after which there occurs "irregular low-grade fever, malaise, headache, and chilly sensations." The symptoms of malaria follow a

cyclical course. After a time, they lessen and the patient feels better, only to experience recurring episodes, each one more severe. Robert Burkow, ed., *The Merck Manual of Diagnosis and Therapy*, 14th ed. (Rahway, NJ: Merck Company, 1982), 239–40. During the eighteenth and nineteenth centuries, malaria was considered endemic to the mid-Mississippi Valley. Many reported historical cases of "fever" and "ague" might have been cases of malaria. As one epidemiological study of this region notes, "Textbooks of medical geography, memoirs, travel reports, army statistics, and medical journals of the period all agree that malaria was the American disease and, while the older states had emerged from its worst vexation, its hotbed was what was up to the 1850s was still called 'the west,' the valley of the Mississippi and its tributaries." Erwin H. Ackerkenecht, *Malaria in the Upper Mississippi Valley, 1760–1900* (Baltimore: Johns Hopkins University Press, 1945), 16.

[16] Jonas Viles, "Population and Extent of Settlement in Missouri before 1804," *Missouri Historical Review* 5, no. 4 (July 1911): 209; Ekberg, *French Roots in the Illinois Country*, 93. See also Bonnie Stepenoff, *From French Community to Missouri Town: Ste. Genevieve in the Nineteenth Century* (Columbia: University of Missouri Press, 2006).

[17] Ekberg, *Colonial Ste. Genevieve*, 197–238. Historian Bonnie Stepenoff has denominated the unique architectural style of Ste. Genevieve as a metaphor for its cultural distinctness: "The people of Ste. Genevieve built the walls of their houses with logs upended from holes in the ground (*poteaux en terre*) or mounted on heavy timber sills (*poteaux sur soles*) in a manner reminiscent of homes in medieval Normandy or in colonial Quebec. These vertical log houses visually signaled the differences between French settlers and their Anglo-American counterparts, who laid the logs horizontally one on top of the other." Stepenoff, *From French Community to Missouri Town*, 3–4. Diane Mutti Burke, "Mah Pappy Belong to a Neighbor: The Effects of Abroad Marriages on Missouri Slave Families," in *Searching for Their Places: Women in the South Across Four Centuries*, ed. Thomas H. Appleton Jr. and Angela Boswell (Columbia: University of Missouri Press, 2003), 59–60.

[18] Jonas Viles, "Missouri in 1820," *Missouri Historical Review* 15, no. 1 (October 1920): 40; Gardner, *Lead King*, 68–69, 180.

[19] Emily Margaret Austin File, Brazoria County Historical Museum, Angleton, TX. Quote comes from Louise Chilton Bryan, "Emily Margaret Austin," Emily Margaret Austin File.

[20] Gracy, *Moses Austin*, 79, 91; Ekberg, *Colonial Ste. Genevieve*, 153; Paul R. Richeson, "The Perrys of Potosi," typescript, Western Historical Manuscript Collection, Missouri University of Science and Technology (also located in the Mary and John W. Beretta Texana Collection, Coates Library, Trinity University), 5. For a detailed study of the influx of Anglo-Americans into the mining areas of Missouri and the role played by Moses Austin in these events, see Schroeder, *Opening the Ozarks*.

[21] Rath, "Moses Austin," 68; Henry R. Schoolcraft, *Journal of a Tour into the*

Interior of Missouri and Arkansaw (London: Sir Richard Phillips, 1821), 48; Jones, *Peach Point Plantation,* 5.

[22] "Genealogical Notes," *Austin Papers,* 1:1–6; Alphonso Wetmore, *Gazetteer of Missouri* (St. Louis, MO: C. Keemle, 1837), 32.

[23] Cantrell, *Stephen F. Austin,* 33–35.

[24] Anya Jabour, "'Grown Girls, Highly Cultivated': Female Education in an Antebellum Southern Family," *Journal of Southern History* 64 (February 1998): 25; Anya Jabour, "'College Girls': The Female Academy and Female Identity in the Old South," in *"Lives Full of Struggle and Triumph": Southern Women, Their Institutions and Their Communities,* ed. Bruce L. Clayton and John A. Salmond (Gainesville: University Press of Florida, 2003), 74–92; "Memoir," *Portfolio* 9 (August 1813): 117–22; Edna Talbert Whitley, "George Beck: An Eighteenth Century Painter," *Register of the Kentucky Historical Society* 67 (January 1969): 20–36; Clinton, *Plantation Mistress,* 12; Kierner, *Beyond the Household,* 147.

[25] Whitley, "George Beck," 33–35. Historian Laura F. Edwards provides an extensive discussion of education for adolescent females of the elite class in the South. She notes, "Parents began emphasizing discipline as their daughters approached their teens to prepare them for their future roles as wives, mothers, and mistresses of their own household. At this point, many girls left home for the more structured routine of boarding or day schools." Edwards, *Scarlett Doesn't Live Here Anymore,* 18. For additional literature on the importance of boarding schools for upper-class girls in the antebellum South, see Christie Anne Farnham, *The Education of the Southern Belle: Higher Education and Student Socialization in the Antebellum South* (New York: New York University Press, 1994). See also Steven M. Stowe, "The Not-So-Cloistered Academy: Elite Women's Education and Family Feeling in the Old South," in *The Web of Southern Social Relations: Women, Family, and Education,* ed. Walter J. Frazer Jr., R. Frank Saunders Jr., and Jon L. Wakelyn (Athens: University of Georgia Press, 1985), 90–106.

[26] Stowe, "Not-So-Cloistered Academy," 34.

[27] The historical record notes various birth dates for Bryan. Historian David B. Gracy II believes that Bryan was almost twice Emily's age, being a man in his thirties during her teenage years. See Gracy, *Moses Austin,* 131. The Austin family Bible notes that Bryan was born in 1789, meaning that he was approximately seventeen years of age when he first came to Missouri. Bryan's newspaper obituary also notes his birth year as 1789, as do Austin family records, including Emily's Bible. This would make him only six years older than Emily. See John L. Trevebaugh, "Merchant on the Western Frontier: William Morrison of Kaskaskia, 1790–1837" (PhD dissertation, University of Illinois, 1962), iv, 3–4, 7. All accounts agree that he was older, and at least to Moses and Maria, the age difference of six years may have seemed inappropriate during the early years of Emily and James' courtship. The median age of southern

brides in the 1810s was twenty, while the median age of grooms was twenty-eight, so Emily was young for marriage given the sensibilities of the era. Clinton, *Plantation Mistress,* 60.

[28] The first quotation about romantic love comes from Jabour, *Scarlett's Sisters,* 158. The second quote is reproduced in Trevebaugh, "Merchant on the Western Frontier," 196–99. Between 1809 and 1815, 65 percent of the firm's shipments to New Orleans consisted of smelted lead. Ruby Johnson Swartzlow, "Early History of Lead Mining in Missouri," *Missouri Historical Quarterly* 29 (July 1935): 195–205; James Bryan Papers, 1820–1870, Center for American History, University of Texas at Austin. For an early inventory from the store, see "Store at Mines for Mr. Bryan," box 2N248, James Bryan Papers.

[29] Trevebaugh, "Merchant on the Western Frontier," 68–69, 196–99. James Bryan also began to acquire real estate holdings in the area. For examples, see records at the Clerk of Courts, Ste. Genevieve County, Ste. Genevieve, Missouri: Indentures of James Bryan, February 6, 1810, Book B39; December 14, 1810, Book B100; and July 7, 1812, Book B185. See also William Morrison Ledger, Chester Public Library, Chester, Illinois, 7. The remains of Bryan's homestead and mill have been destroyed by modern construction. In August 2006, the author visited the areas inhabited by Bryan along Hazel Run, east of modern Bonne Terre, Missouri. Bryan's home site is now the location of a small lake along Saffell Road, a few miles north of where it crosses State Highway K. Mr. William Saffell graciously showed the author the location of Bryan's mill and his mining operations.

[30] Edwards drives home the importance of family by noting that "in a time when illness and early death were common, when commerce operated through personal connections, and when no public safety net assisted individuals who fell on hard times, even the wealthiest slave owners leaned heavily on their families." Edwards, *Scarlett Doesn't Live Here Anymore,* 19.

CHAPTER TWO: A MISSOURI MARRIAGE

[1] Cantrell, *Stephen F. Austin,* 44–46.

[2] Gardner, *Lead King,* 125; Moses Austin to James Bryan, June 4, 1811, *Austin Papers,* 1:192.

[3] Gracy, *Moses Austin,* 143; Perry, "Family Notes by Request"; Bryan, "Emily Margaret Austin."

[4] Gracy, *Moses Austin,* 132–42.

[5] Ibid., 141.

[6] Elisha Austin died in 1794, the year before Emily's birth. He had moved to New Haven as a young man, first keeping store as a budding merchant. During

the American Revolution, he went into partnership with another of Moses' brothers, Archibald, in order to outfit privateers to harass the British navy. This introduced Elisha to the potential profits of maritime commerce. He began sending his own ships to the West Indies and various ports in Europe. His crowning moment came in 1793 when he became the first American ship owner to send a trading vessel to Canton, thus opening the United States trade with China. Rebecca Smith Lee, *Mary Austin Holley: A Biography* (Austin: University of Texas Press, 1962), 7–9.

[7] William Ransom Hogan, comp., "Henry Austin," *Southwestern Historical Quarterly* 37, no. 3 (January 1934): 187.

[8] Ibid., 187–88.

[9] Lee, *Mary Austin Holley,* 86.

[10] See Henry Brown Collins, ed. *Valentine's Manual of Old New York* (New York: Valentine Publishing, 1919), image number 805396.

[11] Moses Austin to Emily Austin, June 20, 1812, *Austin Papers*, 1:210–11. Emily would be a person of strong religious belief for her entire life, although she had decidedly ecumenical tastes regarding particular denominations. Her mother's Anglicanism greatly influenced her, as did her father's Congregationalism. At later times in her life, she belonged to the Episcopal Church and attended the Presbyterian Church. Perry, "Family Notes by Request."

[12] Hogan, "Henry Austin," 187.

[13] Moses Austin's instructions to his son Stephen in April of 1812 clearly indicate that James Bryan made the trip to New Orleans in the company of young Austin. Moses, for example, advised his son to keep careful accounts on the journey so that he could settle with Bryan. He also advised the two men to stay with James Rumsey when they arrived in New York City. Moses Austin to Stephen F. Austin, April 28, 1812, *Austin Papers*, 1:204. Edwards, *Scarlett Doesn't Live Here Anymore,* 20–21.

[14] Moses Austin to James Bryan, December 4, 1812, *Austin Papers*, 1:220; Guy Bryan to James Bryan, September 1, 1812, box 2N248, James Bryan Papers; Bryan, "Emily Margaret Austin"; Gracy, *Moses Austin,* 143.

[15] Mary Austin Holley Papers, 1784–1846, Center for American History, University of Texas at Austin; Marriage Certificate of James and Emily Bryan, August 31, 1813, box 3C55, Mary Austin Holley Papers. The courtship and marriage of Emily and James proved a typical one for the era. See Nancy F. Cott, *Public Vows: A History of Marriage and the Nation* (Cambridge, MA: Harvard University Press, 2000).

[16] Gracy, *Moses Austin,* 154–55. Sally McMillen, who has extensively studied childbirth in the antebellum South, characterizes the death of a child as devastating, even though infant mortality was high and most parents did not expect all of their children to live. She notes that "when a child died, mothers found that an open grief was healing. Antebellum southern society could not offer mothers psychiatric counseling, institutionalized support groups, or the swift travel that might let women

talk out their sadness face to face with a distant family member. But it did allow mothers to mourn, and many women willingly shared their pain and sorrow with relatives and friends." This Emily did in the months after the death of her baby. See Sally G. McMillen, *Motherhood in the Old South: Pregnancy, Childbirth, and Infant Rearing* (Baton Rouge: Louisiana State University Press, 1990). Look especially at the chapter "Their Sorrowing Hearts, Infant Mortality and Material Bereavement," 165–79. For additional perspectives on childbirth and infant mortality in the era, consult Jane Turner Censer, *North Carolina Planters and Their Children, 1800–1860* (Baton Rouge: Louisiana State University Press, 1984); Richard W. and Dorothy C. Wertz, *Lying in: A History of Childbirth in America* (New York: Schocken Books, 1979); and Judith Walzer Leavitt, *Brought to Bed: Childbearing in America, 1750 to 1950* (New York: Oxford University Press, 1986).

[17] Moses Austin to James Bryan, December 4, 1812, *Austin Papers*, 1:220–21; Clinton, *Plantation Mistress,* 37.

[18] Cantrell, *Stephen F. Austin,* 28–29; Moses Austin to Stephen F. Austin, December 16, 1804, *Austin Papers*, 1:94; Moses Austin to Miss Emily Austin, June 20, 1812, *Austin Papers*, 1:210–11.

[19] Cantrell, *Stephen F. Austin,* 45, 71; J.E.B. Austin to Emily Austin, February 28, 1826, *Austin Papers*, 2:1269.

[20] James F. and Stephen S. Perry Papers, 1785–1942, Center for American History, University of Texas at Austin (hereafter cited as Perry Papers); Moses Austin to James Bryan, December 18, 1816, Perry Papers, Series B; Gracy, *Moses Austin,* 168, 175; Moses Austin to James Bryan, July 5, 1817, *Austin Papers*, 1:316–17.

[21] Gracy, *Moses Austin,* 157–58; Cantrell, *Stephen F. Austin,* 54; Moses Austin to James Bryan, November 25, 1814, *Austin Papers*, 1:243; Cantrell, *Stephen F. Austin,* 56; Gardner, *Lead King,* 146–47.

[22] Moses Austin to James Bryan, September 6, 1817, *Austin Papers*, 1:320–21; Gracy, *Moses Austin,* 174.

[23] Gracy, *Moses Austin,* 165–67.

[24] Account Book, 1815, box 2N249, James Bryan Papers; Moses Austin to James Bryan, August 31, 1817, *Austin Papers*, 1:319–20; Moses Austin to James Bryan, June 30, 1817, *Austin Papers*, 1:316; Moses Austin to James Bryan, July 21, 1817, *Austin Papers*, 1:317; James Cox Jr. to James Bryan, January 23, 1818, Perry Papers, Series B.

[25] Aron, *American Confluence,* 166; Robert L. Jones and Pauline H. Jones, "Stephen F. Austin in Arkansas," *Arkansas Historical Quarterly* 25, no. 4 (Winter 1966): 336–53.

[26] "Stephen F. Austin and the Preemption Claims at Little Rock, 1819," SMF 009, Southwestern Regional Archives (SRA), Washington, Arkansas; Receipt of James Bryan, SMF 489, SRA; Ibid.; James Cummins to James Bryan, July 15, 1819, SMF

489, SRA; Ibid.; Stephen F. Austin to James Bryan, January 8, 1818, SMF 489, SRA; Stephen F. Austin to James Bryan, November 2, 1818, *Austin Papers*, 1:333–34; James Cummins to James Bryan, July 15, 1819, *Austin Papers*, 1:345–46. See also Donald P. McNeilly, *The Old South Frontier: Cotton Plantations and the Formation of Arkansas Society, 1819–1861* (Fayetteville: University of Arkansas Press, 2000), 33–52.

[27] Guy M. Bryan Papers, 1821–1901, Center for American History, University of Texas at Austin; Emily M. Bryan Songbook, January 11, 1819, box 3N140, Guy M. Bryan Papers.

[28] Cantrell, *Stephen F. Austin*, 80–81; Jones, "Stephen F. Austin in Arkansas," 351; Stephen F. Austin to his Mother, January 20, 1821, *Austin Papers*, 1:373.

[29] Gracy, *Moses Austin*, 206.

[30] Gracy, *Moses Austin*, 209–210; Moses Austin to James Bryan, April 21, 1821, *Austin Papers*, 1:387–88; Moses Austin to James Bryan, April 22, 1821, *Austin Papers*, 1:388–89; "Moses Austin Genealogy," *Austin Papers*, 1:1–6.

[31] Maria Austin to Stephen F. Austin, June 8, 1821, *Austin Papers*, 1:394–95; Gracy, *Moses Austin*, 215.

[32] Gracy, *Moses Austin*, 213–14.

CHAPTER THREE: THE YEARS AT HAZEL RUN AND POTOSI

[1] Jones, *Peach Point Plantation*, 68; Perry Family File 75, Brazoria County Historical Museum, Angleton, TX; James Bryan to Stephen F. Austin, January 15, 1822, *Austin Papers*, 1:465–66; Maria Austin to Stephen F. Austin, January 19, 1822, *Austin Papers*, 1:467–69.

[2] One of these house slaves was named Milley. She would accompany Emily to Texas and outlive her into the 1850s. The two women had a close relationship in which Emily proved to be a benevolent mistress. Guy M. Bryan would later recall as an adult that Milley lived with Emily and the children almost as if she were a member of the family. William F. Bryan to James F. Perry, June 10, 1825, box 2N248, James Bryan Papers. The loan came in two installments, the first in the amount of $3,600 with an additional $1,400 later. Indenture of Emily Austin with Guy Bryan, August 20, 1823, Book D3, Clerk of Courts, Ste. Genevieve, Missouri; Jones, *Peach Point Plantation*, 3; Gracy, *Moses Austin*, 220.

[3] James Bryan's obituary noted that Bryan "departed this life at Herculaneum on the 16th July, inst., after a short but painful illness, which he bore with great Christian fortitude…Mr. Bryan has left a widowed mother-in-law, a distressed wife, and four helpless children to mourn their great and irreparable loss." Obituary of James Bryan, *St. Louis Missouri Republican*, July 24, 1822, State Historical Society of Missouri, Columbia; Gracy, *Moses Austin*, 218.

[4] Cantrell, *Stephen F. Austin*, 165. Guy Bryan did nothing to take possession of the Hazel Run property. However, once Emily was remarried, Guy Bryan charged his son with collecting the note from James F. Perry, Emily's new husband. J. M. Bryan to James F. Perry, January 10, 1835, box 2N249, James Bryan Papers; Bryan, "Emily Margaret Austin"; Gracy, *Moses Austin*, 218. Catherine Clinton notes, "Widowhood, of course, was especially devastating in a society so predicated upon the centrality of the male; to the loss of a husband was added the alienating loss of that central core which gave definition to everything else in a woman's life." Clinton, *Plantation Mistress*, 170; Wood, *Slaveholding Widows*, 84.

[5] Gracy, *Moses Austin*, 220; James A. Creighton, *A Narrative History of Brazoria County* (Waco, TX: Texian Press, 1975), 24; Jones, *Peach Point Plantation*, 6.

[6] J.E.B. Austin to Stephen F. Austin, September 6, 1824, *Austin Papers*, 1:890–92.

[7] Ibid.; Richeson, "Perrys of Potosi," 20; Jones, *Peach Point Plantation*, 9–10; Note by Emily Perry in J.E.B. Austin to Stephen F. Austin, September 6, 1824, *Austin Papers*, 1:890–92; J.E.B. Austin to Stephen F. Austin, September 6, 1824, *Austin Papers*, 1:890–92.

[8] See Salmon Giddings, *The Gospel, the power of God unto salvation a sermon preached at the installation of the Rev. Thomas Donnell to the pastoral office in Concord Church, and congregation of Belleview, April 25th, 1818* (St. Louis, MO: Henry and Maury, 1818); Adella B. Moore, *History of the Bellevue Presbyterian Church* (Farmington, MO: Elmwood Press, 1955); William Stevenson, Autobiography, typescript, Bridwell Library, Southern Methodist University, Dallas, Texas. The Perry family was Presbyterian, including James. Emily had been raised an Episcopalian, and some of her Bryan children, especially Guy M. Bryan, would remain in that denomination as adults. Nonetheless, James Perry's Presbyterianism prevailed in the family among the children who came from his union with Emily. As his wife, she supported both the Episcopal and Presbyterian Churches for the remainder of her lifetime.

[9] Certificate of Discharge, February 5, 1814, Perry Papers, vol. A-1; John Baldwin to James F. Perry Jr., February 4, 1817, Perry Papers, vol. A-1.

[10] Richeson, "Perrys of Potosi," 2–3.

[11] Lela Ethel McKinley, "The Life of James F. Perry" (master's thesis, University of Texas at Austin, 1934), 2–5. By 1830, James had bought out his cousin's interest, and the store became his sole property. Washington County Land Patents, M000010–260, General Land Office Records, Bureau of Land Management, Missouri.

[12] For a discussion of companionate marriage, see Nancy F. Cott, *Public Vows*, 11–12. The first quotation comes from Suzanne Lebsock, who has written of companionate marriage in the antebellum era, "The result for women was enhanced status, greater power, greater autonomy, and a strong, even equal status, in family affairs." Suzanne Lebsock, *The Free Women of Petersburg: Status and Culture in an*

Antebellum Southern Town, 1784–1860 (New York: W. W. Norton, 1984), 17. The second quotation comes from Catherine Kerrison, *Claiming the Pen: Women and Intellectual Life in the Early American South* (Ithaca, NY: Cornell University Press, 2006), 150. For more on the concept of companionate marriage, see Lawrence Stone, *The Family, Sex, and Marriage in England, 1500–1800* (New York: Harper and Row, 1979), 325–495; Carl N. Degler, *At Odds: Women and the Family in America from the Revolution to the Present* (New York: Oxford University Press, 1980).

[13] This was Maria Austin's opinion of Emily. Jones, *Peach Point Plantation,* 68.

[14] J.E.B. Austin to Emily Perry, November 10, 1825, *Austin Papers,* 2:1232–33. Family tradition holds that Emily instructed her sons to remove both rings as quickly as possible after the moment of her death. Her son Guy did this, keeping the Bryan ring for his line of descendants while Stephen Perry kept James' ring for his line. Both rings remained in possession of family members as prized heirlooms. Bryan, "Emily Margaret Austin," Emily Margaret Austin File.

[15] Jones, *Peach Point Plantation,* 28; Bryan, "Emily Margaret Austin," Emily Margaret Austin File. In some respects, Emily became used to acting as if she were a man in the areas of family decision-making, and it did not bother James F. Perry when she occasionally continued to do so after their marriage. For the southern norms regarding how men treated their wives, see Friend and Glover, *Southern Manhood*; and Stowe, *Intimacy and Power in the Old South.*

[16] Emily Perry to Stephen F. Austin, December 18, 1825, *Austin Papers,* 2:1239–40; Stephen F. Austin to Emily Perry, January 28, 1826, *Austin Papers,* 2:1260–62.

[17] Stephen F. Austin to Emily Perry, August 21, 1826, *Austin Papers,* 2:1239–40; Emily Perry to Stephen F. Austin, December 1825, *Austin Papers,* 2:1427–28; J.E.B. Austin to Emily, November 10, 1825, *Austin Papers,* 2:1232–33; Emily Perry to Stephen F. Austin, December 18, 1825, *Austin Papers,* 2:1239–40; Ibid.

[18] Stephen F. Austin to Emily Perry, October 22, 1826, *Austin Papers,* 2:1228–29; Stephen F. Austin to Emily Perry, August 21, 1826, *Austin Papers,* 2:1427–28; J.E.B. Austin to Emily Perry, February 28, 1826, *Austin Papers,* 2:1268–69.

[19] Stephen F. Austin to Emily Perry, December 17, 1824, *Austin Papers,* 2:991–92.

[20] Emily Perry to J.E.B. Austin, April 10, 1825, *Austin Papers,* 2:1072–74.

[21] James F. Perry to Stephen F. Austin, February 14, 1825, *Austin Papers,* 1:1041–43.

[22] J.E.B. Austin to Emily, June 3, 1825, *Austin Papers,* 2:1113–14.

[23] Emily to J.E.B. Austin, October 12, 1825, *Austin Papers,* 2:1072–74; Stephen F. Austin to Emily, October 22, 1825, *Austin Papers,* 2:1228–29; Stephen F. Austin to Emily, December 12, 1825, *Austin Papers,* 2:1238–39; Stephen F. Austin to Emily, January 28, 1826, *Austin Papers,* 2:1260–62.

[24] J.E.B. Austin to Emily, February 28, 1826, *Austin Papers,* 2:1260–62; Emily to Stephen F. Austin, December 18, 1825, *Austin Papers,* 2:1239–40; James F. Perry to Stephen F. Austin, November 5, 1826, *Austin Papers,* 2:1490–93.

[25] Cantrell, *Stephen F. Austin,* 19; McKinley, "Life of James F. Perry," 14; Randolph B. Campbell, *An Empire for Slavery: The Peculiar Institution in Texas, 1821–1865* (Baton Rouge: Louisiana State University Press, 1989), 21.

[26] Campbell, *Empire for Slavery,* 22, 26; Stephen F. Austin to James F. Perry, May 26, 1827, *Austin Papers,* 2:1645–46. For a general discussion about the westward movement of slavery, see Michael A. Morrison, *Slavery and the American West: The Eclipse of Manifest Destiny and the Coming of the Civil War* (Chapel Hill: University of North Carolina Press, 1997).

[27] For a discussion of the westward movement of southern planters during the antebellum era, see James David Miller, *South By Southwest: Planter Emigration and Identity in the Slave South* (Charlottesville: University of Virginia Press, 2002), 18–38. Randolph B. Campbell's book, *Empire for Slavery,* is a landmark study that provides the only state-based analysis of slavery in Texas. Campbell postulates that Texas was culturally part of the South and the values of the southerners gave the state its basic social and cultural milieu during the nineteenth century. The quotation comes from Campbell, *Empire for Slavery,* 18.

[28] Westall would die in the cholera epidemic of 1833 that devastated the Brazoria region.

[29] Margaret S. Henson, *Samuel May Williams: Early Texas Entrepreneur* (College Station: Texas A&M University Press, 1976), 22; Jones, *Peach Point Plantation,* 12.

[30] Cantrell, *Stephen F. Austin,* 215; Jones, *Peach Point Plantation,* 89.

[31] Jones, *Peach Point Plantation,* 12; Cantrell, *Stephen F. Austin,* 216; McKinley, "Life of James F. Perry," 17–19.

[32] Abigail Curlee, "The History of a Texas Slave Plantation, 1831–1863," *Southwestern Historical Quarterly* 26 (1922): 80; McKinley, "Life of James F. Perry," 67.

CHAPTER FOUR: THE MOVE TO TEXAS

[1] McKinley, "Life of James F. Perry," 25–26; Cantrell, *Stephen F. Austin,* 227; Fannie Baker Sholars, "The Life and Services of Guy M. Bryan" (master's thesis, University of Texas at Austin, 1930), 5; Creighton, *History of Brazoria County,* 45; Receipt, May 29 and June 4, 1830, Perry Papers, vol. A-1.

[2] Historian Joan E. Cashin has noted that "women, with few exceptions, opposed migration because they thought it would undermine or even destroy the family and take their loved ones to a distant, dangerous place." Cashin, *Family Venture,* 32.

[3] The Perrys owned this grant of land for rest of their lives, although it did not become their permanent residence, Peach Point Plantation. They would own much more land in Texas than this property, and the original terms of this grant created an additionally unusual situation in the settlement of their respective estates during the 1850s. Probate eventually determined that Emily's holding constituted three-quarters of this property: one-half share under the original terms of the grant itself, and one-half share of the community property shared with James. For a full discussion of women's property rights as practiced by Spain and Mexico in Texas land law, see Jean Stuntz, *Hers, His, and Theirs: Community Property Law in Spain and Early Texas* (Lubbock: Texas Tech University Press, 2005); Cantrell, *Stephen F. Austin*, 220; Jones, *Peach Point Plantation*, 16; McKinley, "Life of James F. Perry," 3; Agreement between Perry and Hunter, March 20, 1830, Perry Papers, vol. A-1.

[4] Agreement between Perry and Hunter, March 20, 1830, Perry Papers, vol. A-1.

[5] Quotations come from Reminiscences of Moses Austin Bryan, Austin College Archives, Abell Library, Sherman, TX; Bill of Ladling, April 20, 1831, Perry Papers, vol. A-1.

[6] Emily Perry to Austin Bryan, February 20, 1831, Perry Papers, vol. A-3.

[7] Jones, *Peach Point Plantation,* 21; Receipt of John Hutchins, June 17, 1830, *Austin Papers,* 1:738.

[8] Some historians have incorrectly concluded that Moses Austin Bryan traveled with this entourage, not realizing that he was already in Texas. The children who made the trip with them were William Joel Bryan, Guy M. Bryan, Mary Elizabeth Bryan, Stephen Samuel Perry, and Eliza Margaret Perry.

[9] In later years, Guy M. Bryan was very proud of his having ridden a mule all the way to Texas from Potosi. The mule lived for ten years after their arrival and took young Bryan to school for most of the time he lived at Peach Point Plantation. Perry, "Family Notes by Request." The bed is still in possession of Emily's descendants. The piano did not survive, although a sidepiece is conserved in collections of the Brazoria County Historical Museum in Angleton, Texas. Jones, *Peach Point Plantation*, 4.

[10] McKinley, "Life of James F. Perry," 32; Reminiscences of Moses Austin Bryan, Austin College Archives.

[11] Rosa eventually married Robert Justus Kleberg. See the reminiscences of Rosa von Roeder Kleberg in Crystal Sasse Ragsdale, ed., *The Golden Free Land: The Reminiscences and Letters of Women on an American Frontier* (Austin, TX: Landmark Press, 1976), 25. McKinley, "Life of James F. Perry," 43; Jones, *Peach Point Plantation*, 5; Cantrell, *Stephen F. Austin*, 240.

[12] McKinley, "Life of James F. Perry," 35. The Perry family thereafter referred to this parcel of land as "Pleasant Bayou" since the plantation complex at that location fronted on the smaller stream. The point where Chocolate and Pleasant Bayous meet is

located in eastern Brazoria County today. There are no remains of the Perry plantation in the vicinity. A small settlement known as Chocolate Bayou, Texas, did eventually spring up near the Perrys' land. It was a small crossroads that received the United States Post Office in 1911, but it ceased to exist in the 1940s. Today there are no commercial establishments at that location, and only a few families live in the crossroads neighborhood there. Jones, *Peach Point Plantation,* 26.

[13] Jones, *Peach Point Plantation,* 57. As historian Stephanie Cole has noted, influential southern women such as Catharine Beecher believed that "mothers were essential in the rearing of well-disciplined adults. Only a mother had the 'natural' kindness and good temper that suited her to be the most important person in a child's life; and only the natural mother had the qualities necessary to raise a child correctly." Emily and James Perry subscribed to this viewpoint. See Stephanie Cole, "A White Woman, of Middle Age, Would Be Preferred: Children's Nurses in the Old South," in *Neither Lady nor Slave: Working Women of the Old South,* ed. Susanna Delfino and Michelle Gillespie (Chapel Hill: University of North Carolina Press, 2002), 77.

[14] Allen Platter, "Educational, Social and Economic Characteristics of the Plantation Culture of Brazoria County, Texas" (PhD dissertation, University of Houston, 1961), 27. The spartan nature of the main house at Peach Point was typical of many Texas plantations. Historian Clement Eaton has noted, "Many of the planters particularly of the Southwest did not live nearly as well as thrifty farmers of the North, although their property was much greater...Some of the owners of numerous slaves and large plantations lived in log cabins." Clement Eaton, *A History of the Old South: The Emergence of a Reluctant Nation,* 3rd ed. (1975; repr., Prospect Heights, IL: Waveland Press, 1987), 394–95.

[15] Jones, *Peach Point Plantation,* 49.

[16] Curlee, "Texas Slave Plantation," 112.

[17] It eventually had twelve rooms, and by the 1850s, all of the exterior log walls had been covered with milled lumber. Curlee, "Texas Slave Plantation," 12; Jones, *Peach Point Plantation,* 31.

[18] Perry had bought out Hunter's interest in the store and served as its sole owner until 1833, when Somervell became involved as a partner. Somervell arrived in Texas during May of 1833 from Missouri. McKinley, "Life of James F. Perry," 65–67; Austin Bryan to Emily Perry, June 18, 1833, Perry Papers, Series 3. According to Annette Kolodny, a modern critic of Mrs. Holley's writings, the commitment to the concept of family informed many of Mary's views about Texas, which she manifested within her self-concept as an Austin. "What excited Holley about Texas," Kolodny notes about the general opinion of the whole colony, "we come to understand was less its promise of a toilless garden than its simulation of an extended family." Annette Kolodny, *The Land Before Her: Fantasy and Experience of the American Frontiers, 1630–1860* (Chapel Hill: University of North Carolina Press, 1984), 102.

[19] Cousin James Perry died on June 2, 1833. Platter, "Plantation Culture of Brazoria County," 33; Jones, *Peach Point Plantation,* 36–37. Munson is buried today in the churchyard of the Gulf Prairie Presbyterian Church, near the Perry family plot (ibid.).

[20] Jones, *Peach Point Plantation,* 35. The section of the cemetery where her parents buried Mary Elizabeth Bryan is today at the center of the Perry and Bryan family plots. Emily and subsequent generations of her descendants rest nearby.

[21] Lee, *Mary Austin Holley,* 198; Cantrell, *Stephen F. Austin,* 271; Jones, *Peach Point Plantation,* 37.

[22] Randolph B. Campbell, *Gone to Texas: A History of the Lone Star State* (New York: Oxford University Press, 2003), 125; Cantrell, *Stephen F. Austin,* 271, 275–79.

[23] McKinley, "Life of James F. Perry," 79; Stephen F. Austin to James F. Perry, October 6, 1834, *Austin Papers,* 2:1. These small portraits were painted by an artist who occupied a cell near Austin's chamber in the prison where both were incarcerated. Austin to Samuel May Williams, October 6, 1834, *Austin Papers,* 2:7.

[24] Henry Austin to Perry, November 24, 1834, *Austin Papers,* 2:29; Austin to Perry, November 6, 1834, *Austin Papers,* 2:21.

[25] Creighton, *History of Brazoria County,* 36, 41; Jones, *Peach Point Plantation,* 90; Stephen F. Austin to James F. Perry, November 6, 1934, *Austin Papers,* 2:21.

[26] McKinley, "Life of James F. Perry," 80.

[27] Stephen F. Austin to James F. Perry, November 6, 1834, *Austin Papers,* 3:17–22.

[28] Lee, *Mary Austin Holley,* 198; Cantrell, *Stephen F. Austin,* 271; Jones, *Peach Point Plantation,* 37.

[29] J. P. Bryan, ed., *Mary Austin Holley: The Texas Diary, 1835–1838* (Austin: University of Texas Press, 1965), 29–30. Mary Austin Holley is considered to be one of the significant popularizers of the guitar as a musical instrument during the nineteenth century.

[30] Stephen F. Austin to James F. Perry, February 6, 1835, *Austin Papers,* 3:41–42; James F. Perry to Stephen F. Austin, December 7, 1834, *Austin Papers,* 3:32–35. For an articulate discussion of cotton production on a typical plantation of the era, especially dealing with Mississippi, see David J. Libby, *Slavery and Frontier in Mississippi, 1720–1835* (Jackson: University Press of Mississippi, 2004).

[31] Platter, "Plantation Culture of Brazoria County," 32; James F. Perry to Lastrsaps and Desmare, January 15, 1835, *Austin Papers,* 3:39–40. Andrew J. Torget, a graduate student at the University of Virginia, has assembled a database of slavery statistics for antebellum Texas that may be the most accurate available. The figures above come from it. "Brazoria County Totals by County and Year 1837–1845," Texas Slavery Project, http://www.texasslaveryproject.org/ (accessed January 11, 2007). After the death of Stephen F. Austin in 1836, Emily purchased slaves for the plantation with

resources she had inherited from him. Title to these slaves remained in her name rather than that of James. By the time of her death in 1851, she owned almost three dozen slaves who were so acquired, in addition to those owned by James Perry, who had been purchased with funds generated by Peach Point profits. See "Last Will and Testament of Emily Austin Perry," Emily Margaret Austin File.

[32] Curlee, "Texas Slave Plantation," 93, 104–5; Jones, *Peach Point Plantation,* 121; James F. Perry to Stephen F. Austin, May 5, 1835, *Austin Papers,* 3:71–72.

[33] J. G. McNeel to James F. Perry, June 22, 1835, *Austin Papers,* 3:77; McKinley, "Life of James F. Perry," 88–89.

CHAPTER FIVE: PEACH POINT AND REVOLUTION

[1] Stephen F. Austin to James F. Perry, July 13, 1835, *Austin Papers,* 3:90–91; Cantrell, *Stephen F. Austin,* 297–98, 305; Austin to Mary Austin Holley, August 21, 1835, *Austin Papers,* 3:101; "Bought of Hotchkiss and Company," *Austin Papers,* 3:101.

[2] Cantrell, *Stephen F. Austin,* 309; Perry, "Family Notes by Request"; Reminiscences of Moses Austin Bryan, Austin College Archives.

[3] Gerald S. Piece, ed., "Some Early Letters of Moses Austin Bryan," *Southwestern Historical Quarterly* 70 (January 1967): 463–64; Creighton, *History of Brazoria County,* 101–3. Emily's initiative in organizing this dinner clearly had politically oriented motives. It would be the event that reintroduced her brother to active involvement in the political troubles of Anglo Texas. In so doing, she followed an important, yet sublimated, role that antebellum women played at many levels of American politics: namely, they created a social atmosphere as a forum for important and significantly politicized activities. For analogous actions by women in early nineteenth-century Washington, D.C., see Catherine Allgor, "A Lady Will Have More Influence: Women and Patronage in Early Washington City," in *Women and the Unstable State in Nineteenth-Century America,* ed. Alison M. Parker and Stephanie Cole (College Station: Texas A&M University Press for the University of Texas at Arlington, 2000), 37–60.

[4] Stephen F. Austin to James F. Perry, September 30, 1835, *Austin Papers,* 3:140–42.

[5] Stephen F. Austin to James F. Perry, October 27, 1835, *Austin Papers,* 3:211.

[6] Stephen L. Hardin, *Texian Iliad: A Military History of the Texas Revolution, 1835–1836* (Austin: University of Texas Press, 1994), 60–61; Jones, *Peach Point Plantation,* 88; Moses Austin Bryan to James F. Perry, November 18, 1835, *Austin Papers,* 3:260–61; Stephen F. Austin to James F. Perry, November 22, 1835, *Austin Papers,* 3:262–64.

[7] Moses Austin Bryan to James F. Perry, November 30, 1835, *Austin Papers,* 3:268–69.

[8] Stephen F. Austin to James F. Perry, December 17, 1835, *Austin Papers,* 3:286–87; Moses Austin Bryan to James F. Perry, November 30, 1835, *Austin Papers,* 3:268–69; Moses Austin Bryan to James F. Perry, December 30, 1835, *Austin Papers,* 3:295–97.

[9] Stephen F. Austin to James Perry, December 25, 1835, *Austin Papers,* 3:295–97.

[10] McKinley, "Life of James F. Perry," 98–99; Lee, *Mary Austin Holley,* 269; Mary Austin Holley to Stephen F. Austin, April 21, 1836, *Austin Papers,* 3:335–36.

[11] Today, Bell's Landing is in East Columbia, Texas. Sholars, "Life and Services of Guy M. Bryan," 10–11. Because of this exploit, Guy M. Bryan later enjoyed a reputation as the "Paul Revere" of the Texas Revolution.

[12] Henry Austin to James Perry, March 6, 1836, *Austin Papers,* 3:318–19.

[13] Sholars, "Life and Services of Guy M. Bryan," 12–13. This incident became a happy family memory for Emily and her children. Forever thereafter, they would repeat the catchphrase "Up, Buck and Ball, do your best" whenever they sought to encourage each other. Many years later, when Guy M. Bryan was campaigning after the Civil War for a seat in the United States Congress, he came upon a woman who asked him, "Mr. Bryan, do you remember the two little girls and a stalled wagon in the Runaway Scrape? I am one of those little girls, and my mother taught us that whenever we could do for Mrs. Perry or any of her family a favor, we must do it." Perry, "Family Notes by Request"; McKinley, "Life of James F. Perry," 102; James F. Perry to Stephen F. Austin, April 8, 1836, *Austin Papers,* 3:326–27.

[14] McKinley, "Life of James F. Perry," 102–3.

[15] Sholars, "Life and Services of Guy M. Bryan," 12; McKinley, "Life of James F. Perry," 102–3.

[16] For the remainder of his life, Austin Bryan took great delight recounting for his children and grandchildren the conversation between Santa Anna and Houston that he translated. He greatly embellished it with pronounced histrionics. A descendant recalled that Bryan would intone, "I am Antonio López de Santa Anna, President of Mexico, Commander in Chief of the Army of Operations, and I put myself at the disposition of the valiant General Houston and expect to be treated as a general should be when a prisoner of war." Always, when retelling this story, Bryan would pause at the words "I put myself" in order to interject his own comment, "Thinks I to myself, that's a lie. You did not put yourself." Perry, "Family Notes by Request." Later, after the Civil War, the state legislature commissioned a regal painting of Santa Anna's surrender to hang in the capitol building in Austin. Due to a series of miscommunications, the artist failed to put Moses Austin Bryan in the painting. The legislature refused to accept it until Bryan had been added. The artist thus secured a recent picture of an elderly, bearded Bryan. It was that bearded likeness of Austin Bryan that found its way

into the painting, making him appear much older than he had been on the battlefield that day in 1836. Paul G. Bell Papers, 1912, 1937–2002, Center for American History, University of Texas at Austin; Memo for File by Paul Gervais Bell, April 26, 1963, box 4Ac108, Paul G. Bell Papers; Sholars, "Life and Services of Guy M. Bryan," 14.

[17] Harris, Dilue Rose. "Reminiscences of Mrs. Dilue Rose Harris," pts. 1–3, *Quarterly of the Texas State Historical Association* 4 (October 1900): 85–127, 4 (January 1901): 155–89, 7 (January 1904): 214–22. Bryan, *Mary Austin Holley Diary,* 52; Jones, *Peach Point Plantation,* 67. For a biographical sketch of Harris, see Jeanette Hastedt Flachmeier, "Dilue Rose Harris (1825–1914)," in *Women in Early Texas,* ed. Evelyn M. Carrington (Austin, TX: Jenkins Publishing, 1975), 101–7.

[18] Curlee, "Texas Slave Plantation," 94. Although the historical record does not explicitly note if this loan was granted, Perry's expenditures for the next year indicate that it most likely was made by this New Orleans agent. Jones, *Peach Point Plantation,* 45.

[19] Jones, *Peach Point Plantation,* 68; Mary Austin Holley to Stephen F. Austin, June 1, 1836, *Austin Papers,* 3:362.

[20] Cantrell, *Stephen F. Austin,* 347–50; Jones, *Peach Point Plantation,* 69; Stephen F. Austin to Henry Austin, June 27, 1836, *Austin Papers,* 3:371. Stephen clearly employed the abstract notion of "home" in defining civic virtue, basing it on domesticity. Home and hearth became a metaphor to be expanded in defining larger social constructs and identities, especially the civic polity. Austin saw the home as the conceptual building block of his colony, which was an aggregate of families. Since Peach Point was his specific home and Emily was its mistress, his sister thus served as a generic example, in the civic sense, to all those living in the Republic of Texas. Although she most certainly did not appreciate Stephen objecting to her trip, she eventually adopted this view of herself when, after Stephen's death, she took it upon herself to keep his memory alive in Texas. This civically imbued notion about the nature of home as a way to construct larger identities was typical of the time. As Amy Kaplan has pointed out, "If domesticity plays a key role in imagining the nation as home, then women, positioned as the center of the home, played a major role in defining the concept of the nation." Amy Kaplan, "Manifest Domesticity," in Davidson and Hatcher, *No More Separate Spheres,* 184.

[21] Cantrell, *Stephen F. Austin,* 351–55.

[22] Stephen F. Austin to James F. Perry, September 2, 1836, *Austin Papers,* 3:428.

[23] Stephen F. Austin to James F. Perry, December 18, 1836, *Austin Papers,* 3:477; Stephen F. Austin to James F. Perry, October 25, 1836, *Austin Papers,* 3:438–39.

[24] Stephen F. Austin to James F. Perry, December 2, 1836, *Austin Papers,* 3:464–65.

25 Cantrell, *Stephen F. Austin,* 362–64; Jones, *Peach Point Plantation,* 74–75.

26 Jones, *Peach Point Plantation,* 75.

27 McKinley, "Life of James F. Perry," 105–6. It would take Perry several years to sort through the various details of Stephen F. Austin's land holdings. Title to all of his land eventually reverted to Emily Austin Bryan Perry in her name as the sole legal owner. It was treated under the provisions of Texas law as if it had been prenuptial ganancial property. With her husband's help, Emily did make an attempt to develop as an investment some of these holdings on San Luis Island in the 1840s, and after her death most parcels of this land went to her sons. Essentially, the three Bryan sons ended up with most of their uncle's undeveloped land, while Peach Point Plantation, along with the other land that had originally been deeded to Emily and James F. Perry in common, went to Eliza and Stephen, the surviving children of their marriage. All of the Bryan and Perry siblings apparently felt this was an equitable division. *Telegraph and Texas Register,* January 6, 1838 and May 19, 1838, Center for American History, University of Texas at Austin; James F. Perry letter book, October 31, 1838, Perry Papers, vol. A-9; McKinley, "Life of James F. Perry," 109.

28 Jones, *Peach Point Plantation,* 90. Emily's inheritance gave her a unique legal status that departed from the legal practice of *feme covert* as it existed in the southern United States at that time. As historian Marylynn Salmon has noted of the United States, "Under the common law, a married woman (feme covert) could not own property, either real or personal . . . Since women could not own property under the common law, they could not exercise legal controls over it. A feme covert could not make a legally binding contract. She could not sell or mortgage property that she brought to the marriage or that she and her husband acquired." However, in the technical point of law, feme covert did not strictly apply to this inheritance because it was under Mexican law, a system of jurisprudence that did not explicitly enunciate this legal doctrine for women. Hence, the management of the Stephen F. Austin estate did not strictly follow the legalities of feme covert, although as longtime residents of the United States, the Perrys were undoubtedly familiar with its philosophical underpinnings as the usual manner in which individual couples dealt with the wife's property. For that reason, all legal documents related to this estate were negotiated in the name of James F. Perry, and Emily clearly participated in the making of them. For a discussion of feme covert as practiced in the British colonies and later the southern United States, see Marylynn Salmon, "Women and Property in South Carolina: The Evidence from Marriage Settlements, 1730 to 1830," *William and Mary Quarterly* 39 (October 1982): 655–56. As Anglo-Americans moved into territory that had operated under Spanish colonial governments, they tended to blend together legal practices from both systems, as was the case of ante nuptial and ganancial property in marriages. See Deborah A. Rosen, "Women and Property Across America: A Comparison of Legal Systems in New Mexico and New York," *William*

and Mary Quarterly 60 (April 2003): 355–81. This was the case for Texas in the 1820s and 1830s. Light Townsend Cummins, "Church Courts, Marriage Breakdown, and Separation in Spanish Louisiana, West Florida, and Texas, 1763–1836," *Journal of Texas Catholic History and Culture* 4 (1993): 97–114. For feme covert in mid-nineteenth century Texas, see Angela Boswell, "Married Women's Property Rights and the Challenge to the Patriarchal Order: Colorado County, Texas," in *Negotiating Boundaries of Southern Womanhood: Dealing with the Powers That Be*, ed. Janet L. Coryell et al. (Columbia: University of Missouri Press, 2000).

[29] Boswell, "Married Women's Property Rights," 86.

[30] The quote comes from Lebsock, *Free Women of Petersburg*, 55–56. See also Norma Basch, "Equity vs. Equality: Emerging Concepts of Women's Political Status in the Age of Jackson," *Journal of the Early Republic* 3 (Fall 1983): 297–318; Kathleen E. Lazarou, "Concealed Under Petticoats: Married Women's Property and the Law of Texas, 1840–1913" (PhD dissertation, Rice University, 1980).

[31] Jones, *Peach Point Plantation*, 76; Cashin, *Family Venture*, 15; James F. Perry to Emily Perry, June 2, 1837, Perry Papers, Series A.S.

[32] Austin Bryan to James F. Perry, June 12, 1837, Perry Papers, Series A.S. The numerous letters exchanged among the family never specially named Eliza's illness. However, physicians who eventually treated the young woman gave her standard remedies employed in the management of epileptic-related disorders; this included Dr. Samuel Jackson, one of the nation's most eminent physicians and a member of the College of Physicians at Philadelphia. Eliza did not necessarily suffer from epilepsy. Other medical conditions can also produce seizures such as she experienced, including vitamin deficiency, birth or cranial trauma, and cardiovascular irregularities. Whatever its specific nature, her illness occurred at a time when seizure-related afflictions were beginning to be treated medically in more enlightened fashion than had formerly been the case. Emily and the rest of the family went to great lengths over the ensuing decades to ensure the young woman's life would be as normal as possible. The period from 1800 to 1860 witnessed great advances in medical treatments, some of which undoubtedly benefited Eliza Perry. For a detailed discussion of these treatments, various of which Eliza would receive over the course of her adult life, see Owsei Temkin, *The Falling Sickness: A History of Epilepsy from the Greeks to the Beginnings of Modern Neurology*, 2nd ed. (Baltimore: Johns Hopkins University Press, 1994), 255–99.

[33] Emily Perry to James F. Perry, June 19, 1837, Perry Papers, Series A.S. Nothing ever came of the suggestion that Moses Austin Bryan change his name, although Emily would make this suggestion several additional times in the future. In a July 1837 letter, she said, "Let Stephen [Perry] be called Stephen Franklin Austin. It will have to be done by Act of Congress, which I see from the public prints will meet in September; Austin [Moses Austin Bryan] will drop the name of Bryan." Emily Perry

to James F. Perry, July 22, 1837, Perry Papers, Series A.S. Obviously, since this never happened, either Austin Bryan (then age twenty) or his stepfather, perhaps both, did not agree with this course of action. Emily's support for this, however, does provide an important clue to how she continued to define her family identity, even after having been married for almost a quarter-century.

[34] Emily Perry to James F. Perry, July 9, 1837, Perry Papers, Series A.S.; Emily Perry to James F. Perry, June 19, 1837, Perry Papers, Series A.S.; Austin Bryan to James F. Perry, July 9, 1837, Perry Papers, Series A.S.

[35] Austin Bryan to James F. Perry, July 21, 1837, Perry Papers, Series A.S.; "Outline of Seminary History," in *1883 Catalog of Steubenville Female Academy,* http://digitalshoebox.org/cdm4/document.php (accessed December 12, 2006).

[36] Austin Bryan to James F. Perry, July 21, 1837, Perry Papers, Series A.S.; Emily Perry to James F. Perry, July 22, 1837, Perry Papers, Series A.S.; Austin Bryan to James F. Perry, September 3, 1837, Perry Papers, Series A.S.

[37] Lavinia Perry was born in 1813 and was thus two years older than Emily's oldest son, Joel Bryan. In the summer of 1837, Lavinia was twenty-five and Joel twenty-two. The two step-cousins would marry three years later on April 6, 1840. Although no extant correspondence speaks to a long-distance romance, the timing and circumstances of Lavinia's return to Texas hint at an already existing attachment between the two young people. Austin Bryan to James F. Perry, September 3, 1837, Perry Papers, Series A.S.

[38] Emily Perry to James F. Perry, September 6, 1837, Perry Papers, Series A.S.; Emily Perry to James F. Perry, July 9, 1837, Perry Papers, Series A.S.

[39] Emily Perry to James F. Perry, August 13, 1837, Perry Papers, Series A.S.

[40] Ibid.; Emily Perry to James F. Perry, September 6, 1837, Perry Papers, Series A.S.; Emily Perry to James F. Perry, July 9, 1837, Perry Papers, Series A.S.; Emily Perry to James F. Perry, August 13, 1837, Perry Papers, Series A.S.

CHAPTER SIX: ANTEBELLUM PEACH POINT

[1] Marli F. Weiner, *Mistresses and Slaves: Plantation Women in South Carolina, 1830–1860* (Champaign: University of Illinois Press, 1998), 23. The Clinton quotation comes from Clinton, *Plantation Mistress,* 21.

[2] In many ways, Emily was as much a farmwife as she was a plantation mistress. The dichotomy between the "ideal southern lady" and the farmwife has been a constant in much of the historical literature on antebellum plantation women. See D. Harland Hagler, "The Ideal Woman in the Antebellum South: Lady or Farmwife?" *Journal of Southern History* 46 (August 1980): 416–17. The farmwife interpretive model has its origins in a foundation study of southern women's history: Spruill,

Women's Life and Work in the Southern Colonies. Anne Firor Scott's *The Southern Lady,* published two generations later, counterbalanced the farmwife model by emphasizing the elite southern woman as a "lady." The two models have never been fully reconciled by historians, because examples of both kinds of women can easily be found in the antebellum South. Emily's life clearly had its foundation in both historical viewpoints.

[3] Emily Perry to James F. Perry, July 22, 1837, Perry Papers, Series A.S.; Emily Perry to James F. Perry, November 1, 1837, Perry Papers, Series A.S.; Emily Perry to James F. Perry, September 6, 1837, Perry Papers, Series A.S.; Emily Perry to James F. Perry, July 22, 1837, Perry Papers, Series A.S.; Campbell, *Empire for Slavery,* 128. For a general discussion of the garden's importance as an iconic part of the southern plantation and the role of slaves in maintaining them, see Betty Wood, *Women's Work, Men's Work: The Informal Slave Economics of Lowcountry Georgia* (Athens: University of Georgia Press, 1995), 31–40.

[4] Emily Perry to James F. Perry, July 9, 1837, Perry Papers, Series A.S.; Emily Perry to James F. Perry, September 6, 1837, Perry Papers, Series A.S.; Emily Perry to James F. Perry, July 22, 1837, Perry Papers, Series A.S.; Emily Perry to James F. Perry, November 1, 1837, Perry Papers, Series A.S. Emily's delegation of these various household tasks to the slaves was very typical for that era. For a generic discussion of household duties routinely given to female slaves, see Leslie Howard Owens, *This Species of Property: Slave Life and Culture in the Old South* (New York: Oxford University Press, 1977), 112–20. Many of Emily's concerns about housekeeping reflected the common assumptions of her era about how a home should be maintained. See Susan Strasser, *Never Done: A History of American Housework* (New York: Pantheon Books, 1982).

[5] Emily Perry to James F. Perry, July 22, 1837, Perry Papers, Series A.S.; Emily Perry to James F. Perry, July 9, 1837, Perry Papers, Series A.S.; Emily Perry to James F. Perry, June 19, 1837, Perry Papers, Series A.S. Emily's experiences in helping to establish Peach Point Plantation were similar to those of many other women who lived in all parts of the expanding nineteenth-century frontier. For such examples, see Virginia K. Bartlett, *Keeping House: Women's Lives in Pennsylvania, 1790–1850* (Pittsburg, PA: University of Pittsburg Press, 1994), 19–37; and Joanna L. Stratton, *Pioneer Women: Voices from the Kansas Frontier* (New York: Simon and Schuster,1981), 46–56.

[6] Emily Perry to James F. Perry, September 6, 1837, Perry Papers, Series A.S.; Emily Perry to James F. Perry, July 22, 1837, Perry Papers, Series A.S.; Emily Perry to James F. Perry, August 13, 1837, Perry Papers, Series A.S. Emily's expansive view of her duties at Peach Point proved all too typical for plantation mistresses. Historian Jean E. Friedman has noted, "The agrarian partnership in which women shared economic production with men and assumed dual work roles in the household and the field was as much a product of southern self-sufficiency as it was a consequence of the lack of

an integrated market system." Jean E. Friedman, *The Enclosed Garden: Women and Community in the Evangelical South, 1830–1900* (Chapel Hill: University of North Carolina Press, 1985), 21.

[7] Emily Perry to James F. Perry, July 22, 1837, Perry Papers, Series A.S.; Emily Perry to James F. Perry, September 6, 1837, Perry Papers, Series A.S.; Emily Perry to James F. Perry, August 13, 1837, Perry Papers, Series A.S.

[8] Emily Perry to James F. Perry, August 13, 1837, Perry Papers, Series A.S.; Clinton, *Plantation Mistress,* 184; Edwards, *Scarlett Doesn't Live Here Anymore,* 22; William Ransom Hogan, *The Texas Republic: A Social and Economic History* (Norman: University of Oklahoma Press, 1946), 47. Modern historical scholarship has tended to see significant commonalities between elite southern women and the slave as communally subordinate in the society of the era. Stephanie Cole aptly notes that "many scholars now consider gender and race together, creating a new category they refer to alternately as either 'gendered race' or 'radicalized gender.'" Stephanie Cole, introduction to *Searching for Their Places: Women in the South Across Four Centuries,* ed. Thomas H. Appleton Jr. and Angela Boswell (Columbia: University of Missouri Press, 2003), 3. Historian Jacqueline Jones has contended with justification, based on her research in region-wide antebellum southern historical sources, that some plantation mistresses treated their female slaves harshly and brutally because of their own frustrations as elite white women who were themselves subordinated by society at large. Jones notes, "In their role as labor managers, mistresses lashed out at slave women not only to punish them, but also to vent their anger on victims even more wronged themselves." Jacqueline Jones, *Labor of Love, Labor of Sorrow: Black Women, Work, and the Family from Slavery to the Present* (New York: Basic Books, 1985), 25. For a discussion of the variety of complex relations between white mistresses and female slaves, see Minrose C. Gwin, *Black and White Women of the Old South: The Peculiar Sisterhood in American Literature* (Knoxville: University of Tennessee Press, 1985), 45–109. The historical record is absolutely silent on any sort of ill treatment Emily might have visited upon her slaves. To the contrary, in view of a complete lack of documentary evidence for such hard behavior, it must be submitted that Emily never treated her slaves harshly. She had a nurturing and a positive relationship with them, about which there exists ample evidence throughout the family's correspondence.

[9] Platter, "Plantation Culture of Brazoria County," 43; Curlee, "Texas Slave Plantation," 80.

[10] The quotation comes from Eaton, *History of the Old South,* 253. For Eaton's discussion of the scholarly debate about the treatment of slaves, see 251. Eaton based his opinions on the various studies of Texas plantation slavery made by Abigail Curlee Holbrook, all of which highlighted Peach Point.

[11] The fact that the household at Peach Point existed as a unit of production made it typical for the era, especially in the differentiation of gender roles. See Carol

Lasser, "Gender, Ideology, and Class in the Early Republic," *Journal of the Early Republic* 10, no. 3 (Autumn 1990): 331–37. For correspondence about plantation slaves, see Emily Perry to James F. Perry, June 19, 1837, Perry Papers, Series A.S.; and Emily Perry to James F. Perry, July 22, 1837, Perry Papers, Series A.S. In spite of various later attempts by others to develop Quintana, the town never grew. It has, however, always maintained a precarious existence as a beachfront recreational community. In the census of the year 2000, it enjoyed the distinction of being the incorporated city in Texas with the smallest population, at only thirty-eight people. Some of the undeveloped town lots at Quintana have been owned by Emily's descendants to the present day.

[12] Emily Perry to James F. Perry, November 1, 1837, Perry Papers, Series A.S.; Jones, *Peach Point Plantation,* 87; Emily Perry to James F. Perry, November 1, 1837, Perry Papers, Series A.S.

[13] Cashin, *Family Venture,* 15.

[14] Lee, *Mary Austin Holley,* 288–89. Hammeken was involved in these efforts while Holley traveled to Texas. She wrote Harriet Brand, her daughter, the week before Christmas 1837: "Mr. Hammeken returns to New Orleans on a business scheme relating to Dollar Point after seeing Mr. Perry, the owner. He is offered any sum of money there, New Orleans, to carry on a project at Dollar Point. This is just below my land which is but three miles from the mouth of Dickinson Creek." Mattie Austin Hatcher, *Letters of an Early American Traveler: Mary Austin Holley, Her Life and Her Works, 1784–1846* (Dallas, TX: Southwest Press, 1933), 68; San Luis File, Brazoria County Historical Museum, Angleton, TX.

[15] Hatcher, *Letters of an Early American Traveler,* 68; Lee, *Mary Austin Holley,* 280.

[16] Lee, *Mary Austin Holley,* 280; Jones, *Peach Point Plantation,* 96.

[17] Bryan, *Mary Austin Holley Diary,* 52; Jones, *Peach Point Plantation,* 96; Lee, *Mary Austin Holley,* 294.

[18] Hatcher, *Letters of an Early American Traveler,* 68; Bryan, *Mary Austin Holley Diary,* 52, 54; Hogan, *Texas Republic,* 57.

[19] Hatcher, *Letters of an Early American Traveler,* 72; Lee, *Mary Austin Holley,* 294.

[20] Bryan, *Mary Austin Holley Diary,* 54.

[21] Hatcher, *Letters of an Early American Traveler,* 73; Bryan, *Mary Austin Holley Diary,* 52.

[22] Emily Perry to James F. Perry, August 13, 1837, Perry Papers, Series A.S.; Mirabeau B. Lamar to Gail Borden, January 20, 1837, *Austin Papers,* 3:462–64; Cantrell, *Stephen F. Austin,* 369; Lee, *Mary Austin Holley,* 294.

[23] Lee, *Mary Austin Holley,* 324–25; James F. Perry to the Public, undated, *Austin Papers,* 3:484–87.

[24] Hatcher, *Letters of an Early American Traveler,* 77.

[25] The site of Austinia is currently the location of Texas City, although the modern municipality does not descend from it. "Site of Austinia," Historical Marker Records, Texas State Historical Commission, http://www.9key.com/markers (accessed December 14, 2006); Jesse Ponce, "Austinia: A History," San Luis File; James F. Perry to John S. Brickey, April 19, 1839, Perry Papers, vol. A.S.; James F. Perry Letter Book, Perry Papers, vol. A-1; McKinley, "Life of James F. Perry," 115.

[26] Andrew Forrest Muir, "Railroad Enterprise in Texas, 1836–1841," *Southwestern Historical Quarterly* 47 (April 1944): 339–70; "Power of Attorney of the Stockholders of San Luis Company," August 14, 1840, Perry Papers, vol. A-7; William G. Hill to James F. Perry, July 19, 1839, Perry Papers, vol. A-7; Agreement between James F. Perry, Emily M. Perry his wife, William G. Hill, Eliza M. Hill his wife, of the first part, and A. Jackson of the second part, November 13, 1845, Perry Papers, vol. A-7.

[27] Lee, *Mary Austin Holley,* 306–12. Hatcher, *Letters of an Early American Traveler,* 80; Creighton, *History of Brazoria County,* 158. In 1853, a hurricane destroyed most of San Luis, and it quickly stagnated thereafter.

CHAPTER SEVEN: THE MATURE YEARS

[1] Perry, "Family Notes by Request"; William J. Bryan Day Book, Durazno, Brazoria County Historical Museum, Angleton, Texas.

[2] Moses Austin Bryan to Father and Mother, August 31, 1840, Perry Papers, vol. A-9.

[3] Moses Austin Bryan to James F. Perry, February 11, 1839, box 4Ac107, Paul G. Bell Papers.

[4] Later, in the early 1850s, the Perrys gave Austin College an additional $3,500 while assigning to it any money that might come in a possible settlement with the Republic government as a reimbursement to Stephen F. Austin's estate for his expenses during the 1836 diplomatic mission to the United States. Those payments eventually came to the college in the 1870s, paid by the state government. Light Townsend Cummins, *Austin College: A Sesquicentennial History* (Austin, TX: Eakin Press, 1999), 12, 16.

[5] Robert F. Pace, *Halls of Honor: College Men in the Old South* (Baton Rouge: Louisiana State University Press, 2004), 16; Guy M. Bryan to James F. Perry, July 28, 1837, Perry Papers, vol. A-5; Guy M. Bryan to Mother, September 26, 1837, Perry Papers, vol. A-5.

[6] A nineteenth-century writer noted of these schools, "Much attention is given to the cause of education in Steubenville. There are five public and four select

schools, a male academy and a female seminary. The male institution, called 'Grove Academy,' is flourishing. It is under the charge of the Rev. John W. SCOTT, has three teachers and eighty scholars. The female seminary is pleasantly situated on the bank of the Ohio, commanding an extensive view of the river and the surrounding hills. It is under the charge of the Rev. Charles C. BEATTY, D. D., superintendent, and Mrs. Hetty E. BEATTY, principal. It was first established in the spring of 1829, and now receives only scholars over twelve years of age. It is in a very high degree flourishing, having a widely extended reputation. The establishment costs nearly $40,000, employs from ten to twelve teachers and usually has 150 pupils, the full number which it can accommodate." Henry Howe, *Historical Collections of Ohio* (1888; repr., Cincinnati, OH: C. H. Krehbeil and Company, 1902), 1:964.

[7] S. S. Perry Papers, Austin College Archives, Abell Library, Sherman, Texas; James F. Perry to Eliza Perry, June 3, 1839, S. S. Perry Papers; Stephen S. Perry to James F. Perry, June 8, 1840, Perry Papers, vol. A-8; James F. Perry to Reverend C. Beatty, September 29, 1840, Perry Papers, vol. A-9; Mary Ellen Doyle, *Pioneer Spirit: Catherine Spalding, Sister of Charity of Nazareth* (Lexington: University Press of Kentucky, 2006); Jones, *Peach Point Plantation,* 100.

[8] Eliza Perry to Emily Perry, October 12, 1840, Perry Papers, vol. A-9; Eliza Perry to Emily Perry, December 12, 1840, Perry Papers, vol. A-9.

[9] Sister Catherine Spalding to Mrs. Perry, December 11, 1840, Perry Papers, vol. A-9; Emily Perry to Sister Catherine Spalding, June 1, 1841, Perry Papers, vol. A-9; James F. Perry to Eliza Perry, March 30, 1841, Perry Papers, vol. A-9.

[10] Sister Catherine Spalding to Emily Perry, October 16, 1841, Perry Papers, vol. A-9; Sister Columba Carroll to Emily Perry, November 9, 1841, Perry Papers, vol. A-9.

[11] The headmistress also added in her letter, "I presume it is unnecessary to mention that Eliza's stay in Louisville and physician's charges, etc, would considerably add to her ordinary expenses." Sister Columba Carroll to Emily Perry, December 2, 1841, Perry Papers, vol. A-9.

[12] Sister Catherine Spalding to Emily Perry, February 22, 1842, Perry Papers, vol. A-1; Sister Catherine Spalding to Emily Perry, April 24, 1842, Perry Papers, vol. A-10; Sister Catherine Spalding to Emily Perry, June 14, 1842, Perry Papers, vol. A-10.

[13] Emily Perry to Stephen Perry, June 13, 1841, Perry Papers, vol. A-9; Emily Perry to Guy M. Bryan, June 13, 1841, Perry Papers, vol. A-9; Guy M. Bryan to My Dear Father and Mother, April 28, 1841, Perry Papers, vol. A-9.

[14] Catherine Clinton, *Plantation Mistress,* 7, 32. By the 1840s, Peach Point had become a stereotypical southern plantation. Although not one of the largest slave-owning planters in the South, James F. Perry enjoyed most of the business and agricultural successes of the southern planter. See William K. Scarborough, *Masters of*

the Big House: Elite Slave-Holders of the Mid-Nineteenth-Century South (Baton Rouge: Louisiana State University Press, 2003).

[15] Charles Richard Williams, ed., *The Diary and Letters of Rutherford B. Hayes, Nineteenth President of the United States,* vol. 1 (Columbus: Ohio State Archeological and Historical Society, 1922), 255. The first quotation comes from Clinton, *Plantation Mistress,* 139. The second quotation is from Sally G. McMillen, "Antebellum Southern Fathers and the Health Care of Children," *Journal of Southern History* 60, no. 3 (August 1994): 515.

[16] Joel Bryan to James F. Perry, October 7, 1840, Perry Papers, vol. A-10; James F. Perry to Stephen F. Perry, February 29, 1844, Perry Papers, vol. A-10; Platter, "Plantation Culture of Brazoria County," 43. This was consistent with practices on many other larger southern plantations. See Steven M. Stowe, *Doctoring the South: Southern Physicians and Everyday Medicine in the Mid-Nineteenth Century* (Chapel Hill: University of North Carolina Press, 2004); Marie Jenkins Schwartz, *Birthing a Slave: Motherhood and Medicine in the Antebellum South* (Cambridge, MA: Harvard University Press, 2006), 143–86; Robert Hancock Hunter, *Narrative of Robert Hancock Hunter,* 2nd ed. (Austin, TX: Cook Printing, 1936; Austin: Encino, 1966); Platter, "Plantation Culture of Brazoria County," 43; Campbell, *Empire for Slavery,* 142. Today, the Medical College of Louisiana is Tulane University. John P. Dyer, *Tulane: The Biography of a University, 1834–1965* (New York: Harper and Row, 1965). For a history of treating slaves at Tulane, see John Duffy, *The Rudolph Matas History of Medicine in Louisiana,* 2 vols. (Baton Rouge: Louisiana State University Press, 1962). Richard C. Wade, *Slavery in the Cities: The South, 1820–1860* (New York: Oxford University Press, 1964), 138.

[17] Campbell, *Empire for Slavery,* 136. For a biographical discussion of Tait, see Miller, *South by Southwest,* 3–6, 71–75, 124–25. Tait recommended, "Serve out to every working hand once a week from two & a half to three and a half pounds of bacon according to circumstances. If milk & butter is plenty, then less meat; if molasses is served out, then one quart in place of one pound of meat. Of dried-beef five or six pounds is the weekly allowance, also one peck of meal. Lying-in women to be allowed one quart of coffee and two quarts of sugar, & fed from the overseer's kitchen 2 weeks." Tait Plantation Slave Rules, Version 1, Charles William Tait Papers, 1844–1865, Center for American History, University of Texas at Austin; Jones, *Peach Point Plantation,* 51; Elizabeth Silverthorne, *Plantation Life in Texas* (College Station: Texas A&M University Press, 1986). For various schools of thought regarding slave management on the part of southern planters, see James O. Breeden, ed., *Advice Among Masters: The Ideal in Slave Management in the Old South* (Westport, CT: Greenwood Press, 1980).

[18] Clinton, *Plantation Mistress,* 6–7; Campbell, *Empire for Slavery,* 136. The production figures are noted in Curlee, "Texas Slave Plantation,"103.

[19] With this herd of cattle, Borden began the experimentation that eventually allowed him to produce condensed milk, "which was a forerunner to a dairy products country company that would make his name known over a wide area." Jones, *Peach Point Plantation,* 99, 123; Platter, "Plantation Culture of Brazoria County," 46–48; Curlee, "Texas Slave Plantation," 101–2; Creighton, *History of Brazoria County,* 196.

[20] Sam W. Haynes, *Soldiers of Misfortune: The Somervell and Mier Expeditions* (Austin: University of Texas Press, 1997).

[21] Guy would eventually marry Jack's daughter Laura in the late 1850s after Emily's death. Moses Austin Bryan to his Wife, August 31, 1844, box 2N252, Paul G. Bell Papers; Emily Perry to Stephen S. Perry, April 27, 1845, Perry Papers, vol. A-12.

[22] Stephen S. Perry Diary, 1843, Perry Papers, vol. A-11; Eliza Perry to Stephen S. Perry, April 16, 1844, Perry Papers, vol. A-11; Stephen S. Perry to James F. Perry, March 11, 1845, Perry Papers, vol. A-1; Guy M. Bryan to Stephen S. Perry, December 27, 1844, Perry Papers, vol. A-11.

[23] Lawrence L. Brown, *The Episcopal Church in Texas, 1838–1874* (Austin, TX: Church Historical Society, 1963), 7–11; Eliza Perry to Stephen S. Perry, April 16, 1844, Perry Papers, vol. A-11; Ibid.; Murphy DuBose, "Early Days of the Protestant Episcopal Church in Texas," *Southwestern Historical Quarterly* 34 (April 1931): 293–316. The quotation comes from Williams, *Diary and Letters of Rutherford B. Hayes:* 1:250. Ministers of various denominations held church services at the Gulf Prairie Church from the 1830s until after the Civil War. Emily Perry, as noted, invited Episcopal priests, while James Perry favored Presbyterian ministers. Another local planter, James Caldwell, was a devout Methodist and encouraged pastors from that denomination to also hold services there. In fact, for the most part, circuit-riding Methodist preachers appeared at Gulf Prairie in greatest numbers during Emily's lifetime. The Gulf Prairie Church organized as a Presbyterian congregation in 1877, which it has remained to the present day.

[24] The quotation is from Catherine Clinton, *Plantation Mistress,* 177. For the reminiscences of Emily's granddaughter, see Perry, "Family Notes by Request"; Receipt of Hyde and Goodrich, March 20, 1849, in the amount of $647, Perry Papers, vol. A-15; Jones, *Peach Point Plantation,* 115; George L. Hammeken to Emily Perry, September 22, 1848, Perry Papers, vol. A-11; George L. Hammeken to Emily Perry, December 18, 1849, S. S. Perry Papers.

[25] For a biography of Hayes, see Ari A. Hoogenboom, *Rutherford B. Hayes: Warrior and President* (Lawrence: University of Kansas Press, 1995).

[26] All quotations in this and the following paragraphs related to Hayes' observations come from Williams, *The Diary and Letters of Rutherford B. Hayes,* 246–58.

[27] Henry Austin to James Perry, March 22, 1850, Perry Papers, vol. A-11. Mrs. Holley had long since given up her project of writing a biography of Stephen F. Austin.

She died on August 2, 1846. Henry Austin to James Perry, April 7, 1850, Perry Papers, vol. A-11.

28 Hugh J. McLeod to James F. Perry, April 13, 1851, Perry Papers, vol. A-17; Hugh J. McLeod to Mrs. Perry, April 19, 1851, Perry Papers, vol. A-17.

29 Henry Austin to My Dear Father, March 22, 1850, Perry Papers, vol. A-17; "Last Will and Testament of Emily Austin Perry," Emily Margaret Austin File; James F. Perry to Emily Perry, May 25, 1851, Perry Papers, vol. A-18. Emily's will was more typical of a man's last will and testament than one probated for a southern plantation mistress, as these women often did not have formal wills of their own. For a discussion of planters' wills, see Joan E. Cashin, "According to His Wish and Desire: Female Kin and Female Slaves in Planter Wills," in *Women of the American South: A Multicultural Reader,* ed. Christie Anne Farnham (New York: New York University Press, 1997), 90–119.

30 Emily Perry to James F. Perry, May 11, 1851, Perry Papers, vol. A-18; Emily Perry to James F. Perry, May 5, 1851, Perry Papers, vol. A-18; Eliza Perry to James F. Perry, May 30, 1851, Perry Papers, vol. A-18; Richard Harrison Shyrock, "Trends in American Medical Research During the Nineteenth Century," *Proceedings of the American Philosophical Society* 91, no. 1 (February 1947): 58–63; Oliver Wendell Holmes, "The Contagiousness of Puerperal Fever" (1843; repr., Baltimore: Williams and Wilkin, 1936), 195–268.

31 Eliza Perry to James F. Perry, May 30, 1851, Perry Papers, vol. A-18.

32 As one study notes, "Chronic obstructive pulmonary disease (COPD) is characterized by the progressive development of airflow limitation that is not fully reversible." It presents today predominantly in individuals who have been heavy smokers of tobacco products. In modern times, largely because of present-day controls on environmental pollution, industrial and atmospheric etiologies related to provocative agents in the environment are secondary and less observed as causes of COPD. Peter J. Barnes, "Chronic Obstructive Pulmonary Disease," *New England Journal of Medicine* 343 (July 2000): 269–80; Paul Kelleher, Karin Pacheco, and Lee S. Newman, "Inorganic Dust Pneumonias: The Metal-Related Parenchymal Disorders," *Environmental Health Perspectives Supplements* 108, no. 4 (August 2000): S686; Robert Walter, Daniel J. Gottlieb, and George T. O'Conner, "Environmental and Genetic Risk Factors and Gene-Environment Factors in the Pathogenesis of Chronic Obstructive Pulmonary Disease," *Environmental Health Perspectives Supplements* 108 (4): S733–S742.

33 Modern medical diagnosis and treatments available in the United States and throughout the world today seldom permit patients presenting with COPD to experience anything approaching the full range of symptoms that are theoretically possible if the syndrome remains undiagnosed and unmanaged by conventional medical therapies. Michael Fleischer et al., "Environmental Impact of Cadmium:

A Review by the Panel on Hazardous Trace Substances," *Environmental Health Perspectives* 7 (May 1974): 253–323; Kaye H. Kilburn, "Particles Causing Lung Disease," *Environmental Health Perspectives* 55 (April 1984): 97–109; Burkow, "Chronic Obstructive Pulmonary Disease," *Merck Manual,* 628–35; Agency for Toxic Substances and Disease Registry, "A Toxicology Curriculum for Communities Trainer's Manual," Center for Disease Control and Prevention, Department of Health and Human Services, http://www.astdr.cdc,gov/toxmanual/modules/4/lecturenotes.html (accessed January 25, 2008). Two physicians, Watson Arnold, MD/PhD, and Anne LeMaistre, MD, reviewed the foregoing discussion, in which I suggest that a possible aerosol ingestion of heavy metal traces by the Moses Austin family while living at Austinville and Potosi was a cause of lifelong medical conditions, thereby producing in these four individuals consistent symptoms from the 1810s to their respective deaths. Both physicians concurred that heavy metal poisoning from substances other than lead, such as cadmium, could have been a realistic possibility, although each physician stressed that the historical evidence does not provide enough information to permit an informed diagnosis. Dr. Arnold wondered if tuberculosis might also have been involved, while Dr. LeMaistre suggested that congestive heart failure (which itself might result from chronic cadmium poisoning) may have played a role in the death of Moses Austin. Watson Arnold, MD/PhD, to the author, January 8, 2008, letter in possession of the author; and Anne LeMaistre, MD, to the author, January 25, 2008, letter in possession of the author.

[34] Eliza Perry to James F. Perry, July 18, 1851, Perry Papers, vol. A-18.

Epilogue

[1] "Last Will and Testament of Emily Austin Perry," Emily Margaret Austin File.

[2] The last will and testament indicates that the monetary value of Emily's estate was approximately $450,000 in 1851 United States dollars. Although the translation of dollar amounts from earlier periods of history to the present is very inexact by necessity, a rough conversion of the 1851 dollar value of Emily's estate to 2008 values (adjusted for inflation) places it at approximately twelve million dollars in terms of purchasing power based on the Consumer Price Index. See Samuel H. Williamson, "Five Ways to Compute the Relative Value of a U.S. Dollar Amount, 1790–2005," http://measuringworth.com/ (accessed December 1, 2006); "A list of William J. Bryan Out of the Estate of Emily M. Perry, Deceased and Final Settlement and Division of Said Estate," box 2N2534, Perry Papers.

BIBLIOGRAPHY

I. Primary Source

A. Manuscript Collections

A Note on the Austin Family Papers

Much of this volume is based on several archival collections that today comprise the Austin family papers generated during the lifetimes of Moses Austin, Stephen F. Austin, and Emily Austin. These materials, currently divided into several different collections, are mostly located at the Center for American History of the University of Texas at Austin. Of these, the collection called the Moses and Stephen F. Austin Papers is the best known. This particular collection has been in the possession of the University of Texas at Austin for over one hundred years and has formed the documentary foundation for a considerable number of historical studies dealing with the early history of Anglo-American Texas. Eugene C. Barker edited a three-volume published collection of the Moses and Stephen F. Austin Papers in the era of World War I, while he also used these papers extensively in writing his classic biography of Stephen F. Austin. Gregg Cantrell's biography of Stephen F. Austin contains a comprehensive historical discussion about the history and provenance of the Moses and Stephen F. Austin Papers, and Cantrell delineates how several generations of historians have used these materials in their research. This biography of Emily Austin has also used the Moses and Stephen F. Austin Papers extensively, especially the volumes edited by Barker. Unlike many previous studies, my interests have focused mostly on the personal family information to the exclusion of political and institutionally oriented concerns. In addition, Emily's biography has made extensive use of the James Franklin and Stephen Samuel Perry Papers, also located at the Center for American History. This collection constitutes the manuscripts and documents saved by Emily and James F. Perry during their years of marriage, along with additional items from the lifetimes of their adult children, especially Stephen Samuel Perry and his descendants. The Perry Papers have not heretofore been systematically mined by historians to the same extent as the Moses and Stephen F. Austin Papers. This biography is the first to survey all of them in an effort to provide a detailed picture of Emily's life. It is therefore useful to comment on the historical provenance of the Perry Papers and how this collection relates to the Moses and Stephen F. Austin Papers.

During her own lifetime, Emily took great care to conserve family papers that related to her father, her brother, and her husbands. It was her desire that someone would eventually write a biography of Stephen F. Austin from these materials. For that reason, she and James Perry maintained a constantly growing collection of family papers at the Peach Point Plantation starting in the 1830s. Both Mirabeau B. Lamar and Mary Austin Holley had access to some of these papers during the time when they respectively contemplated writing a biography of Stephen F. Austin. They reported that the materials were then stored in a large trunk in Emily's home, probably in the bedroom used by Stephen F. Austin during his lifetime. These family papers remained at Peach Point until the years after the Civil War. By that time, they had come to include not only the papers of Moses and Stephen F. Austin, but also the papers relating to James Bryan, James F. Perry, Emily, and the adult children. At some point prior to the 1890s, the Bryan and Perry descendants divided the papers among themselves. This probably occurred after Stephen S. Perry's death in 1874. The division of these papers was most likely done at the motivation of Guy M. Bryan, who was historically minded and actively sought to advance the memory of his famous uncle, Stephen. For that reason, all of the papers dealing with Moses and Stephen F. Austin were separated from the corpus of Perry family correspondence. For the most part, this was a chronological division. Any materials from the lifetime of Moses or Stephen became part of the documents that went to Guy M. Bryan.

Generally, Guy M. Bryan took almost all of the papers from Peach Point dated prior to 1836, except for those papers that distinctly and explicitly pertained to James Bryan, James F. Perry, or Emily after her marriage to Perry. As well, each of the three Bryan brothers apparently, at that time, took from the papers various items that related to them individually, especially to their adult years after the early 1840s. Guy M. Bryan referred to the main corpus of historical papers that he acquired as the Moses and Stephen F. Austin Papers. He kept these items at his residence for a number of years. By the 1890s, they had found their way to Austin, Texas, where Bryan housed them in a storage room at the State Capitol building. After several false starts during which Bryan attempted to find a historian to write the desired biography of Stephen F. Austin, these papers were eventually donated to the archives of the University of Texas, where they have remained ever since.

Whatever materials the three Bryan brothers did not take remained at Peach Point with the descendants of their half brother Stephen Samuel Perry. These are the papers that today comprise the James F. and Stephen S. Perry Papers, and unlike the Moses and Stephen F. Austin Papers, they have been available for scholarly use for a much shorter period of time, having been open for unrestricted usage since the 1970s. Eugene C. Barker wanted the family to donate these papers to the University of Texas as well. He visited with various family members during the 1920s in an effort to secure this donation, but his efforts proved unsuccessful. The Perry family did permit Barker to consult these papers under their personal supervision and thereafter occasionally permitted some of his graduate students to do the same on special application. For example, both Lela Ethel McKinley and Abigail Curlee used the papers as part of their graduate student research in the 1930s. It was at this point that Miss Winnie Allen entered the picture. A native of Henrietta, Texas, Miss Allen graduated from the University of Texas with an undergraduate history degree in 1920. Five years later, she earned an MA and joined the staff of the university as an assistant archivist. In 1936, upon the death of Mattie Austin Hatcher, Miss Allen became the university's chief archivist, a position she would hold for the next thirty-five years. She spent her career aggressively expanding the holdings of the university archives.

Most likely on the advice of Eugene C. Barker, Miss Allen made acquisition of the Perry Papers an important goal upon becoming chief archivist. During the late 1930s, she traveled several times to Houston, Angleton, Freeport, and Peach Point Plantation, where she visited with various members of the Perry and Bryan families, winning their confidence and trust. Although the historical record contains only a few hints regarding the family's apparent reluctance to donate the Perry Papers, it can be surmised today that they had several reasons for their hesitation. Several family members were apparently embarrassed by the references to slavery in the papers, while others worried that unscrupulous individuals might use information from the papers in bringing ill-served mineral right litigation, which was then a general occurrence all across the Texas legal landscape. Additionally, some members of the Perry family worried about the frankly personal and very human portrayal of Emily and the family in the many personal letters of the collection, especially regarding Eliza Perry's illness and the frustrations expressed about her medical condition. The 1930s and 1940s were an era when political history reigned supreme, and many educated people in those years did not consider the sort of familial matters reflected in the papers to be valid subject matter for historical interest.

Nonetheless, Miss Allen maintained her persistent efforts to secure the papers for the University of Texas, since she realized that they would serve as an important archival complement to the Moses and Stephen F. Austin Papers. By 1939, she had won an ally in the person of S. S. Perry, who was then the proprietor of Peach Point and part owner of the papers. In that year, he promised Miss Allen that he would work to secure permission for the donation from other members of his family. Miss Allen continued to visit with the family, and they eventually came to an agreement in 1940. The University of Texas would take possession of the papers in return for Miss Allen's staff preparing typescripts of all the materials. One copy of the typescripts would remain in the archives along with the original documents, while four complete copies of the transcripts would be bound into volumes and furnished to various members of the Bryan and Perry families. Mr. J. P. Bryan Sr., a family member who was then an attorney in Brazoria County, would make a survey of the papers on behalf of the Perrys and approve each item for donation to the university. Mr. Bryan decided to "go over the old papers and take out such materials and personal things that would not be of use to the university." He also permitted family members to take souvenir copies of letters, most likely as autograph collections bearing the signatures of their forebears. Recently, in 2005, a small and previously unknown group of several dozen items (most likely culled by a family member in the early 1940s as one of the autograph collections) was donated to the Austin College Archives by Ann Ross, a descendant of the first Stephen S. Perry.

In April of 1942, Mr. Bryan had completed this organizing process, and Miss Allen drove to Angleton, where she took delivery of the main body of the papers. She accessioned them in the university archives as the James Franklin and Stephen Samuel Papers. She apparently separated out from these materials the papers pertaining to James

Bryan's business interests in Missouri, which today exist at the Center for American History as the James Bryan Papers. The Perry family retained legal ownership of all the papers they had sent to Austin with Miss Allen until 1951, when they made a formal donation of title to the University of Texas. However, under the terms of this donation, the Perry Papers had significant restrictions on them that limited their usage. Any historian who wished to consult them had to first secure advance permission of attorney J. P. Bryan Sr., who represented the interests of his Perry relations. To his credit, Mr. Bryan had a deep understanding of Texas history, which included his editing of Mary Austin Holley's diary and his serving as president of the Texas State Historical Association. He therefore understood the nature of historical research and approved applications from a number of historians who wished to consult the collection. Finally, at Mr. Bryan's urging, the Perry family removed all restrictions from the papers in 1970, and thereafter the collection has been freely consulted by any person wishing to see it. The visibility of this collection greatly expanded a decade later when it became part of a massive microfilm project edited by historian Kenneth M. Stampp. The Perry Papers now comprise part of the *Records of Ante-Bellum Plantations from the Revolution through the Civil War*, Series G, published in microform by University Publications of America. As such, they may be consulted in any library or archive that has purchased a copy, including the Austin College Library in Sherman, Texas. The microfilm edition of the James F. and Stephen S. Perry Papers contains microform images of both the original documents and the typescripts prepared by Miss Allen's staff at the University of Texas in the 1940s and early 1950s. The Lois Brock Adriance Library at the Brazoria County Historical Museum also has a complete set of the University of Texas typescripts bound into volumes. A docent member of the staff at that facility prepared an extensive index of the typescripts, and this valuable finding aid is available to researchers who consult the transcribed Perry Papers at that location in Angleton, Texas.

The research conducted for this volume has used and compared all versions: the originals at the Center for American History, the microfilm edition, and the bound volumes of typescripts. This presents a problem for citation, since each version employs a different system of organization. Every document of the Perry Papers thus has the potential to be cited in three different ways, depending upon which version is being noted. Since each of the three versions contain the same bound typescripts as the only organizational commonality, the method of citation employed in the footnotes of this study uses the number of the bound volume. Additionally, the onomastic and topical index located at the Brazoria County Historical Museum is keyed only to the bound volumes, thereby making that method of citation potentially more useful to researchers. Any researcher wishing to extrapolate bound transcript volumes with the box numbers of the originals at the University of Texas or the microfilm roll numbers can do so by comparing the findings aids for the three versions of the Perry Papers.

MANUSCRIPT COLLECTIONS CONSULTED

Austin, Emily Margaret, File. Brazoria County Historical Museum, Angleton, TX.

Austin-Learning Letters. Center for American History, University of Texas at Austin.

Austin, Moses and Stephen F., Papers, 1676, 1765–1889. Center for American History, University of Texas at Austin.

Bell, Paul G., Papers, 1912, 1937–2002. Center for American History, University of Texas at Austin.

Bryan, Guy M., Papers, 1821–1901. Center for American History, University of Texas at Austin.

Bryan, James, Papers, 1820–1870. Center for American History, University of Texas at Austin.

Bryan, James, Papers. Texas State Library. Austin.

Bryan, Moses Austin, Papers, 1817–1895. Center for American History, University of Texas at Austin.

Bryan v. Kennett. 113 U.S. 197, 1885. United States Supreme Court Reports.

Bryan, William J., Day Book, Durazno. Brazoria County Historical Museum, Angleton, TX.

Buehler, H. A. "The Wythe Lead Mines." 1917. Typescript. Western Historical Manuscript Collection. University of Missouri at Columbia.

Holley, Mary Austin, Papers, 1784–1846. Center for American History, University of Texas at Austin.

Morrison, William, Ledger. Chester Public Library, Chester, IL.

Perry Family File 75. Brazoria County Historical Museum, Angleton, TX.

Perry, Hally Bryan. "Family Notes by Request." Typescript. Texas State Library, Austin.

Perry, James F. and Stephen S., Papers, 1785–1942. Center for American History, University of Texas at Austin.

Perry, James F. and Stephen S., Papers. Typescript. Brazoria County Historical Museum, Angleton, TX.

Perry, S. S., Family Papers. Abell Library, Austin College, Sherman, TX.

Reminiscences of Moses Austin Bryan. Abell Library, Austin College, Sherman, TX.

Richeson, Paul R. "The Perrys of Potosi." Typescript. Western Historical Manuscript Collection. Missouri University of Science and Technology. Also located in the Mary and John W. Beretta Texana Collection. Coates Library, Trinity University.

San Luis File. Brazoria County Historical Museum, Angleton, TX.

Stampp, Kenneth M., ed. *Records of Ante-Bellum Southern Plantations from the Revolution through the Civil War.* Series G. *Selections from the Barker Texas*

History Center, University of Texas at Austin. Part 1. Frederick, MD: University
    Publications of America, 1987.
Stevenson, William, Autobiography. Typescript. Bridwell Library, Southern Methodist
    University, Dallas, TX.
St. Francis County Circuit Court Records. Farmington, Missouri.
Ste. Genevieve County Clerk of Courts Records. Ste. Genevieve, Missouri.
Southwest Regional Archives. Washington, Arkansas.
Tait, Charles William, Papers. 1844–1865. Center for American History, University of
    Texas at Austin.
Washington County Circuit Court Records. Potosi, Missouri.
Washington County Land Patents, M000010–260. General Land Office Records.
    Bureau of Land Management, Missouri.
William Robinson v. James Bryan. 1820. Territorial Briefs and Records. William R.
    Bowen School of Law, University of Arkansas at Little Rock.

B. Newspapers

Houston Telegraph and Texas Register, 1837–1855. Center for American History,
    University of Texas at Austin.
Fayette (MO) Intelligencer, 1819–1835. State Historical Society of Missouri, Columbia.
St. Louis Missouri Gazette, 1808–1822. State Historical Society of Missouri, Columbia.
St. Louis Missouri Republican, 1822–1828. State Historical Society of Missouri,
    Columbia.

C. Published Documents

Almonte, Juan N. "Statistical Report on Texas, 1835." Translated by Carlos E.
    Castaneda. *Southwestern Historical Quarterly* 28 (1925): 177–222.
———. *"Almonte's Texas: Juan N. Almonte's 1834 Inspection, Secret Report, and Role in
    the 1836 Campaign.* Edited by Jack Jackson. Translated by John Wheat.
    Austin: Texas State Historical Association, 2003.
Barker, Eugene C., ed. *The Austin Papers.* Vol. 1 and 2. Washington DC: American
    Historical Association, 1919–22. Vol. 3. Austin: University of Texas, 1927.
Bryan, J. P., ed. *Mary Austin Holley: The Texas Diary, 1835–1838.* Austin: University of
    Texas Press, 1965.
Garrison, George P., ed. "A Memorandum of M. Austin's Journey from the Lead Mines
    in the County of Wythe in the State of Virginia to the Lead Mines in the
    Province of Louisiana West of the Mississippi, 1796–1797." *American
    Historical Review* 5, no. 3 (April 1900): 518–23.

Giddings, Salmon. *The Gospel, the power of God unto salvation a sermon preached at the installation of the Rev. Thomas Donnell to the pastoral office in Concord Church, and congregation of Belleview, April 25th, 1818.* St. Louis, MO: Henry and Maury, 1818.

Harris, Dilue Rose. "The Reminiscences of Mrs. Dilue Harris." *Quarterly of the Texas State Historical Association* 4 (October 1900): 85–127; 4 (January 1901): 155–89; 7 (January 1904): 214–22.

Hatcher, Mattie Austin. *Letters of an Early American Traveler: Mary Austin Holley, Her Life and Her Works, 1784–1846.* Dallas, TX: Southwest Press, 1933.

Hogan, William R., comp. "Henry Austin." *Southwestern Historical Quarterly* 37, no. 3 (January 1934): 185–214.

Holmes, Oliver Wendell. "The Contagiousness of Puerperal Fever." 1843. Reprint, Baltimore: Williams and Wilkin, 1936.

Howe, Henry. *Historical Collections of Ohio.* Vol. 1. 1888. Reprint, Cincinnati, OH: C. H. Krehbeil and Company, 1902.

Hunter, Robert Hancock. *Narrative of Robert Hancock Hunter.* 2nd ed. Austin, TX: Cook Printing, 1936.

Jefferson, Thomas. *Notes on the State of Virginia, 1746–1786.* Richmond, VA: J. L. Hill, 1903.

Marshall, Thomas Maitland. *The Life and Papers of Frederick Bates.* 2 vols. St. Louis: Missouri Historical Society, 1926.

Piece, Gerald S., ed. "Some Early Letters of Moses Austin Bryan." *Southwestern Historical Quarterly* 70 (January 1967): 461–71.

Reichstein, Andreas, ed. "The Austin-Learning Correspondence, 1828–1836." *Southwestern Historical Quarterly* 88 (1985): 247–82.

Schoolcraft, Henry R. *Journal of a Tour into the Interior of Missouri and Arkansaw.* London: Sir Richard Phillips, 1821.

Tomerlin, Jacqueline Beretta, comp. *Fugitive Letters, 1829–1836: Stephen F. Austin to David G. Burnet.* San Antonio, TX: Trinity University Press, 1981.

Wallis, Mrs. Jonnie, and Laurance L. Hill, eds. *Sixty Years on the Brazos: The Life and Letters of Dr. John Washington Lockhart, 1824–1900.* 1930. Reprint, New York: Argonaut Press, 1966.

Wetmore, Alphonso. *Gazetteer of Missouri.* St. Louis, MO: C. Keemle, 1837.

Williams, Charles Richard, ed. *Diary and Letters of Rutherford B. Hayes, Nineteenth President of the United States.* 5 vols. Columbus: Ohio State Archeological and Historical Society, 1922–1926.

Winkler, E. W., ed. "The Bryan-Hayes Correspondence." *Southwestern Historical Quarterly* 25, no. 2 (October 1921): 98–120; 25, no. 3 (January 1922): 121–36; 25, no. 4 (April 1922): 274–99.

Wooten, Dudley G., ed. *A Comprehensive History of Texas, 1685–1897.* 2 vols. Dallas, TX: W. G. Scarff, 1898.

II.   SECONDARY SOURCES

A. BOOKS

Ackerkenecht, Erwin H. *Malaria in the Upper Mississippi Valley, 1760–1900.* Baltimore: Johns Hopkins University Press, 1945.

Anzilotti, Cara. *In the Affairs of the World: Women, Patriarchy, and Power in Colonial South Carolina.* Westport, CT: Greenwood Press, 2002.

Aron, Stephen. *American Confluence: The Missouri Frontier from Borderland to Border State.* Bloomington: University of Indiana Press, 2006.

Austin, Richard R. *Austins to Wisconsin.* Wilmington, DE: William N. Cann, 1964.

Bakken, Gordon. *Law in the Western United States.* Norman: University of Oklahoma Press, 2000.

———. *Rocky Mountain Constitution Making, 1850–1912.* Westport, CT: Greenwood Press, 1987.

Bardaglio, Peter W. *Reconstructing the Household: Families, Sex, and the Law in the Nineteenth-Century South.* Chapel Hill: University of North Carolina Press, 1995.

Barker-Benfield, G. J. *The Horrors of the Half-Known Life: Male Attitudes Toward Women and Sexuality in Nineteenth-Century America.* New York: W.W. Norton, 1976.

Barker, Eugene C. *The Life of Stephen F. Austin, Founder of Texas, 1793–1836: A Chapter in the Westward Movement of the Anglo-American People.* Revised edition. 1925. Reprint, Austin: University of Texas Press, 1949.

Bartlett, Virginia K. *Keeping House: Women's Lives in Pennsylvania, 1790–1850.* Pittsburg, PA: University of Pittsburg Press, 1994.

Boatwright, Eleanor Miot. *Status of Women in Georgia, 1783–1860.* Brooklyn, NY: Carlson Publishing, 1994.

Boswell, Angela. *Her Act and Deed: Women's Lives in a Rural Southern County, 1837–1873.* College Station: Texas A&M University Press, 2001.

Boydston, Jeanne. *Home and Work: Housework, Wages, and the Ideology of Labor in the Early Republic.* New York: Oxford University Press, 1990.

Boydston, Jeanne, Mary Kelley, and Anne Margolis. *The Limits of Sisterhood: The Beecher Sisters on Women's Rights and Woman's Sphere.* Chapel Hill: University of North Carolina Press, 1988.

Bredbenner, Candice Lewis. *A Nationality of Her Own: Women, Marriage, and the Law of Citizenship*. Berkeley: University of California Press, 1998.

Breeden, James O., ed. *Advice Among Masters: The Ideal in Slave Management in the Old South*. Westport, CT: Greenwood Press, 1980.

Brown, Kathleen M. *Good Wives, Nasty Wenches, and Anxious Patriarchs: Gender, Race, and Power in Colonial Virginia*. Chapel Hill: University of North Carolina Press, 1996.

Brown, Lawrence L. *The Episcopal Church in Texas, 1838–1874*. Austin, TX: Church Historical Society, 1963.

Burkow, Robert, ed. *The Merck Manual of Diagnosis and Therapy*, 14th ed. Rahway, NJ: Merck Company, 1982.

Burton, Orville Vernon. *In My Father's House Are Many Mansions: Family and Community in Edgefield, South Carolina*. 1942. Reprint, New York: De Capo Press, 1970.

Bynum, Victoria E. *Unruly Women: The Politics of Social and Sexual Control in the Old South*. Chapel Hill: University of North Carolina Press, 1992.

Campbell, Randolph B. *An Empire for Slavery: The Peculiar Institution in Texas, 1821–1865*. Baton Rouge: Louisiana State University Press, 1989.

————. *Gone to Texas: A History of the Lone Star State*. New York: Oxford University Press, 2003.

Cantrell, Gregg. *Stephen F. Austin: Empresario of Texas*. New Haven, CT: Yale University Press, 1999.

Carlin, Jim, and Liz Austin Carlin. *Some Descendants of Richard Austin of Charlestown, Massachusetts, 1638*. Green River, WY: Gateway Press for the Austin Families Association of America, 1998.

Cashin, Joan E. *A Family Venture: Men and Women on the Southern Frontier*. New York: Oxford University Press, 1991.

Caughfield, Adrienne. *True Women and Westward Expansion*. College Station: Texas A&M University Press, 2005.

Censer, Jane Turner. *North Carolina Planters and Their Children, 1800–1860*. Baton Rouge: Louisiana State University Press, 1984.

Chambers-Schiller, Lee Virginia. *Liberty, A Better Husband: Single Women in America, the Generations of 1780–1840*. New Haven, CT: Yale University Press, 1984.

Christian, William A. *Richmond: Her Past and Present*. 1911. Reprint, Spartanburg, SC: Reprint Company, 1972.

Clark, Clifford Edward, Jr. *The American Family Home, 1800–1960*. Chapel Hill: University of North Carolina Press, 1986.

Clinton, Catherine. *The Plantation Mistress: Woman's World in the Old South*. New York: Pantheon Books, 1982.

———. *Tara Revisited: Women, War, and the Plantation Legend.* New York: Abbeville Press, 1995.

Clinton, Catherine, and Michele Gillespie, eds. *The Devil's Lane: Sex and Race in the Early South.* New York: Oxford University Press, 1998.

Clinton, Catherine, and Nina Silber, eds. *Divided Houses: Gender and the Civil War.* New York: Oxford University Press, 1992.

Clugston, Katherine, and Richard Stevenson. *Wilderness Road (Virginia).* New York: Blue Ribbon Books, 1937.

Collins, Henry Brown, ed. *Valentine's Manual of Old New York.* New York: Valentine Publishing, 1919.

Cott, Nancy F. *The Bonds of Womanhood: "Woman's Sphere" in New England, 1790–1835.* New Haven, CT: Yale University Press, 1978.

———. *Public Vows: A History of Marriage and the Nation.* Cambridge, MA: Harvard University Press, 2000.

Crawford, Anne Fears, and Crystal Sasse Ragsdale. *Women in Texas History: Their Lives, Their Experiences, Their Accomplishments.* Burnett, TX: Eakin Press, 1982.

Creighton, James A. *A Narrative History of Brazoria County.* Waco, TX: Texian Press, 1975.

Crocket, George Louis. *Two Centuries in East Texas: A History of San Augustine County and Surrounding Territory from 1685.* 1932. A facsimile reproduction for the Christ Episcopal Church, San Augustine. Austin, TX: Hart Graphics, 1982.

Cummins, Light Townsend. *Austin College: A Sesquicentennial History.* Austin, TX: Eakin Press, 1999.

Davidson, Cathy N., and Jessamyn Hatchers, eds. *No More Separate Spheres!: A Next Wave American Studies Reader.* Durham, NC: Duke University Press, 2002.

Degler, Carl N. *At Odds: Women and the Family in America from the Revolution to the Present.* New York: Oxford University Press, 1980.

———. *Place Over Time: The Continuity of Southern Distinctiveness.* Baton Rouge: Louisiana State University Press, 1977.

Douglas, Ann. *The Feminization of American Culture.* New York: Alfred A. Knopf, 1977.

Douglas, Robert Sidney. *History of Southeast Missouri: An Account of its Historical Progress, Its People, and Its Principal Interests.* 2 Vols. Chicago: Lewis Publishing, 1912.

Doyle, Mary Ellen. *Pioneer Spirit: Catherine Spalding, Sister of Charity of Nazareth.* Lexington: University of Kentucky Press, 2006.

Duffy, John. *The Rudolph Matas History of Medicine in Louisiana.* 2 vols. Baton Rouge: Louisiana State University Press, 1962.

Dyer, John P. *Tulane: The Biography of a University, 1834–1965.* New York: Harper and Row, 1965.

Eaton, Clement. *A History of the Old South: The Emergence of a Reluctant Nation.* 3rd ed. 1975. Reprint, Prospect Heights, IL: Waveland Press, 1987.

Edwards, Laura F. *Scarlett Doesn't Live Here Anymore: Southern Women in the Civil War Era.* Champaign: University of Illinois Press, 2000.

Ekberg, Carl J. *Louis Bolduc: His Family and His House.* Tucson, AZ: Patrice Press, 2002.

———. *Colonial Ste. Genevieve.* Tucson, AZ: Patrice Press, 1996.

———. *French Roots in the Illinois Country: The Mississippi Frontier in Colonial Times.* Champaign: University of Illinois Press, 1998.

Epstein, Barbara Leslie. *The Politics of Domesticity: Women, Evangelism, and Temperance in Nineteenth-Century America.* Middletown, CT: Wesleyan University Press, 1981.

Exley, Jo Ella Powell, ed. *Texas Tears and Texas Sunshine: Voices of Frontier Women.* College Station: Texas A&M University Press, 1985.

Farnham, Christie Anne. *The Education of the Southern Belle: Higher Education and Student Socialization in the Antebellum South.* New York: New York University Press, 1994.

Faust, Drew Gilpin. *A Sacred Circle: The Dilemma of the Intellectual in the Old South, 1840–1860.* Baltimore: Johns Hopkins University Press, 1977.

———. *Mothers of Invention: Women of the Slaveholding South in the American Civil War.* Chapel Hill: University of North Carolina Press, 1996.

Fletcher, John Gould. *Arkansas.* Chapel Hill: University of North Carolina Press, 1947.

Foley, William E. *The Genesis of Missouri: From Wilderness Outpost to Statehood.* Columbia: University of Missouri Press, 1989.

Fox-Genovese, Elizabeth. *Within the Plantation Household: Black and White Women of the Old South.* Chapel Hill: University of North Carolina Press, 1988.

Friedman, Jean E. *The Enclosed Garden: Women and Community in the Evangelical South, 1830–1900.* Chapel Hill: University of North Carolina Press, 1985.

Friend, Craig Thompson, and Lorri Glover, eds. *Southern Manhood: Perspectives on Masculinity in the Old South.* Athens: University of Georgia Press, 2004.

Gardner, James Alexander. *Lead King: Moses Austin.* St. Louis, MO: Sunrise Publishing, 1980.

Genovese, Eugene D. *Roll, Jordan, Roll: The World the Slaves Made.* New York: Pantheon Books, 1976.

Ginsberg, Lori. *Women and the Work of Benevolence: Morality, Politics, and Class in the Nineteenth-Century United Sates.* New Haven, CT: Yale University Press, 1990.

Goodspeed's History of Franklin, Jefferson, Washington, Crawford, & Gasconade Counties, Missouri. Chicago: Goodspeed Publishing Company, 1888.

Gracy, David B., II. *Moses Austin: His Life.* San Antonio, TX: Trinity University Press, 1987.

Gray, Lewis Cecil. *A History of Agriculture in the Southern United States to 1860.* 2 vols.

Washington, DC: Carnegie Institution, 1933.

Greenberg, Kenneth. *Masters and Statesmen: The Political Culture of American Slavery.* Baltimore: Johns Hopkins University Press, 1985.

Griswold, Robert L. *Fatherhood in America: A History.* New York: Basic Books, 1993.

Gutman, Herbert. *The Black Family in Slavery and Freedom, 1750–1925.* New York: Pantheon Books, 1976.

Gwin, Minrose C. *Black and White Women of the Old South: The Peculiar Sisterhood in American Literature.* Knoxville: University of Tennessee Press, 1985.

Halttunen, Karen. *Confidence Men and Painted Women: A Study of Middle-Class Culture in America, 1830–1870.* New Haven, CT: Yale University Press, 1982.

Hardin, Stephen L. *Texian Iliad: A Military History of the Texas Revolution, 1835–1836.* Austin: University of Texas Press, 1994.

Hartog, Hendrik. *Man and Wife in America: A History.* Cambridge, MA: Harvard University Press, 2000.

Haynes, Sam W. *Soldiers of Misfortune: The Somervell and Mier Expeditions.* Austin: University of Texas Press, 1997.

Henson, Margaret S. *Samuel May Williams: Early Texas Entrepreneur.* College Station: Texas A&M University Press, 1976.

Hoff, Joan. *Law, Gender, and Injustice: A Legal history of U.S. Women.* New York: New York University Press, 1991.

Hogan, William Ransom. *The Texas Republic: A Social and Economic History.* Norman: University of Oklahoma Press, 1946.

Hoogenboom, Ari A. *Rutherford B. Hayes: Warrior and President.* Lawrence: University of Kansas Press, 1995.

Horowitz, Helen Lefkowitz. *Campus Life: Undergraduate Cultures from the End of the Eighteenth-Century to the Present.* New York: Knopf, 1987.

Hudson, Larry E. *To Have and to Hold: Slave Work and Family Life in Antebellum South Carolina.* Athens: University of Georgia Press, 1997.

Isenberg, Nancy. *Sex and Citizenship in Antebellum America.* Chapel Hill: University of North Carolina Press, 1998.

Jabour, Anya. *Marriage in the Early Republic: Elizabeth and William Wirt and the Companionate Ideal.* Baltimore: Johns Hopkins University Press, 1998.

———. *Scarlett's Sisters: Young Women in the Old South.* Chapel Hill: University of North Carolina Press, 2007.

Jeffrey, Julie Roy. *Frontier Women: The Trans-Mississippi West, 1840–1880.* New York: Hill and Wang, 1979.

Jensen, Joan M. *Loosening the Bonds: Mid-Atlantic Farm Women, 1750–1850.* New Haven, CT: Yale University Press, 1986.

Jones, Anne Goodwyn, and Susan Van D'Elden Donaldson. *Haunted Bodies: Gender and Southern Tests.* Charlottesville: University of Virginia Press, 1997.

Jones, Jacqueline. *Labor of Love, Labor of Sorrow: Black Women, Work, and the Family from Slavery to the Present.* New York: Basic Books, 1985.

Jones, Marie Beth. *Peach Point Plantation: The First 150 Years.* Waco, TX: Texian Press, 1982.

Kegley, Mary B. *Wythe County, Virginia: A Bicentennial History.* Wytheville, VA: Wythe County Board of Supervisors, 1981.

Kelley, Mary. *Private Woman, Public Stage: Literary Domesticity in Nineteenth-Century America.* New York: Oxford University Press, 1984.

Kerber, Linda K. *No Constitution Right to be Ladies: Women and the Obligations of Citizenship.* New York: Hill and Wang, 1998.

———. *Women of the Republic: Intellect and Ideology in Revolutionary America.* Chapel Hill: University of North Carolina Press for the Institute of Early American History and Culture, 1980.

Kerber, Linda K., and Jane Sherron de Hart. *Women's America: Refocusing the Past.* New York: Oxford University Press, 2004.

Kerrison, Catherine. *Claiming the Pen: Women and Intellectual Life in the Early American South.* Ithaca, NY: Cornell University Press, 2006.

Kett, Joseph F. *Rites of Passage: Adolescence in America, 1790 to the Present.* New York: Basic Books, 1977.

Kierner, Cynthia A. *Beyond the Household: Women's Place in the Early South, 1700–1853.* Ithaca, NY: Cornell University Press, 1998.

Kolodny, Annette. *The Land Before Her: Fantasy and Experience of the American Frontiers, 1630–1860.* Chapel Hill: University of North Carolina Press, 1984.

Leavitt, Judith Walzer. *Brought to Bed: Childbearing in America, 1750 to 1950.* New York: Oxford University Press, 1986.

Lebsock, Suzanne. *The Free Women of Petersburg: Status and Culture in an Antebellum Southern Town, 1784–1860.* New York: W. W. Norton, 1984.

———. *"A Share of Honour": Virginia Women, 1600–1945.* Richmond: Virginia Women's History Project, 1984.

Lee, Rebecca Smith. *Mary Austin Holley: A Biography.* Austin: University of Texas Press, 1962.

Lerner, Gerda. *The Creation of Patriarchy.* New York: Oxford University Press, 1986.

Libby, David J. *Slavery and Frontier in Mississippi, 1720–1835.* Jackson: University Press of Mississippi, 2004.

Loveland, Anne C. *Southern Evangelicals and the Social Order, 1800–1860.* Baton Rouge: Louisiana State University Press, 1980.

Lystra, Karen. *Searching the Heart: Women, Men, and Romantic Love in Nineteenth-Century America.* New York: Oxford University Press, 1989.

Malone, Ann Paton. *Sweet Chariot: Slave Family and Household Structure in Nineteenth-Century Louisiana.* Chapel Hill: University of North Carolina Press, 1992.

Massey, Mary Elizabeth. *Ersatz in the Confederacy.* Columbia: University of South Carolina Press, 1952.

Mathews, Donald G. *Religion in the Old South.* Chicago: University of Chicago Press, 1977.

Matthews, Glenna. *"Just a Housewife": The Rise and Fall of Domesticity in America.* New York: Oxford University Press, 1987.

McCurry, Stephanie. *Masters of Small Worlds: Yeoman Households, Gender Relations, and the Political Culture of the Antebellum South Carolina Low Country.* New York: Oxford University Press, 1995.

McMillen, Sally G. *Motherhood in the Old South: Pregnancy, Childbirth, and Infant Rearing.* Baton Rouge: Louisiana State University Press, 1990.

———. *Southern Women: Black and White in the Old South.* Arlington Heights, IL: Harland Davidson, 1992.

McNeilly, Donald P. *The Old South Frontier: Cotton Plantations and the Formation of Arkansas Society, 1819–1861.* Fayetteville: University of Arkansas Press, 2000.

Miller, James David. *South by Southwest: Planter Emigration and Identity in the Slave South.* Charlottesville: University of Virginia Press, 2002.

Moore, Adella B. *History of the Bellevue Presbyterian Church.* Farmington, MO: Elmwood Press, 1955.

Mordecai, Samuel. *Richmond in By-Gone Days.* 1856. Reprint, New York: Arno, 1975.

Morrison, Michael A. *Slavery and the American West: The Eclipse of Manifest Destiny and the Coming of the Civil War.* Chapel Hill: University of North Carolina Press, 1997.

Myres, Sandra L. *Westering Women and the Frontier Experience, 1800—1915.* Albuquerque: University of New Mexico Press, 1982.

Norton, Mary Beth. *Founding Mothers and Fathers: Gendered Power and the Forming of American Society.* New York: Vintage Books, 1996.

———. *Liberty's Daughters: The Revolutionary Experience of American Women, 1750–1800.* Boston: Little, Brown & Company, 1980.

Oakes, James. *The Ruling Race: A History of American Slaveholders.* New York: Alfred A. Knopf, 1982.

———. *Slavery and Freedom: An Interpretation of the Old South.* New York: Alfred A. Knopf, 1990.

Osterud, Nancy Grey. *Bonds of Community: The Lives of Farm Women in Nineteenth-Century New York.* Ithaca, NY: Cornell University Press, 1991.

Owens, Leslie Howard. *This Species of Property: Slave Life and Culture in the Old South.* New York: Oxford University Press, 1977.

Pace, Robert F. *Halls of Honor: College Men in the Old South.* Baton Rouge:
 Louisiana State University Press, 2004.

Perry, Carolyn, and Mary Louise Weaks, eds. *The History of Southern Women's
 Literature.* Baton Rouge: Louisiana State University Press, 2002.

Peterson, Charles E. *Colonial St. Louis: Building a Creole Community.* Tucson, AZ:
 Patrice Press, 2001.

Pettus, Mrs. Lon. *Big River Mills: Then and Now.* Bonne Terre, MO:
 Bonne Terre Printing, n.d.

Pugh, David G. *Sons of Liberty: The Masculine Mind in Nineteenth-Century America.*
 Westport, CT: Greenwood Press, 1983.

Puryear, Pamela Ashworth, and Nath Winfield Jr. *Sandbars and Steamwheelers: Steam
 Navigation on the Brazos.* College Station: Texas A&M University Press, 1976.

Pusey, William Allen. *The Wilderness Road to Kentucky: Its Location and Features.*
 New York: George Doran and Company, 1921.

Rable, George C. *Civil Wars: Women and the Crisis of Southern Nationalism.*
 Champaign: University of Illinois Press, 1989.

Ragsdale, Crystal Sasse, ed. *The Golden Free Land: The Reminiscences and Letters of
 Women on an American Frontier.* Austin, TX: Landmark Press, 1976.

Red, William Stuart. *A History of the Presbyterian Church in Texas.* Austin, TX:
 Steck, 1936.

Reinier, Jacqueline S. *From Virtue to Character: American Childhood, 1775–1850.*
 New York: Twayne Publishers, 1996.

Risse, Guenter B., Ronald L. Numbers, and Judith Walzer Leavitt, eds.
 Medicine Without Doctors: Home Health Care in American History. New York:
 Science History Publications, 1977.

Roberts, Brian. *American Alchemy: The California Gold Rush and Middle-Class Culture.*
 Chapel Hill: University of North Carolina Press, 2000.

Rothman, Ellen K. *Hands and Hearts: A History of Courtship in America.* New York:
 Basic Books, 1984.

Ryan, Mary P. *The Empire of the Mother: American Writing about Domesticity,
 1830–1860.* New York: Harrington Park Press, 1985.

———. *Women in Public: Between Banners and Ballots, 1825–1880.* Baltimore:
 Johns Hopkins University Press, 1990.

Salmon, Marylynn. *Women and the Law of Property in Early America.* Chapel Hill:
 University of North Carolina Press, 1986.

Saville, Max. *George Morgan: Colony Builder.* 1932. Reprint, New York:
 AMS Publishing, 1967.

EMILY AUSTIN of TEXAS

Scarborough, William K. *Masters of the Big House: Elite Slave-Holders of the Mid-Nineteenth-Century South*. Baton Rouge: Louisiana State University Press, 2003.

Schmitz, Joseph William. *Thus They Lived: Social Life in the Republic of Texas*. San Antonio, TX: Naylor, 1935.

Schroeder, Walter A. *Opening the Ozarks: A Historical Geography of Missouri's Ste. Genevieve District, 1760–1830*. Columbia: University of Missouri Press, 2002.

Schwartz, Marie Jenkins. *Birthing a Slave: Motherhood and Medicine in the Antebellum South*. Cambridge, MA: Harvard University Press, 2006.

Scott, Anne Firor. *Making the Invisible Woman Visible*. Champaign: University of Illinois Press, 1984.

———. *The Southern Lady: From Pedestal to Politics, 1830–1930*. Chicago: University of Chicago Press, 1970.

Scott, Joan Wallach. *Feminism and History*. New York: Oxford University Press, 1996.

———. *Gender and the Politics of History*. New York: Columbia University Press, 1988.

Sharpless, Rebecca. *Fertile Ground, Narrow Choices, 1900–1940*. Chapel Hill: University of North Carolina Press, 1999.

Shore, Laurence. *Southern Capitalists: The Ideological Leadership of an Elite, 1832–1885*. Chapel Hill: University of North Carolina Press, 1986.

Sibley, Marilyn McAdams. *Lone Stars and State Gazettes: Texas Newspapers before the Civil War*. College Station: Texas A&M University Press, 1983.

Silverthorne, Elizabeth. *Plantation Life in Texas*. College Station: Texas A&M University Press, 1986.

Simpson, Henry. *The Lives of Eminent Philadelphians*. Philadelphia: William Brotherhead, 1859.

Smith, Daniel Blake. *Inside the Great House: Planter Family Life in Eighteenth-Century Chesapeake Society*. Ithaca, NY: Cornell University Press, 1980.

Smith, Rebecca Lee. *Mary Austin Holley: A Biography*. Austin: University of Texas Press, 1962.

Smith-Rosenberg, Carroll. *Disorderly Conduct: Visions of Gender in Victorian America*. New York: Oxford University Press, 1986.

Spruill, Julia Cherry. *Women's Life and Work in the Southern Colonies*. 1983. Reprint, New York: W. W. Norton, 1972.

Stepenoff, Bonnie. *From French Community to Missouri Town: Ste. Genevieve in the Nineteenth Century*. Columbia: University of Missouri Press, 2006.

Stevenson, Brenda E. *Life in Black and White: Family and Community in the Slave South*. New York: Oxford University Press, 1996.

Stone, Lawrence. *The Family, Sex, and Marriage in England, 1500–1800*. New York: Harper and Row, 1979.

Stowe, Steven M. *Doctoring the South: Southern Physicians and Everyday Medicine in the Mid-Nineteenth Century.* Chapel Hill: University of North Carolina Press, 2004.

———. *Intimacy and Power in the Old South: Ritual in the Lives of the Planters.* Baltimore: Johns Hopkins University Press, 1987.

Strasser, Susan. *Never Done: A History of American Housework.* New York: Pantheon Books, 1982.

Stratton, Joanna L. *Pioneer Women: Voices from the Kansas Frontier.* New York: Simon and Schuster, 1981.

Stuntz, Jean. *Hers, His, and Theirs: Community Property Law in Spain and Early Texas.* Lubbock: Texas Tech University Press, 2005.

Summers, Lewis P. *History of Southwestern Virginia, 1746–1786.* Richmond, VA: J. C. Hill, 1903.

Taylor, Joe Gray. *Eating, Drinking and Visiting in the South: An Informal History.* Baton Rouge: Louisiana State University Press, 1982.

Temkin, Owsei. *The Falling Sickness: A History of Epilepsy from the Greeks to the Beginnings of Modern Neurology.* 2nd ed. Baltimore: Johns Hopkins University Press, 1994.

Theriot, Nancy M. *Mothers and Daughters in Nineteenth-Century America: The Biosocial Construction of Femininity.* Lexington: University Press of Kentucky, 1996.

Verbrugge, Martha H. *Able-Bodied Womanhood: Personal Health and Social Change in Nineteenth-Century Boston.* New York: Oxford University Press, 1978.

Vernon, Walter N. *William Stevenson: Riding Preacher.* Dallas, TX: Southern Methodist University Press, 1964.

Vlach, John Michael. *Back of the Big House: The Architecture of Plantation Slavery.* Chapel Hill: University of North Carolina Press, 1993.

Wade, Richard C. *Slavery in the Cities: The South, 1820–1860.* New York: Oxford University Press, 1964.

Wall, Bennett H., Light T. Cummins, Judith K. Schafer, Edward F. Hass, and Michael Kurtz. *Louisiana: A History.* 4th ed. Chicago: Harlan Davidson, 1997.

Warbasse, Elizabeth Bowles. *The Changing Legal Rights of Married Women, 1800–1861.* New York: Garland, 1987.

Weiner, Marli F. *Mistresses and Slaves: Plantation Women in South Carolina, 1830–1860.* Champaign: University of Illinois Press, 1998.

Wertz, Richard W., and Dorothy C. Wertz. *Lying-In: A History of Childbirth in America.* New York: Schocken Books, 1979.

White, Deborah Gray. *Ar'n't I a Woman?: Female Slaves in the Plantation South.* New York: W. W. Norton, 1985.

Wiley, Bell Irvin. *Confederate Women.* Westport, CT: Greenwood, 1975.

Wolfe, Margaret Ripley. *Daughters of Canaan: A Sage of Southern Women.* Lexington: University of Kentucky Press, 1995.

Wood, Betty. *Women's Work, Men's Work: The Informal Slave Economics of Lowcountry Georgia.* Athens: University of Georgia Press, 1995.

Wood, Kirsten E. *Masterful Women: Slaveholding Widows from the American Revolution through the Civil War.* Chapel Hill: University of North Carolina Press, 2004.

Wright, Gavin. *The Political Economy of the Cotton South: Households, Markets, and Wealth in the Nineteenth Century.* New York: W. W. Norton, 1978.

Wyatt-Brown, Bertram. *Southern Honor: Ethics and Behavior in the Old South.* New York: Oxford University Press, 1982.

B. ARTICLES

Allgor, Catherine. "A Lady Will Have More Influence: Women and Patronage in Early Washington City." In *Women and the Unstable State in Nineteenth-Century America*, edited by Alison M. Parker and Stephanie Cole, 37–60. College Station: Texas A&M University Press for the University of Texas at Arlington, 2000.

Anderson, Hattie M. "Frontier Economic Problems in Missouri, 1815–1828." *Missouri Historical Review* 34 (October 1939): 38–70.

Baker, Paula. "The Domestication of Politics: Women and American Political Society, 1780–1920." *American Historical Review* 89 (1984): 620–47.

Barnes, Peter J. "Chronic Obstructive Pulmonary Disease." *New England Journal of Medicine* 343 (July 2000): 269–80.

Basch, Norma. "The Emerging Legal History of Women in the Unites States: Property, Divorce, and the Constitution." *Signs: Journal of Women in Culture and Society* 12 (Autumn 1986): 97–117.

———. "Equity vs. Equality: Emerging Concepts of Women's Political Status in the Age of Jackson." *Journal of the Early Republic* 3 (1983): 297–318.

Blake, John B. "Women and Medicine in Ante-Bellum America." *Bulletin of the History of Medicine* 39 (March–April 1965): 99–123.

Boswell, Angela. "Married Women's Property Rights and the Challenge to the Patriarchal Order: Colorado County, Texas." In *Negotiating Boundaries of Southern Womanhood: Dealing with the Powers that Be*, edited by Janet L. Coryell, Thomas H. Appleton Jr., Anastatia Sims, Sandra Gioia Treadway, 89–109. Columbia: University of Missouri Press, 2000.

Burke, Diane Mutti. "Mah Pappy Belong to a Neighbor: The Effects of Abroad Marriages on Missouri Slave Families." In *Searching for Their Places: Women in the South across Four Centuries*, edited by Thomas H. Appleton Jr. and Angela Boswell, 57–78. Columbia: University of Missouri Press, 2003.

Cash, Marie. "Arkansas in Territorial Days." *Arkansas Historical Quarterly* 1, no. 3 (September 1942): 223–34.

Cashin, Joan E. "According to His Wish and Desire: Female Kin and Female Slaves in Planter Wills." In *Women of the American South: A Multicultural Reader*, edited by Christie Anne Farnham, 90–119. New York: New York University Press, 1997.

———. "Culture of Resignation." Introduction to *Our Common Affair: Texts from Women in the Old South*, edited by Joan E. Cashin, 1–41. Baltimore: Johns Hopkins University Press, 1996.

———. "The Structure of Antebellum Families: 'The Ties That Bound Us Was Strong.'" *Journal of Southern History* 56 (February 1990): 55–70.

Censer, Jane Turner. "Southwestern Migration among North Carolina Planter Families." *Journal of Southern History* 57 (1991): 407–26.

Christie, John. "Living with History." *Middletown (CT) Press*, February 19, 2004.

Chused, Richard H. "Married Women's Property Law: 1800–1850." *Georgetown Law Journal* 71 (June 1983): 1359–1425.

Clinton, Catherine. "Caught in the Web of the Big House: Women and Slavery." In *The Web of Southern Social Relations: Women, Family, and Education*, edited by Walter J. Fraser Jr., R. Frank Saunders Jr., and Jon L. Wakelyn, 19–34. Athens: University of Georgia Press, 1985.

———. "Equally Their Due: The Education of the Planter Daughter in the Early Republic." *Journal of the Early Republic* 2 (1982): 39–60.

Cole, Stephanie. Introduction to *Searching for Their Places: Women in the South Across Four Centuries*, edited by Thomas H. Appleton Jr. and Angela Boswell, 1–12. Columbia: University of Missouri Press, 2003.

———. "A White Woman, of Middle Age, Would Be Preferred: Children's Nurses in the Old South." In *Neither Lady nor Slave: Working Women of the Old South*, edited by Susanna Delfino and Michelle Gillespie, 75–101. Chapel Hill: University of North Carolina Press, 2002.

Conner, Paul. "Patriarchy: Old World and New." *American Quarterly* 17, no. 1 (Spring 1965): 48–62.

Cummins, Light Townsend. "Church Courts, Marriage Breakdown, and Separation in Spanish Louisiana, West Florida, and Texas, 1763–1836." *Journal of Texas Catholic History and Culture* 4 (1993): 97–114.

———. "Her Weary Pilgrimage: The Remarkable Mississippi River Adventures of Anne McMeans." *Louisiana History* 47 (Fall 2006): 389–415.

Curlee, Abigail. "The History of a Texas Slave Plantation, 1831–1863." *Southwestern Historical Quarterly* 26 (1922): 79–127.

Deckler, Edna Perry, and Winne Allen, comps. "Memorandum Relating to the Heirship of Stephen Fuller Austin and his sister Emily Margaret Bryan Perry." *Stirpes: Texas State Genealogical Quarterly* 7, no. 2 (June 1967): 44–51; 7, no. 3 (September 1967): 109–15; 7, no 4 (December 1967): 150–52; 8, no. 1 (March 1968): 21–26; 9, no. 2 (June 1968): 71–74; 9, no. 3 (September 1968): 116–18; 9, no. 4 (December 1968): 148–49; 9, no. 1 (March 1969): 39–40; 9, no. 2 (June 1969): 65.

Edwards, Laura F. "The People's Sovereignty and the Law: Defining Gender, Race, and Class Differences in the Antebellum South." In *Beyond Black and White: Race, Ethnicity, and Gender in the U.S. South and Southwest*, edited by Stephanie Cole and Alison M. Parker, 3–34. College Station: Texas A&M University Press for the University of Texas at Arlington, 2004.

Faust, Drew Gilpin. "'Trying to do a Man's Business': Gender, Violence, and Slave Management in Civil War Texas." *Gender History* 4 (Summer 1992): 197–214.

———. "Coming to Terms with Scarlett." *Southern Culture* 5 (1990): 1–48.

Flachmeier, Jeanette Hastedt. "Dilue Rose Harris (1825–1914)." In *Women in Early Texas*, edited by Evelyn M. Carrington, 101–7. Austin, TX: Jenkins Publishing, 1975.

Fleischer, Michael, Adel F. Sarofim, David W. Fassett, Paul Hammond, Hansford T. Shacklette, Ian C. Nisbet, and Samuel Epstein. "Environmental Impact of Cadmium: A Review by the Panel on Hazardous Trace Substances." *Environmental Health Perspectives* 7 (May 1974): 253–323.

Fox-Genovese, Elizabeth. "Family and Female Identity in the Antebellum South: Sarah Gayle and Her Family." In *In Joy and in Sorrow: Women, Family, and Marriage in the Victorian South, 1830–1900*, edited by Carol Bleser, 15–30. New York: Oxford, University Press, 1991.

———. "Scarlett O'Hara: The Southern Lady as a New Woman." *American Quarterly* 33, no. 4 (Autumn 1981): 391–411.

———. "Texas Women and the Writing of Women's History." In *Women and Texas History: Selected Essays*, edited by Fane Downs and Nancy Baker Jones, 3–14. Austin: Texas State Historical Association, 1993.

Freedman, Estelle B. "Sexuality in Nineteenth-Century America: Behavior, Ideology, and Politics." *Reviews in American History* 10, no. 4, The Promise of American History: Progress and Prospects (December 1982): 196–215.

Goodman, Dena. "Public Sphere and Private Life: Toward a Synthesis of Current Historiographical Approaches to the Old Regime." *History and Theory* 31 (1991): 1–20.

Gray, Virginia Gearhart. "Activities of Southern Women, 1840–1860." In *Unheard Voices: The First Historians of Southern Women,* edited by Anne Firor Scott, 76–91. Charlottesville: University Press of Virginia, 1993.

Hagler, D. Harland. "The Ideal Woman in the Antebellum South: Lady or Farmwife?" *Journal of Southern History* 46 (August 1890): 405–18.

Hartog, Hendrik. "Lawyering, Husbands' Rights, and 'the Unwritten Law' in Nineteenth-Century America." *Journal of American History* 84, no. 1 (June 1997): 67–96.

Hoffschwelle, Mary S. "Women's Sphere and the Creation of Female Community in the Antebellum South: Three Tennessee Slaveholding Women." *Tennessee Historical Quarterly* 50 (Summer 1991): 80–89.

Hogan, William Ransom, comp. "Henry Austin," *Southwestern Historical Quarterly* 37, no. 3 (January 1934): 185–214.

Holbrook, Abigail Curlee. "A Glimpse of Life on Antebellum Slave Plantations in Texas." *Southwestern Historical Quarterly* 76 (April 1973): 361–83.

Isenberg, Nancy. "The Personal is Political: Gender, Feminism, and the Politics of Discourse Theory." *American Quarterly* 44 (Sept 1992): 449–58.

———. "Second Thoughts on Gender and Women's History." *American Studies* 36 (Spring 1995): 93–104.

Jabour, Anya. "'College Girls': The Female Academy and Female Identity in the Old South." In *"Lives Full of Struggle and Triumph": Southern Women, Their Institutions and Their Communities*, edited by Bruce L. Clayton and John A. Salmond, 74–92. Gainesville: University Press of Florida, 2003.

———. "'Grown Girls, Highly Cultivated': Female Education in an Antebellum Southern Family." *Journal of Southern History* 64 (February 1998): 22–64.

———. "Marriage and Family in the Nineteenth-Century South." In *Major Problems in the History of American Families and Children,* edited by Anya Jabour, 121–30. Boston: Houghton Mifflin, 2005.

Johnson, Michael P. "Planters and Patriarchy: Charleston, 1800–1860." *Journal of Southern History* 46, no. 1 (February 1980): 45–72.

Jones, Robert L., and Pauline H. Jones. "Stephen F. Austin in Arkansas." *Arkansas Historical Quarterly* 25, no. 4 (Winter 1966): 336–53.

Kelleher, Paul, Karin Pacheco, and Lee S. Newman. "Inorganic Dust Pneumonias: The Metal-Related Parenchymal Disorders." *Environmental Health Perspectives Supplements* 108, no. 4 (August 2000): S685–S696.

Kelley, Mary. "Beyond the Boundaries." *Journal of the Early Republic* 21 (Spring 2001): 73–78.

Kerber, Linda K. "Separate Spheres, Female Worlds, Woman's Place: The Rhetoric of Women's History." *Journal of American History* 75 (June 1988): 9–39.

Kilburn, Kaye H. "Particles Causing Lung Disease." *Environmental Health Perspectives* 55 (April 1984): 97–109.

King, Wilma. "The Mistress and Her Maids: White and Black Women in a Louisiana Household, 1858–1868." In *Discovering the Women in Slavery: Emancipating Perspectives on the American Past*, edited by Patricia Morton, 82–106. Athens: University of Georgia Press, 1996.

———. "Within the Professional Household: Slave Children in the Antebellum South." *Historian* 59 (Spring 1997): 523–40.

Lasser, Carol. "Gender, Ideology, and Class in the Early Republic." *Journal of the Early Republic* 10, no. 3 (Autumn 1990): 331–37.

Leslie, Kent Anderson. "A Myth of the Southern Lady: Antebellum Proslavery Rhetoric and the Proper Place of Woman." *Sociological Spectrum* 6 (1986): 31–49.

Malone, Anne Patton. "Women in Texas History." In *A Guide to the History of Texas,* edited by Light Townsend Cummins and Alvin Bailey Jr., 96–102. New York: Greenwood Press, 1988.

May, Robert. "Southern Elite Women, Sectional Extremism, and the Male Political Sphere." *Journal of Mississippi History* 50 (November 1988): 251–85.

McDermott, John Francis., ed. "The Diary of Charles de Hault de Lassus." *Louisiana Historical Quarterly* 30 (1947): 359–438.

McMillen, Sally G. "Antebellum Southern Fathers and the Health Care of Children." *Journal of Southern History* 60, no. 3 (August 1994): 513–32.

———. "Mothers' Sacred Duty: Breast-feeding Patterns among Middle- and Upper-Class Women in the Antebellum South." *Journal of Southern History* 51, no. 3 (August 1985): 333–56.

"Memoir." *Portfolio* 9 (August 1813): 117–22.

Morris, Christopher. "The Articulation of Two Worlds: The Master-Slave Relationship Reconsidered." *Journal of American History* 85 (December 1998): 982–1007.

Muir, Andrew Forrest. "Railroad Enterprise in Texas, 1836–1841." *Southwestern Historical Quarterly* 47 (April 1944): 339–70.

Murphy, DuBose. "Early Days of the Protestant Episcopal Church in Texas." *Southwestern Historical Quarterly* 34 (April 1931): 293–316.

Pugh, Nina Nichols. "The Spanish Community of Gains in 1803: *Sociedad de Gananciales.*" *Louisiana Law Review* 30 (December 1969): 1–43.

Reynolds, Suzanne. "Increases in Separate Property and the Evolving Marital Partnership." *Wake Forest Law Review* 24 (Summer 1989): 240–333.

Rosen, Deborah A. "Women and Property across America: A Comparison of Legal Systems in New Mexico and New York." *William and Mary Quarterly* 60 (April 2003): 355–81.

Ross, Margaret Smith. "Cadron: An Early Town That Failed." *Arkansas Historical Quarterly* 16, no 1 (Spring 1957): 3–27.

Salmon, Marylynn. "Women and Property in South Carolina: The Evidence from Marriage Settlements, 1730 to 1830." *William and Mary Quarterly* 39 (October 1982): 655–85.

Scott, Anne Firor. "Women's Perspective on Patriarchy in the 1850s." In *Half Sisters of History: Southern Women and the American Past*, edited by Catherine Clinton, 76–92. Durham, NC: Duke University Press, 1994.

———. "Writing the History of Southern Women." In *Half Sisters of History: Southern Women and the American Past*, edited by Catherine Clinton, 1–7. Durham, NC: Duke University Press, 1997.

Shorter, Edward. "Women's Work: What Difference Did Capitalism Make?" *Theory and Society* 3, no. 4 (Winter 1976): 513–27.

Shyrock, Richard Harrison. "Trends in American Medical Research During the Nineteenth Century." *Proceedings of the American Philosophical Society* 91, no. 1 (February 1947): 58–63.

Sides, Sudie Duncan. "Southern Women and Slavery." *History Today* 20 (1970): 54–60, 124–30.

Sikes, Art. "Who is Anthony Austin?" Paper presented to the Austin Convention, Pittsfield, MA, 2001.

Smith, Bea Ann. "The Partnership Theory of Marriage: A Borrowed Solution Fails." *Texas Law Review* 68 (March 1990): 689–735.

Stowe, Steven M. "Growing Up Female in the Planter Class." *Helicon Nine* 17 (1987): 194–205.

———. "The Not-So-Cloistered Academy: Elite Women's Education and Family Feeling in the Old South." In *The Web of Southern Social Relations: Women, Family, and Education,* edited by Walter J. Fraser Jr., R. Frank Saunders Jr., and Jon L. Wakelyn, 90–106. Athens: University of Georgia Press, 1985.

Swartzlow, Ruby Johnson. "Early History of Lead Mining in Missouri." *Missouri Historical Quarterly* 29 (July 1935): 195–205.

Talbot, Gayle. "John Rice Jones." *Southwestern Historical Quarterly* 35, no. 2 (October 1931), 146–50.

Vernon, Walter N. "Beginnings of Methodism in Arkansas." *Arkansas Historical Quarterly* 21, no 4 (Winter 1972): 356–72.

Viles, Jonas. "Missouri in 1820." *Missouri Historical Review* 15, no. 1 (October 1920): 36–52.

———. "Population and Extent of Settlement in Missouri before 1804." *Missouri Historical Review* 5, no. 4 (July 1911): 189–213.

Walsh, Lorena S. "The Experience and Status of White Women in Chesapeake." In *The Web of Southern Social Relations: Women, Family, and Education,* edited by Walter J. Fraser Jr., R. Frank Saunders Jr., and Jon L. Wakelyn, 1–18. Athens: University of Georgia Press, 1985.

Walter, Robert, Daniel J. Gottlieb, and George T. O'Conner. "Environmental and Genetic Risk Factors and Gene-Environmental Factors in the Pathogenesis of Chronic Obstructive Pulmonary Disease." *Environmental Health Perspectives Supplements* 108, no. 4 (August 2000): S733–S742.

Weiner, Jonathan M. "Female Planters and Planters' Wives in Civil War and Reconstruction Alabama, 1850–1870." *Alabama Review* 30 (April 1977): 135–49.

Welter, Barbara. "The Cult of True Womanhood: 1820–1860." *American Quarterly* 18 (Summer 1966): 151–74.

Whisonant, Robert C. "Geology and the Civil War in Southwestern Virginia: The Smyth County Saltworks." *Virginia Minerals* 42, no. 3 (April 1996): 21–31.

Whitley, Edna Talbot. "George Beck: An Eighteenth Century Painter." *Register of the Kentucky Historical Society* 67 (January 1969): 20–36.

Zeigler, Sara L. "Wifely Duties: Marriage, Labor, and the Common Law in Nineteenth-Century America." *Social Science History* 20, no. 1 (Spring 1996): 63–96.

C. Dissertations and Theses

Bornholst, Jacquelyn Wooley. "Plantation Settlement in the Brazos River Valley, 1820–1860." MA thesis, Texas A&M University, 1971.

Curlee, Abigail. "A Study of Texas Slave Plantations, 1822–1865." PhD diss., University of Texas at Austin, 1932.

Gracy, David B., II. "George Washington Littlefield: A Biography in Business." PhD diss., Texas Tech University, 1971.

Hanley, Lucy Elizabeth. "Lead Mining in the Mississippi Valley during the Colonial Period." MA thesis, Saint Louis University, 1942.

Kilbride, Dan. "Philadelphia and the Southern Elite: Class, Kinship, and Culture in Antebellum America." PhD diss., University of Florida, 1997.

Lazarou, Kathleen E. "Concealed Under Petticoats: Married Women's Property and the Law of Texas, 1840–1913." PhD diss., Rice University, 1980.

McKinley, Lela Ethel. "Life of James F. Perry." MA thesis, University of Texas at Austin, 1934.

Platter, Allen. "Educational, Social and Economic Characteristics of the Plantation Culture of Brazoria County, Texas." PhD diss., University of Houston, 1961.

Rath, Gertrud R. "The Life and Times of Moses Austin in Missouri." MA thesis, Hollins College, 1934.

Sedevie, Donna. "Women and the Law of Property in the Old Southwest: The Anecdotes of the Mississippi Married Woman's Law, 1798–1839." MA thesis, University of Southern Mississippi, 1996.

Sholars, Fannie Baker. "The Life and Services of Guy M. Bryan." MA thesis, University of Texas at Austin, 1930.

Trevebaugh, John L. "Merchant on the Western Frontier: William Morrison of Kaskaskia, 1790–1837." PhD diss., University of Illinois, 1962.

Weiner, Marli Frances. "Plantation Mistresses and Female Slaves: Gender, Race, and South Carolina Women, 1830–1880." PhD diss., University of Rochester, 1985.

Wilson, Ruthe Anderson. "The Story of Fulton: The Oldest Town in Arkansas." MS thesis, East Texas State Teachers College, 1952.

D. ONLINE SOURCES

Agency for Toxic Substances and Disease Registry. "A Toxicology Curriculum for Communities Trainer's Manual." Center for Disease Control and Prevention, Department of Health and Human Services. http://astdr.cdc.gov/toxmanual/modules/4/lecturenotes.html (accessed January 25, 2008).

"Brazoria County Totals by County and Year 1837–1845." Texas Slavery Project. http://www.texasslaveryproject.org/ (accessed January 11, 2007).

"Outline of Seminary History." In 1883 Catalog of Steubenville Female Academy. http://www.digitalshoebox.org/cdm4/document.php (accessed December 12, 2006).

Samuel H. Williamson. "Five Ways to Compute the Relative Value of a U.S. Dollar Amount, 1790–2005." http://measuringworth.com/ (accessed December 1, 2006).

"Site of Austinia." Historical Marker Records. Texas State Historical Commission. http://www.9key.com/markers (accessed December 14, 2006).

INDEX

Locators in *italics* indicate illustrations.

ISBN 0-87565-351-8

5 2 7 9 5

9 780875 653518

$27.95

TCU Press • Fort Worth, Texas
http://www.prs.tcu.edu